D0049278

THE GUMSHOE
AND THE SHRINK

GUENTHER REINHARDT, DR. ARNOLD HUTSCHNECKER, AND
THE SECRET HISTORY OF THE 1960 KENNEDY/NIXON ELECTION

DAVID L. ROBB

SANTA
MONICA
PRESS

Published by:

Santa Monica Press LLC
P.O. Box 850
Solana Beach, CA 92075
1-800-784-9553
www.santamonicapress.com
books@santamonicapress.com

Printed in the United States

Santa Monica Press books are available at special quantity discounts when purchased in bulk by corporations, organizations, or groups. Please call our Special Sales department at 1-800-784-9553.

ISBN-13 978-1-59580-066-4

Library of Congress Cataloging-in-Publication Data

Robb, David L.
 The gumshoe and the shrink : Guenther Reinhardt, Dr. Arnold Hutschnecker, and the secret history of the 1960 Kennedy-Nixon election / by David L. Robb.
   p. cm.
 Includes bibliographical references and index.
 ISBN 978-1-59580-066-4
 1. Presidents–United States–Election–1960. 2. Nixon, Richard M. (Richard Milhous), 1913-1994–Pyschology. 3. Nixon, Richard M. (Richard Milhous), 1913-1994–Health. 4. Presidential candidates–United States–Biography. 5. Political campaigns–United States–History–20th century. 6. United States– Politics and government–1953-1961. 7. Kennedy, John F. (John Fitzgerald), 1917-1963. 8. Reinhardt, Guenther. 9. Hutschnecker, Arnold A., 1898- 10. Private investigators–United States–Biography. I. Title.
 E837.7.R63 2012
 973.92–dc23
                              2011049062

Cover design by Michael Kellner
Interior design and production by Future Studio

MIX
Paper from
responsible sources
FSC
www.fsc.org
FSC® C011935

This book is dedicated
to the memory of Milt Ebbins,
a good man, a great friend, and a dapper dresser.

Contents

CHAPTER 1

The Urgent Call to Nixon

It was a warm and humid September afternoon on the Upper East Side of Manhattan as Guenther Reinhardt, one of the nation's strangest and most mysterious private detectives, stood at the door of the swank Park Avenue offices of Dr. Arnold A. Hutschnecker, Vice President Richard Nixon's psychotherapist. It was 1960, and the most storied presidential election in American history was only two months away.

Few real-life private detectives have careened through life with more adventure, intrigue, and misery than Guenther Reinhardt. By his own account, he'd covered the 1924 treason trial of Adolf Hitler, predicted the Japanese attack on Pearl Harbor, witnessed the outbreak of the Spanish Civil War, busted the German-American Bund, interviewed Leon Trotsky's assassin in a Mexican jail, uncovered the theft of billions of dollars of Reichsbank gold, and chased Communist and Nazi spies all over Europe and North America.

But he was always broke, always scrambling for money, and not above concocting a few facts to make a better story—or selling the information he'd gathered along the way to the highest bidder.

Cut from the Sam Spade school of private detecting and the *One Flew Over the Cuckoo's Nest* school of personal behavior, Reinhardt was a bipolar Don Quixote, a manic-depressive knight-errant in search of adventure and a fast buck.

Standing at Dr. Hutschnecker's door, Reinhardt hesitated a moment, looking up and down the taxi-filled, tree-lined street to make sure no one was following him. He almost always thought *someone* was following him. But not today—at least, not now. He'd taken a circuitous route from his apartment three miles to the south in Greenwich Village just to be sure.

He took one last drag on his Chesterfield and flicked it, still lit, into the street. There was barely a breeze; the leaves on the old elms, which were just starting to turn their autumnal shades, were barely moving. But a storm was coming. At that very moment, 1,600 miles to the south, Hurricane Donna was ravaging Puerto Rico, and in a few days, the Category Five hurricane—one of the strongest in recorded history—would roar up the Eastern Seaboard, ravaging New York City with 90-mile-per-hour winds and leaving this stretch of Park Avenue littered with the broken branches of its beautiful old trees.

Reinhardt had made an appointment to see Dr. Hutschnecker on the pretext of seeking a consultation, and was now about to spring the trap that could destroy Nixon's chance of winning the upcoming election.

There had been rumors for years that Nixon was seeing a therapist. Back in 1955, Walter Winchell, the legendary columnist (and Reinhardt's good friend), wrote that Nixon was seeing a psychiatrist. But Winchell hadn't learned the doctor's name, and without that, the story died for lack of corroboration. No one before Reinhardt had discovered the identity of "Nixon's shrink." Now, on the eve of the 1960 presidential election, Reinhardt was about to meet him.

Guenther was on a secret mission to collect information about Nixon's relationship with Dr. Hutschnecker and turn it over to Frank Sinatra, who had hired the detective on behalf of John F. Kennedy's father, old man Joe Kennedy.

Reinhardt took a deep breath, rang the bell at 829 Park Avenue, Apartment 1-A, and switched on the wire recorder hidden in his coat pocket.

Five days earlier, Loie Gaunt answered the phone in Vice President Richard Nixon's office in the Senate Office Building in Washington. It was Nora de Toledano on the line, and she wanted to speak to "the Boss." It was urgent, she said.

But Nixon wasn't in. He was laid up in bed at Walter Reed Army Hospital with a badly infected left knee that he'd banged on a car door while campaigning in North Carolina. It was Friday, September 2, 1960, and the presidential election was only two months away.

Nora was in a panic. She told Loie she'd just gotten off the phone with a strange acquaintance of hers, a private detective named Guenther Reinhardt, who was asking a lot of odd questions about the vice president. Loie jotted down everything Nora said in a memo, revealed here for the first time.

Nora had known Guenther for years. They ran in the same anti-Communist circles, he as a crusading anti-Communist investigator, and she as an advisor to the Committee for One Million, a group dedicated to keeping Red China out of the United Nations. Nora had met Guenther through her husband, Ralph de Toledano, a co-founder of the conservative *National Review* and a Nixon admirer and biographer.

Ralph liked Guenther, and in the early '50s had written a flattering promo for him when Guenther was trying to make a living as a lecturer.

"Guenther Reinhardt brings to any assignment not only a wide journalistic background but a decade of top-level intelligence experience," Ralph de Toledano wrote. "Many of the exposés now making headlines were wrapped up in his files many years ago. Through his work with the FBI and the U.S. Counterintelligence Corps, he has amassed a tremendous knowledge of the secret world of espionage and subversion which few Americans ever glimpse. He has repeatedly broken through the security curtain of Nazi and Communist operations, both here and abroad. The story he has to tell is of vital importance to the nation."[1]

But Guenther gave Nora de Toledano the creeps. Her son, Jim, would later recall that whenever she mentioned Guenther's name, "her upper lip would curl."

Guenther knew that Nora was close to Nixon, and when he got her on the phone that day in September 1960, he asked her if she was aware that Nixon was seeing a psychiatrist named Arnold Hutschnecker.

"I'm sure it's not true," she told him emphatically, and after hanging up, immediately called Nixon's office to find out. She knew that if it were true and it became public, Nixon's presidential campaign would be over.

"I was Vice President Nixon's office manager," Loie Gaunt recalled nearly 50 years later. "I took maybe 100 calls a day in the vice president's office. Nora was always passing things on. She called about a lot of things. I just took messages. I told Rose [Nixon's secretary], and she told me what to do."[2]

Nora and her husband, Ralph, were ardent supporters of Nixon and were eager to do whatever they could to help him. "Just say the word," Nora once told Nixon. "We are always available for anything we can do for you."[3]

In 1956, Ralph de Toledano had written an admiring book about the vice president titled *Nixon*, and many years later would write another flattering book titled *One Man Alone: Richard Nixon*. As an editor at *Newsweek*, de Toledano secretly alerted Nixon to articles that were being written about him before their publication in the magazine.

In August of 1957, one of Nixon's top aides told the vice president that Ralph de Toledano had offered to send him an advance copy of a story about him that was being worked on at *Newsweek*. The aide noted, however, that de Toledano had advised him that this had to be kept confidential because it "could cost him his job if it were known that he had done so."[4]

It certainly would have cost him his job if anybody found out. It's highly unethical for a magazine editor to leak the contents of a story before its publication. But de Toledano knew Nixon's hunger for inside information, and he was only too happy to provide it to him on the sly.

Pretty and petite, his wife, Nora, was a brilliant researcher whom Nixon often counted on when he needed ammunition to use against his many enemies or to defend his shabby record of name-calling and hurling false accusations.

In 1958, with an eye clearly on the 1960 presidential race, Nixon asked Nora to write up a report answering all the charges that had ever been leveled against him.

What she produced was a 45-page report that gave detailed answers to dozens of allegations that had been brought against Nixon over the years, including charges, she noted, that "he calls his opponents crooks and Communists; that he equates the Communist and Democratic Parties; that he called President Harry Truman 'a traitor'...that he is vindictive; and that Nixon is more immoderate than other campaigners in his language and characterizations."[5]

According to Nora's report, all of these charges were false.

In fact, they were all true. Nixon did call his political opponents crooks and Communists, he had been very immoderate in his language and characterizations, he had referred to President Truman as a "traitor," and he was very, very vindictive.

Nora's report contained detailed descriptions of dozens of hateful things Nixon had said over the years, and a passionate defense of each one of them. But by 1958, when she had finished writing the report, the nation's mood was changing. Nixon's old friend and former ally, Joseph McCarthy—the crazed, red-baiting senator from Wisconsin—had already been censored and disgraced, and had died an alcoholic outcast. Wild, unsubstantiated accusations weren't as popular as they had been only a few years earlier. So Nixon ordered that Nora's report be kept tightly under wraps. After all, not everyone would grasp the subtleties that Nora had found in Nixon's inflammatory rhetoric. There was no need for any of this old news to come out now—not with the 1960 election only two years away.

In August of 1958, when one of Nixon's aides asked if it would be all right to send Nora's report to the Republican National Committee, Nixon's office manager wrote: "RN [Richard Nixon] was definite in saying that he did not want the Nora de Toledano material in the files of the RNC. He said, 'This is for us,' and said there were too many people down at the RNC who might get their hands on it and he did not want that."[6]

After talking to Nora about the private detective, Loie Gaunt wrote a memo to Nixon's trusted secretary, Rose Mary Woods, who many years later would become famous during the Watergate scandal for "accidentally" erasing 18½ minutes of Nixon's White House tapes.

In her memo to Woods, Gaunt wrote: "[Nora] said that a rather strange friend of theirs, Gunther Rinehart [sic], who has a rather 'spotty' record, had called her to say that in his work as an undercover investigator…he had learned that a New York psychiatrist by the 'funny' name of Hutschnecker…was claiming that RN was a patient of his and that he enjoyed a very close relationship with the vice president.

"Nora approached it…on the basis that this was probably just a wild rumor, particularly coming from the person it did, and she would like to call him right back and say that RN had never heard of him."[7]

Gaunt, however, cautioned Nora to be careful about what she told the private detective.

"I told her I did not think she should do that until she had confirmation that this was the case," Gaunt wrote in her memo to Woods, "and I did not make any comment one way or the other on whether I had ever heard the [doctor's] name before."[8]

Gaunt, in fact, was well aware of Nixon's long relationship with Dr. Hutschnecker.

The next day, September 3, Reinhardt called Nora again, telling her this time that Hutschnecker was threatening to expose Nixon as one of his patients. After hanging up with Reinhardt, Nora once again dutifully called Nixon's office. It was a Saturday, but Loie Gaunt was at her desk.

"In the second call," Gaunt wrote in a memo to Woods, "Nora said she had some additional information." Nora told Gaunt that Reinhardt had informed her that Dr. Hutschnecker was "in trouble with the law," and that if prosecuted, would "announce to the world that he is an intimate of RN and that RN has been a patient of his."[9]

This was not good news for the Nixon campaign, although the charge that Dr. Hutschnecker was "in trouble with the law" and was threatening to expose Nixon as one of his patients was a lie concocted by Reinhardt to provide a cover story for what he was really up to.

At the end of her typewritten memo, Gaunt asked Woods: "How to handle at this point with Nora??"

Rose Mary Woods didn't get back to Gaunt until Tuesday, September 6—the same day Hutschnecker returned to New York from a vacation at his summer home in Sherman, Connecticut. Nixon was still in the hospital with his knee problem, but Woods got word to him about the private detective's inquires about Dr. Hutschnecker.

"The boss suggested we just file it," Woods told Gaunt, "and if Nora calls again I think all you can say is that you passed it on to me."[10]

Dr. Hutschnecker was not alerted, and the next day, Wednesday, September 7, 1960, Guenther Reinhardt showed up at the doctor's office for a consultation.

CHAPTER 2

The Will to Live

Richard Nixon first met Arnold Hutschnecker in July of 1952 after a former senator had given him Dr. Hutschnecker's book, *The Will to Live*, a best-selling layman's guide to psychological and physical fitness.

Nixon had been putting in long hours in the Senate, working himself to the brink of exhaustion. He was having trouble sleeping and complained of persistent back and neck pain. And now he was being considered as Dwight D. Eisenhower's running mate in the upcoming 1952 presidential election.

"Dick, get that book. You will learn a lot," urged Sheridan Downey, the California Democrat whom Nixon had succeeded in the U.S. Senate two years earlier.[1]

Nixon read the book and liked it so much that he had his young secretary, Rose Mary Woods, call the book's author and make an appointment for a consultation.

There was something special about Arnold Hutschnecker's first book that appealed to a wide cross-section of the general public, and to Richard Nixon in particular. Filled with optimism and practical wisdom, it was one of the most widely read self-help books of its day.

Dr. Hutschnecker, many readers believed, was decades ahead of his time in his approach to psychosomatic and holistic medicine. He believed that the way to prevent or reverse illness was to understand the emotional disturbances that cause it, and that Western doctors, not fully comprehending that the mind and body are one, had for too long separated the emotional from the physical well being of their patients.

"From the first," Dr. Hutschnecker wrote in the preface, "this book aimed to present a physician's view of the interrelationship of mind and body."

Chronically ill, Nixon's mind and body were never working in harmony.

"People who are at odds with themselves have a narrower margin of safety and are ready victims of illness at critical times," Hutschnecker wrote.[2]

And Richard Nixon, Dr. Hutschnecker would later discover, was definitely a man at odds with himself. Many years later, in an unpublished, 211-page manuscript about his treatment of Nixon, titled *Richard Nixon: His Rise to Power, His Self-Defeat*, Dr. Hutschnecker would write that Nixon was "filled with unknown hungers and conflicts within himself."[3]

Dr. Hutschnecker was particularly insightful about the role anxiety can play in undermining an individual's health. As he would later learn, Nixon was filled with anxiety and the fear of failure.

"Anxiety," Hutschnecker wrote in *The Will to Live*, "is a whisper of danger from the unconscious; whether the danger is real or imagined, the threat to health is real."[4]

Dr. Hutschnecker was also a big believer in the healing powers of peace and love, though Nixon didn't share his thoughts on love.

"People react to fear, not love," Nixon once said. "They don't teach that in Sunday school, but it's true."

"Love has never had priority in Nixon's life," Dr. Hutschnecker observed in his unpublished memoirs about treating Nixon, "and he always convinced himself that he did not need to be loved as a human being, only respected as a man."[5]

But Nixon certainly saw himself as a man of peace. In his first inaugural address, Nixon said, without a hint of irony, that "the greatest honor history can bestow is the title of peacemaker."[6]

Dr. Hutschnecker also warned against the destructive powers of hatred. "To hate is easy," he wrote in *The Will to Live*, "but it is healthier to love."[7]

Nixon believed that, too—except for the "love" part. In his farewell address to his staff, just before leaving the White House in disgrace, he said: "Always remember, others may hate you, but those who hate you don't win unless you hate them, and then you destroy yourself."[8]

But it was probably Dr. Hutschnecker's thinking on stress that most appealed to Nixon, since Nixon himself was under a lot of stress.

"Under stress the unconscious gives warning signs to be heeded by those who wish to live in health," Hutschnecker wrote in the little book that drew Nixon to him. "To allow oneself to become run-down under stress is self-destructive...Life confronts everyone with stressful situations and stress causes wear-and-tear in the body...whether the stress is external or emotional, the wear-and-tear is real."[9]

Dr. Hutschnecker believed that emotional stress, like physical stress, lowers resistance to disease. He seemed to know how to help his patients deal with stress, which was just what Nixon needed.

"A regime for stress," he wrote, "is different for each individual and each situation, but the goals are the same: to reduce tension and keep up energy."[10]

As the first book by an unknown author, *The Will to Live* "had a somewhat unusual history," Dr. Hutschnecker wrote in the book's acknowledgements. He didn't explain what that unusual history was, but through public records we now know that he started writing this hopeful and optimistic little book at the lowest point in his life.

When Rose Mary Woods called to make Nixon's first appointment with the doctor, Hutschnecker, a Democrat and lifelong pacifist, wasn't sure if he wanted to treat someone whose reputation was as bad as Nixon's. He knew Nixon's history as a right-wing redbaiter and was disturbed about his close ties to Joseph McCarthy, the deranged anti-Communist senator from Wisconsin. He was also shocked by Nixon's obsession with Alger Hiss, the former State Department official whom Nixon had famously accused of being a Communist spy.

The call from Nixon's secretary, Dr. Hutschnecker wrote, "startled and intrigued" him because Nixon's association with McCarthy and his very public and televised persecution of Hiss—which propelled Nixon onto the national stage—made him wonder if Nixon "hadn't gone overboard."[11]

Hiss, after all, had been one of Dr. Hutschnecker's personal heroes. He had helped establish the United Nations and was president of the Carnegie Endowment for International Peace, two organizations dedicated to world peace that Dr. Hutschnecker believed in very deeply. Up until 1948, Hiss' reputation had been impeccable. He had been a protégé of the great U.S. Supreme Court Judge Oliver Wendell Holmes, and in February of 1945 he had been with President Roosevelt at the Yalta Conference, where the fate of post-war Europe was determined.

Even after Hiss was accused of espionage in 1948 and convicted on two counts of perjury in 1950, many people, including Dr. Hutschnecker, felt that Hiss was a still great man who had been wrongly accused and victimized by Nixon.

"I too felt something was not quite 'right' about it all," Dr. Hutschnecker later wrote. "I suspected ambition was the culprit and I tried to remain impartial about Nixon, but his friendship with Senator Joseph McCarthy greatly troubled me. Because of Hiss and McCarthy, at the time, it was difficult not to perceive Nixon in a negative context."[12]

But Dr. Hutschnecker, who had many famous and prominent patients, was about to have one more. As an immigrant from Nazi Germany, he felt it was his patriotic duty to try to help this important American statesman. And as a citizen, he wanted to find out if Nixon was as terrible as the reputation that preceded him. Besides, politicians fascinated him.

Nixon arrived at Dr. Hutschnecker's Park Avenue office for his first consultation in the first week of July 1952. It was a

sweltering summer day in New York, and in just a few days, he
would be traveling to Chicago to attend the Republican National
Convention, where he would be vying for his party's vice presidential nomination.

During their first consultation, Nixon was friendly but re-
served, courtly but shy, uncomfortable in his own skin. He complained about insomnia, tension, irritability, and neck and back
pains, but made only passing reference to the hardships of political
life in an election year. And despite Nixon's terrible reputation, Dr.
Hutschnecker took an instant liking to him.

"Beneath his correct and even gentlemanly manner," Hutschnecker wrote, "Nixon's shyness surprised me."[13]

Nixon was 39 then, polished and polite, and did not appear to
Dr. Hutschnecker to be the same man he'd heard on the radio during the Hiss trials. There was more to Nixon, he thought, than the
aggressive opportunist portrayed in the media.

Dr. Hutschnecker went through the usual formalities involved
with seeing a patient for the first time. He briefly took Nixon's patient history and gave him a routine examination. As an internist
as well as a psychologist, Dr. Hutschnecker tested Nixon's metabolism and blood chemistry and found everything to be normal. Psychologically, however, Dr. Hutschnecker could tell straight away
that Nixon was anything but normal. His new patient was one of
the most repressed and inhibited men he'd ever examined.

As a psychosomatically-oriented physician, Dr. Hutschnecker
had what was considered at the time to be an unorthodox approach
to examining patients.

"The moment a patient enters my office," he wrote, "I am
guided by my holistic perception of their behavioral traits: type of
walk, voice quality, energy level, the expression of the mouth and
hands—many observations which, when combined with clinical
data, provide a more accurate diagnosis. Body language speaks the
loudest, and all of his movements were a symphony of inhibition."[14]

Like an awkward first date, their initial meeting was tenta-
tive and self-conscious, and Dr. Hutschnecker sensed that Nixon's

inhibitions were so profound that he refrained from probing too deeply into his new patient's psyche.

"His demeanor was so 'correct,' I did not want him to feel uncomfortable during this first meeting so I was reluctant to ask him any intimate questions," Dr. Hutschnecker later wrote. "With another patient, I would have probed more deeply, but with Nixon, it was apparent that he was an unusually private person."[15]

Despite Nixon's resonate voice, indomitable will, and commanding intellect, there was something innocent about him—something almost childlike in his inability to look inward—that appealed to Dr. Hutschnecker and made him want to help and protect his new patient.

"I liked him," Dr. Hutschnecker recalled. "I did not want to lose him as a patient. Nixon would not have responded well to personal questions, so I kept everything technical rather than psychological."[16]

When Nixon left the doctor's office after his first consultation, Hutschnecker turned to his wife Florita and asked her what she thought of him. She said that he had seemed pretty tense.

Dr. Hutschnecker agreed, and though he generally kept his impressions about his patients to himself, told her that with Nixon's intelligence and overriding sense of self-control, he would probably go far in politics.[17]

Of course, Dr. Hutschnecker was right on both counts. Nixon would go far, and he had an almost pathological need to control himself and his emotions.

"I have a fetish about disciplining myself," Nixon once said.[18]

Just a few days after this first office visit with Dr. Hutschnecker, Nixon flew to the 1952 National Republican Convention in Chicago, where he was nominated to run as Dwight D. Eisenhower's vice presidential running mate.

CHAPTER 3

The Private Detective

Dark, intense, and extremely high-strung, Guenther Reinhardt was a strange man in a shady business full of strange men. Even his friends thought he was strange.

"He had some deep-seated psychological problems," recalled Werner Michel, a retired army colonel who worked with Reinhardt in occupied Germany after World War II. "He would go from the height of elation to the depth of depression in a very few moments."[1]

Born in 1905 to a prominent Jewish banking family in Mannheim, Germany, Reinhardt studied economics at Heidelberg University and in 1925 received a bachelor of science degree from Mannheim's State University of Economics. Reinhardt immigrated to the United States after graduating from college, settled in Manhattan and did postgraduate research in economics and statistics at Columbia University. In 1926, he landed a job as a statistician at Ladenburg, Thalmann & Co., the prestigious investment bank and brokerage house in New York City that a few years later would handle the accounts of another German-Jewish émigré—Albert Einstein. In 1931, with Hitler on the rise in Germany, Reinhardt became a U.S. citizen.

"With the approach of Hitler's regime, friends in Wall Street started asking questions about Germany's future international relations," Reinhardt wrote in *Crime Without Punishment*, a book published in 1952 that chronicled his adventures as a spy hunter. "The Nazi ascendancy in Germany, which caused many Americans to be rather unsure of exactly what *was* happening, prompted a group of New York bankers to retain me to interpret for them developments in Germany."[2]

This was his first job as a private investigator.

In 1933, the year Hitler came to power in Germany, Reinhardt began ghostwriting a syndicated foreign-affairs column for the McClure Newspaper Syndicate while still working as a private investigator for the Wall Street bankers. His undercover work, he told friends, involved infiltrating the German-American Bund, the pro-Nazi movement headed by Fritz Kuhn, a fanatical anti-Semite and self-styled "American *führer.*"

Reinhardt's former colleague, Werner Michel, recalled that Reinhardt "was always boasting about how he busted the German-American Bund. He reported on them when nobody else was interested. He would say, 'I knew everything about them and I reported everything to the House Un-American Activities Committee.'"

Michel, who is generally skeptical about Reinhardt's claims, having worked with him in occupied Germany and having seen his strange behavior first-hand, believes that this story was probably true.

"I think that was fairly valid," he said, "although with Guenther, you never knew where fact ended and fiction began."[3]

In *Crime Without Punishment,* Reinhardt wrote that he brought his findings about Fritz Kuhn and the German-American Bund to the attention of the McCormack Committee, the forerunner of the House Un-American Activities Committee, which in 1934 launched a full-scale investigation into the Bund and its leaders. Hired to serve as a liaison with the FBI on the case, Reinhardt had landed his first job as a government investigator.

"I welcomed this assignment," he wrote.

Years later, a political affairs magazine called *Plain Talk,* for which Reinhardt was a contributor, described him as the man "whose evidence helped to convict Fritz Kuhn," the so-called American *führer.*

In 1935, he set off for Europe, using his cover as a journalist to spy on Nazis and Communists.

"I traveled abroad," he wrote, "obtaining, among other things, material for a 10-part Hearst exposé of Nazi operations outside of Germany; leads into an investigation of similar Communist activities—thanks to comrades who felt that my anti-Nazi work could be of benefit to them; a 'scoop' eye-witnessing of the outbreak of the civil war in Spain; and an invaluable accreditation, thanks to an old schoolmate, as a foreign correspondent for *Der Bund* of Berne, one of Switzerland's finest and most respected newspapers."[4]

Upon returning to the U.S. from Europe in 1936, Reinhardt fell in love with a pretty young secretary named Helen Idonea Williams, a descendent of the earliest settlers of West Orange, New Jersey. They got engaged in October and married on August 5, 1937.

Needing a job, Guenther got in touch with his contact at the FBI, Special Agent George J. Starr, one of the bureau's leading experts on the Communist menace who Guenther had worked with on the McCormack Committee. The FBI needed resourceful, German-speaking men like Reinhardt. He was hired as a "special employee" of the FBI in September of 1936 and was put to work as an undercover operative while still writing for various publications, including the *New York Daily News*, *Coronet*, *Life*, and *Look*, and as the American correspondent for the Swiss newspaper *Der Bund*.

Given an internal FBI code name—"Hal Hart"—Guenther's first assignment was to infiltrate the newspaper business and find out which papers were planning to write negative stories about the FBI—and, more importantly, about J. Edgar Hoover. His cover story was that he was writing a hard-hitting investigative piece about Hoover for the left-wing literary magazine, *American Spectator*. His secret purpose was to compile an enemies list for Hoover.

This may have been the worst thing any American journalist has ever done.

Hoover, who loved good publicity and thought that anyone who wrote unfavorably of him was a Communist, had founded the Federal Bureau of Investigation the year before. As the head of its predecessor, the Bureau of Investigation, since 1924, he'd enjoyed a worshipful press that reveled in recounting the adventures of his "G-Men" capturing or killing high-profile gangsters like John

Dillinger, Ma Barker, and Machine Gun Kelly. But in 1936, with war looming in Europe and Japan already overrunning Manchuria, President Franklin Roosevelt assigned counter-espionage duties to the FBI, and the press became more skeptical of Hoover's increasingly heavy-handed and intrusive methods. There was even talk that FDR was going to sack him, and that high-ranking officials in the justice and treasury departments were jockeying to replace him.

Guenther's job was to spy on his fellow reporters, to find out who was working on negative stories about Hoover, and, most importantly, to uncover their sources. His job was to find the names of people in the government—high-ranking, important people—who were saying bad things about the FBI director to reporters. Guenther's job was one of the most important in the Bureau—at least, it was to Hoover.

That's why Hoover was so accommodating when, in November of 1936, Guenther fell ill and had to be rushed to the hospital with a 102-degree fever. As usual, Guenther was broke and couldn't pay rent.

When Edward A. Tamm, the FBI's Assistant Director, informed Hoover of this and suggested advancing Guenther some money, Hoover wrote back in his tiny, cramped scrawl, "See that he is given every assistance," and, "Do all possible to assist him."[5]

Guenther knew hundreds of reporters. Pretending to detest Hoover, he milked them for tidbits of dirt about the FBI director. Many of those reporters even gave Guenther the names of government officials to talk to who could confirm the information they were feeding him. Guenther would then report back to the FBI with the names of these officials, whom Hoover would add to his enemies list and then have them investigated.

One of Guenther's most devious methods of spying on his fellow journalists was to simply hang out at the National Press Building—home of the National Press Club—on 14th Street, just two blocks from the White House, where many newspapers had offices for their Washington bureaus. Guenther's voluminous FBI file shows that he wrote numerous reports about the activities he witnessed there, including a fistfight involving several drunken reporters, and conversations he overheard at the National Press Club bar. He also picked up many valuable pieces of information just by casually glancing at scraps of paper, notes, and mail lying around on reporters' desks while visiting them in their offices. When no one was around, Guenther would go through their trash cans. As he noted in one of his reports to the FBI, "All copy was carefully destroyed but the mimeograph sheets were thrown intact in the large open steel waste basket in the office."[6]

This snooping by an undercover operative of the FBI was a clear-cut violation of the First Amendment protections afforded the press, but that did not appear to have fazed either Guenther or his bosses at the FBI.

One of Guenther's best sources was a former *Boston Globe* reporter named Gardner Jackson, who had some of the best contacts in Washington. Believing Guenther was a Hoover-hater like himself, Jackson gave Guenther numerous leads about the FBI director, including a tip that Hoover was "queer."

While it's widely believed today that Hoover was a closeted homosexual, that was only whispered about back then. Hoover wanted to know who was doing the whispering.

On the afternoon of December 16, 1936, Guenther phoned Edward A. Tamm, his chief contact at the Bureau, and told him about a meeting he'd just had with Jackson, who had told him about a party Hoover had attended the previous summer. Jackson told Guenther that one of his sources in attendance had "noticed at that house party that J. Edgar Hoover was a homosexual pervert."[7]

Guenther, who had only been on the job for three months, had already uncovered Hoover's deepest, darkest secret.

Jackson had told Guenther that if he "wanted additional information on that angle," the "best information that I could possibly get would be if I could get to Stanley Reed, the Solicitor General, but that would be very difficult." He also said that he could "possibly get to Jerome Frank, because Jerome Frank had all of Stanley Reed's notes."[8]

So right there, on that day, Hoover knew that Stanley Reed, the Solicitor General of the United States—a crusading liberal whom President Roosevelt would appoint to the U.S. Supreme Court the very next year—and Jerome Frank, a left-wing lawyer whom FDR would later name as a judge to the United States Court of Appeals for the Second Circuit, were spreading rumors that Hoover was gay.

With that, J. Edgar Hoover's enemies list grew two names longer.

By November, Guenther had only been on the FBI payroll for two month, but his impressive knowledge of the Bureau's inner workings was already beginning to pay dividends. On November 30, he got an offer from a newspaper syndicate to write an upbeat, positive story about Hoover and the FBI. Guenther needed the extra money and was eager to do the job. The Bureau, however, didn't think it was such a good idea; writing favorably about Hoover might blow his cover.

In one of his many memos to Hoover about Guenther, FBI assistant director Tamm said he had told FBI special agent R. Whitley, the agent in charge of the Bureau's New York City field division, to be careful about this.

"I called Mr. Whitley about this matter," Tamm informed Hoover, "and told him it might be well to point out to Hart [Guenther's FBI code name] and caution him against doing or writing anything which would show any friendliness by him towards the Bureau."[9]

Besides, Guenther was supposed to be writing a hatchet piece on Hoover for the *American Spectator*.

"Hart has instructions," Tamm told Hoover, "that his story on the director must be submitted to the *Spectator* immediately."[10]

The FBI was being extra careful not to blow Guenther's cover.

In another memo to Hoover, Tamm wrote that he'd told Special Agent Whitley that "any Agent who goes over to Hart's house to make a contact with him should never be sent in that vicinity on official investigations of any other kind, since Hart is so well known that there would be an immediate association."[11]

Maintaining the appearance of Guenther's charade as a

Hoover-hating journalist was crucial if Guenther was to continue finding names for Hoover to put on his enemies list. And that wasn't always easy.

On December 17, Guenther was having lunch with a couple of reporter friends at the National Press Club. They were drinking cocktails and smoking cigarettes when one of his pals mentioned that J. Edgar Hoover was in the headlines again.

"Well," the pal told Guenther, "did you see your friend Hoover, that lousy son of a bitch, certainly got it in the neck? I hope they crucify him for that."

"What the hell do you mean referring to Hoover as my *friend?*" Guenther shot back in mock indignation. "If you have something in mind, let's have it out!"

"Jeez, I didn't mean it *that* way," the man said, backing down. "I just thought that, you being pals with Walter Winchell and such. Aren't all the boys in that gang working for Hoover? Aren't they all just a bunch of glorified publicity men for that dirty rat?"

"You're cockeyed," Guenther continued, his voice steely. "And you'd better think twice before even joking about something like that because this sort of thing could be taken as a nasty reflection on my journalistic reputation."[12]

After lunch that day at the National Press Club, Reinhardt stopped in to say hello to a reporter friend who had offices upstairs in the building. But his friend wasn't in.

"The only person there was a chap...who said he was working for Drew Pearson," Guenther would later recall.[13]

Pearson, the famous muckraking journalist whose column, "Washington Merry-Go-Round," was syndicated in newspapers all across the country, had a desk, a typewriter, and a phone in the office. But he wasn't there, either.

Sitting down at Pearson's desk to write a note to his friend, Guenther noticed a piece of paper lying on the desk. It was a piece that Pearson had written for his column—one that hadn't been published yet. This was news so hot, it wasn't even hot-off-the-presses yet.

Looking around casually to make sure Pearson's guy at the other desk wasn't watching him, Guenther quickly read over the article, and read it again. He then got up, waved goodbye, and walked nonchalantly out of the office.

Finding an empty office down the hall, Guenther ducked inside and called Edward Tamm at FBI headquarters.

FBI documents show that Tamm took Guenther's call at 2:57 PM, and, as was his custom whenever Guenther called, turned on the wire recorder to record the conversation.[14]

Reinhardt excitedly told Tamm what he'd found, sometimes referring to Hoover as "the Boss."

"The article," Reinhardt said, "is entitled 'Seeing J. Edgar...' The article is about 550 words long. While I could not take a chance on copying, I tried to memorize some of it."

The column, Reinhardt said, was Pearson's account of getting an audience with J. Edgar Hoover.

"It is written in a very satirical vein," Guenther continued. "He puts in the first 250 words on all the gaudiness of the office, on all the pomp and circumstance, so you can finally see him. He takes a crack at the stupid populace that admires the pictures of the heroic deeds and works to be shown around the FBI office. Then he finally comes to the point where he gets into his [Hoover's] office. He describes his office furnishings in a very satirical manner; he pulls the Boss's leg for the efficiency and the crispness with which he barks orders through the telephone, describes the gadgets on his desk, and then he makes fun of his being busy, etc., and ends up with a little note which is somewhat like this. He has a very fine technique by not forbidding you to quote him directly. He [would say instead]: 'Of course, this is something which is outside my department and it is not for direct quotation.'"

Guenther then finished his report to Tamm by saying, "This article is for the 'Merry-Go-Round.'"[15]

This was top-notch spy work, just the kind of thing Hoover liked—being "in the know" before everyone else. For Guenther, it would prove to be a strange and serendipitous introduction to

Drew Pearson, one of the great journalists of his era. Pearson was a crusader whom Guenther would later go to work for, a reporter who, with Guenther's help, would come within a coin toss of stopping Nixon from becoming president of the United States in 1969.

When Guenther wasn't spying on American journalists, he spied on foreign correspondents working in the United States.

In 1937, using his Swiss press credentials as a cover for his FBI work, Reinhardt joined the Association of Foreign Journalists, a prestigious organization of foreign correspondents from newspapers all around the world. Reinhardt, however, had a distinct distaste for and distrust of his Japanese colleagues in the Association. He believed they were nothing but propagandists and spies for Imperial Japan, which had invaded Manchuria in 1931 and mainland China in July 1937. So naturally, he began to spy on them, too.

In April 1938, Reinhardt wrote an article under a fake name for the first issue of *Ken* magazine, a start-up publication run by the editor and publisher of *Esquire* and *Coronet*. His article, titled "A Label for Propaganda," purported to describe how many reporters for Japanese newspapers were spreading subversive propaganda in America. And he was right about that. Many Japanese correspondents working in America for Japan's government-run newspapers were spies, and they all slanted the news to portray Imperial Japan in the most favorable light.

In his 1943 book *Betrayal from the East,* true crime writer Alan Hynd wrote that Reinhardt's article "caused a national sensation" and was "directly responsible for the passage in Congress of a bill that had for a long time taken a severe kicking around—a bill that required agents of foreign powers to register with the State Department."[16]

In October 1938, Reinhardt was elected press secretary of the Association of Foreign Correspondents. There was even a brief article about his election in the *New York Times.*[17]

Reinhardt relished his role as a foreign correspondent—even though he was a naturalized American citizen. In 1939, he was one of 15 such writers invited to pen their impressions of the United

States for a book named *You Americans*. In his chapter, titled "What America Teaches the Foreign Correspondent," Reinhardt praised Walter Winchell, the famed muckraking columnist whom Guenther had known since 1931, as the pinnacle of American journalism.

"I would give my right arm—I can type with my left, anyway—if I could have just one-quarter of the reliable international political information that comes Winchell's way," he wrote.[18]

Reinhardt also took a jab at his Japanese colleagues in the Foreign Press Association, writing with no apparent sense of irony that the great majority of foreign correspondents working in America "are honest and sincere goodwill ambassadors of the highest personal and professional integrity. But unfortunately, there are others too. Theirs is a surreptitious kind of propaganda, artificially cloaked in American terms and designed to implant alien ideas on the American scene for the hidden purpose of benefiting foreign interests."[19]

In October 1940, Reinhardt was elected membership secretary of the Foreign Press Association, and once again, there was a little write-up about it in the *Times*.[20]

War was now raging in Europe, and as the Japanese army was marching across China, Reinhardt grew ever more suspicious of the 16 Japanese members of the Association, all of whom wrote for official Japanese news organs including the *Domei* News Agency, the official news agency for the Empire of Japan, which would be disbanded during Allied occupation of Japan after the war.

The Association required annual membership fees, payable on the first day of October, and Reinhardt often joked that it would be nice if the Japanese reporters would be late with their payments so they could be kicked out of the club. But year in and year out, they were always fastidiously punctual about paying their dues—until one day in mid-October 1941, when Reinhardt noticed that not a single Japanese membership check had come in. On November 1, when reminders were sent out, not one of the Japanese reporters responded. Naturally, Reinhardt began to suspect that something was up.

"Guenther, you're too suspicious," one of his British colleagues told him. "You think there's a spy under every bed."[21]

"But I tell you," replied Reinhardt, "I know these Jap bastards; they're up to something. They know something."[22]

When no membership checks had come in from the Japanese reporters by November 22, Reinhardt took his concerns to the FBI, but his contacts there weren't interested. He then went to the State Department, where he had a few close contacts, but they didn't see anything to be worried about, either. This business with the checks, they told him, was "just a coincidence." Besides, they said, negotiations between the Secretary of State and Imperial Japan to stop the spread of a widening war in the Pacific were "progressing splendidly."[23]

Undeterred, Reinhardt arranged a meeting that night at the Stork Club in Midtown Manhattan with his journalism idol, Walter Winchell, and laid out the membership check scenario for him.

"You're sure of your facts, Guenther?" Winchell asked repeatedly, scribbling notes as they talked and drank coffee. "You're absolutely sure of your facts?"[24]

As recounted in Alan Hynd's *Betrayal from the East*, Reinhardt, who fancied himself a protégé of Winchell's, said he was dead sure, and in the early morning hours, Winchell finally agreed to run an item in his column. "If I didn't know your reputation," Winchell told him, "I wouldn't believe this."[25]

Two days later, on November 24, 1941—13 days before the Japanese attack on Pearl Harbor—Winchell's column appeared in the *New York Daily Mirror* and in syndication in newspapers all across the country, warning that the Japanese were up to something.

"For twenty years the Japs were promptest at paying their dues in the Foreign Press Association," Winchell wrote. "This year they are two months overdue. What's the lowdown? Got some inside news?"[26]

After Pearl Harbor, the Japanese correspondents in the Association were all arrested, and for good measure, kicked out of the Association of Foreign Correspondents. There was a story about that, too, in the *New York Times*.[27]

Two years later, Winchell devoted half of his column to re-counting the night he spent with Guenther Reinhardt at the Stork Club, getting the scoop that the Japanese were up to something no good just before the attack on Pearl Harbor. He gave Reinhardt credit for the scoop.[28]

It was just the beginning of a beautiful friendship that would one day lead him to the door of Dr. Arnold A. Hutschnecker.

CHAPTER 4

Bohemian Grove

Richard Nixon and Guenther Reinhardt crossed paths many times during their lives. The first time was in 1937 when, during the depths of the Great Depression, Reinhardt was working as a "special employee" of the FBI, and Nixon, a law student at Duke University, applied to become an FBI special agent.

Nixon had made it through the FBI's rigorous screening process, passing the physical examination and extensive background check. FBI director J. Edgar Hoover personally approved his application, but when Nixon demurred, telling the Bureau he wanted to wait a month before joining so that he could take the California State Bar exam, his appointment was canceled. Nixon never knew why until, many years later, when he was president, Hoover told him privately that he "would have been made a member of the FBI except for one fact: Congress did not appropriate the necessary funds requested for the FBI in the year 1937."[1]

Hoover put it somewhat differently in 1954 when he introduced then-Vice President Nixon as the commencement speaker at the graduation exercises of the 53rd Session of the FBI National Academy.

"Some years ago," Hoover told the newly graduated crop of FBI agents, "[Nixon] was extended an appointment as special agent of the FBI, but having already embarked upon the practice of law, the FBI's loss ultimately became the country's gain."[2]

Guenther Reinhardt had hoped to become an FBI special agent too, but he was deemed unsuitable because of his erratic behavior and wild mood swings. But he was a brilliant, dogged, and resourceful investigator, and like Nixon and Hoover, a ferocious anti-Communist, so the Bureau put him to work for nearly seven years as a spy who used journalism as his cover.

Nixon and Reinhardt crossed paths again in 1948 when Reinhardt worked briefly as a consultant to the House Un-American Activities Committee (HUAC). The HUAC had become infamous the year before, when it launched its investigation of Communists in the Hollywood movie industry—public hearings that started the Hollywood Blacklist.

Nixon, a first-term congressman, was a junior member of the committee, and can still be seen in old newsreel footage looking gloomily on as HUAC chairman J. Parnell Thomas bangs his gavel and screeches at recalcitrant witnesses, "Are you now or have you ever been a member of the Communist Party?"

Nixon and Reinhardt crossed paths yet again a few years later when they became members of the same private men's club: San Francisco's famed Bohemian Club, which hosts a retreat each summer at the Bohemian Grove among the northern California redwoods for more than 1,000 of the richest and most powerful men in America.

Founded in San Francisco in 1872 as an elite social club for local artists and writers, the Bohemian Club transformed over the years to become one of the most secretive organizations in America. Its members include captains of industry, political titans, and every Republican president since Herbert Hoover.

Many myths and conspiracy theories surround the activities that take place at the Bohemian Grove. Some theorists believe that the course of the world's politics and economy are mapped out there during the annual two-week summer retreats. More likely, it's a place where the rich and powerful let their hair down, commune with nature, and drink vast amounts of alcohol, all the while making invaluable political and business connections.

Songs, pranks, drunkenness, and mock-pagan rituals—including the "Cremation of Care" rite, during which members wear red-hooded robes and cremate an effigy of "Dull Care" at the foot of a giant stone owl altar—are all known parts of the Bohemian Grove experience.

Nixon first attended a Bohemian Grove retreat in the summer of 1950, just a few months before he was elected to the U.S. Senate. It was there that he got his closest look at the man who would become his boss two years later: General Dwight D. Eisenhower.

Nixon had first seen Eisenhower on June 10, 1945, during a parade for the general following his triumphant return to the U.S. after the defeat of Nazi Germany.

"I was doing navy contract termination work on Church Street in Lower Manhattan," Nixon later recalled, "and the window of my twentieth-floor office overlooked the route of his ticker-tape parade up Broadway. I could just make him out through the snowstorm of confetti, sitting in the back of his open car, waving and looking up at the cheering thousands like me who filled every window of the towering buildings."[3]

Nixon got a closer look at Eisenhower three years later, when the general briefed members of the House of Representatives—including Nixon—about the situation in Europe during a meeting held at the Library of Congress.

But it wasn't until his encounter with Eisenhower in the redwoods of northern California that Nixon got his fist close-up look at his future boss.

"In the summer of 1950," Nixon wrote in his memoirs, "I saw him at even closer quarters at the Bohemian Grove, where each year members of the prestigious private men's club and their guests from all over the country gather amidst California's beautiful redwoods. Herbert Hoover used to invite some of the most distinguished of the 1,400 men at the Grove to join him at his 'Cave Man Camp' for lunch each day. On this occasion Eisenhower, then president of Columbia University, was the honored guest. Hoover sat at the head of the table as usual, with Eisenhower at his right."[4]

Later that day, Eisenhower spoke to Hoover's guests at a lakeside amphitheater. "Everyone liked Eisenhower," Nixon recalled, "but the feeling was that he had a long way to go before he would have the experience, the depth, and the understanding to be president."[5]

Publicly, Nixon has written and spoken effusively about the Bohemian Grove, crediting it with helping him to win the presidency in 1968. But privately, he derisively called the Bohemian Club's members a bunch of "fags."

"If I were to choose the speech that gave me the most pleasure and satisfaction in my political career," Nixon wrote nostalgically in his memoirs, "it would be my Lakeside Speech at the Bohemian Grove in July 1967. Because this speech traditionally was off the record, it received no publicity at the time. But in many important ways it marked the first milestone on my road to the presidency.

"The setting is possibly the most dramatic and beautiful I have ever seen. A natural amphitheatre has been built up around a platform on the shore of a small lake. Redwoods tower about the scene, and the weather in July is usually warm and clear. Herbert Hoover had always delivered the Lakeside Speech, but he had died in 1964, and I was asked if I would deliver the 1967 speech in his honor. It was an emotional assignment for me and also an unparalleled opportunity to reach some of the most important and influential men, not just from California but from across the country."[6]

But Nixon expressed his true feelings about the place during a conversation with his two top aides, John Ehrlichman and White House Chief of Staff H. R. "Bob" Haldeman, during a meeting in the Oval Office on May 13, 1971. The conversation was taped on Nixon's secret White House recording system.

"The Bohemian Grove, which I attend from time to time—it is the most faggy goddamned thing you could ever imagine, with that San Francisco crowd," Nixon told his aides. "I can't shake hands with anybody from San Francisco."[7]

Nixon then launched into a Scotch-fueled screed against homosexuals and how they have ruined every great civilization on earth.

"You know what happened to the Greeks!" Nixon bellowed. "Homosexuality destroyed them. Sure, Aristotle was a homo. We all know that. So was Socrates. You know what happened to the

Romans? The last six Roman emperors were fags…You know what happened to the popes? They were layin' the nuns; that's been goin' on for years, centuries. But the Catholic Church went to hell three or four centuries ago. It was homosexual, and it had to be cleaned out. That's what's happened to Britain. It happened earlier to France. Let's look at the strong societies. The Russians. Goddamn, they root 'em out. They don't let 'em around at all. I don't know what they do with them. Look at this country. You think the Russians allow dope? Homosexuality, dope, immorality, are the enemies of strong societies. That's why the Communists and left-wingers are clinging to one another. They're trying to destroy us."[8]

Guenther Reinhardt, who shared Nixon's disdain for "fags"— he later worked as an undercover operative busting gay bars in New York City—became a member of the Bohemian Club on June 21, 1955.[9]

Always looking to infiltrate secret organizations and insinuate himself into groups of powerful men, this was the perfect club for a spy and double agent like Reinhardt, for it not only afforded him the opportunity to make important contacts with influential powerbrokers, but it also put him in a position to gather actionable intelligence that he could use for or against these same powerful men.

Reinhardt's Bohemian Club membership card notes that he was proposed for membership by San Francisco attorney Bartley Crum.[10]

Reinhardt hadn't lasted long as a consultant for the House Un-American Activities Committee, and left there to become Crum's chief investigator. The New York Times would later report that after World War II, Reinhardt had been Crum's "chief private investigator" for 10 years, a strange coupling in light of the fact that Reinhardt was a vehement anti-Communist, and that Crum was one of the lead attorneys for the "Hollywood 10," the first group of motion picture writers and directors who in 1947 were hauled before Nixon and the other HUAC members and accused of being Communists.

In fact, all of the accused were, or had been, members of the

Communist Party. There was even a joke going around Hollywood at the time that acknowledged it: *What's the difference between the Salem Witch Hunt and the witch hunt for Communists in Hollywood?* Answer: *There weren't really any witches in Salem.*

But Crum and the Hollywood 10 believed that the government had no right to compel anyone to reveal or explain their constitutionally protected rights of free speech and association, much less coerce them to reveal the political beliefs of their friends and colleagues, as Nixon and HUAC did when they demanded that witnesses "name names" of other Hollywood members of the Communist Party. And in the end, history and the courts have proved them right.

Crum himself appeared before Nixon and HUAC on numerous occasions as counsel for the accused. And all the while, Reinhardt was his chief investigator.

Ironically, HUAC chairman J. Parnell Thomas would end up serving time in the same federal prison as two of Crum's "Hollywood 10" clients, who'd been sent there for refusing to answer Thomas' questions.

In August 1948, Drew Pearson, the top investigative reporter in the country, revealed that Thomas had claimed to have hired a woman as his clerk, but in eight years she never showed up for work and kicked back her entire salary to Thomas, on which he paid no taxes. Pearson's column, which was based on documents provided to him by Thomas' secretary, led to a trial and Thomas' conviction and imprisonment.

"I remember Guenther," recalled Crum's daughter, Patricia Bosworth. "He was an advisor to my father. I talked to my father about him. He said that Guenther advised him that he might be spied on."[11]

And Guenther was right.

Labeled a subversive, Crum was constantly shadowed by FBI agents who opened his mail and tapped his phones. Finally, unable to cope with the stress of this grinding harassment, Crum killed himself on December 10, 1959, in his Manhattan apartment by washing down an entire bottle of Seconal with Scotch whisky. It was one of the few known suicides attributed to the Hollywood Blacklist.

So what was a fanatical anti-Communist like Guenther Reinhardt doing working as an investigator for Bartley Crum, defender of known Communists and Communist sympathizers? If his past history is any indication, he was almost certainly spying on Crum for the FBI, while getting paid by both sides. It wouldn't be the first time, or the last, that he'd work such a con.

CHAPTER 5

The Firing Squad

Richard Nixon would never have met Dr. Hutschnecker but for a series of chance occurrences, beginning with the miraculously lucky break Hutschnecker got as a young German soldier during World War I. It was 1917, the year of John F. Kennedy's birth, and young Arnold Hutschnecker found himself standing in his tattered German uniform with his back against a wall somewhere in the vast frozen stretches of the Ukraine, facing a Russian firing squad. He was barely 19 years old, and his short life was about to end in a hail of bullets.

Drafted into the Kaiser's army toward the end of the war, Private Hutschnecker had been sent to fight on the front lines in the Ukraine, where German forces were routing the retreating Russian army, which was on the verge of collapse after the Russian Revolution and the fall of Czar Nicholas II.

But in his forward position, Private Hutschnecker found himself trapped behind enemy lines and surrounded by Russian soldiers. Hutschnecker and six members of his unit had taken refuge in a deserted barracks, but it wasn't long before they were captured and quickly lined up against the barracks wall to be summarily executed.

Many years later, Hutschnecker told a friend what happened next: fourteen Russian soldiers, each armed with a rifle, took their positions before the seven condemned German prisoners. There was no escape. No place to run. [1]

Several of the doomed men were offered cigarettes and blindfolds, but Private Hutschnecker declined. As he stood there, about to die in the shivering cold, he could see that the Russian captain in charge of the firing squad seemed to be enjoying this particular duty. Taking a cigarette from his coat pocket, the captain lit it and then ordered his detachment to come to attention in front of the seven condemned men.

"Ready..." commanded the captain as seven of the Russian soldiers fell to one knee, the other seven remaining standing at attention.

"Aim..." ordered the captain as the firing squad raised their rifles in unison, two aimed at each of the shivering Germans.

The air hung heavy with the smoke of nearby burning buildings and the stench of dead horses as young Private Hutschnecker awaited the order to fire. And then, as if to take some last small pleasure in prolonging the agony of his doomed prisoners, the Russian captain took one last long drag on his cigarette, exhaled the smoke into the already smoky air, and tossed the butt to the ground, crushing the dying ember beneath his boot as if to squash the life out of his helpless captives.

But then, just before the captain could give the order to fire, the sound of an approaching engine arose above the din of faraway artillery. The captain looked over his shoulder and saw a motorcycle racing towards them. Several of the soldiers in the firing squad turned their weapons from their captives onto the fast-approaching motorcycle, but before anyone could shoot, the captain ordered them to hold their fire. It was a Russian messenger.

Moments later, the rider skidded his bike to a stop beside the captain, and in a cloud of dust blurted out their new orders. Polish legionnaires—sworn enemies of the Russians—were just down the road and were fast advancing. The Russians had to move out immediately.

The Russian captain and his troops fled on foot, leaving Hutschnecker and his six comrades, some still wearing their blindfolds, standing there with their backs against the wall. One of them spoke Russian, and would later explain to the others what had happened. After removing their blindfolds, they saw the Russians running off down the road, and knew that this was their chance to escape. With Hutschnecker leading the way, they scurried around the barracks and off into the woods to safety.

His last-minute reprieve from the firing squad, and the other horrors of war he'd witnessed as a young man, would make Hutschnecker a lifelong pacifist and skeptic.

"WWI had sown the seed of my discontent with military and political leaders," he wrote in his unpublished memoirs. "Taught to kill, living through such misery, degradation, and hopelessness as a soldier in WWI, I chose a profession to heal. I decided to become a physician...I became determined to devote myself, particularly through my writing, to the study of 'war prevention.'"[2]

Throughout his long life (he lived to age 102) Arnold Hutschnecker would often reflect on the small miracle of circumstance that caused the Russian captain to take that one last drag on his cigarette, giving time for the warning of an advancing army to save a young German private and his comrades from certain death. It was a life lesson that would shape his thinking and his writings, which, many years later, would lead Richard Nixon to seek his counsel.

After the war, Hutschnecker went to medical school, graduating from the Friedrich Wilhelm University in Berlin in 1925, and then trained in psychology at the Charitée, the hospital at the School of Medicine of the University of Berlin. "It was there I first learned of the ability of the human psyche to twist or deny a situation," he wrote.[3]

Those were dark days in Germany. The German economy was in a shambles, but had begun to stabilize after nearly two years of hyperinflation, during which the price of goods doubled every two days. At the height of the economic chaos in 1923, many Germans burned piles of German currency in their fireplaces because the paper money burned longer than the amount of firewood it could buy.

And Adolf Hitler was on the rise. In November 1923, Hitler led the infamous Beer Hall Putsch—a bloody but failed attempt to overthrow the Bavarian government. Hitler was arrested and he and several of his followers were put on trial. Found guilty of treason, Hitler was sentenced to five years in prison, but was released just before Christmas 1924 after serving only eight months. During that time he wrote the Nazi manifesto, *Mein Kampf*.

Against this chaotic backdrop, young Dr. Hutschnecker set out to establish a medical practice—and to see the world. One of his first jobs was as a ship's doctor for the Hamburg–America Line, one of the world's largest shipping and passenger lines.

His voyages gave him a respite from the worsening conditions in Germany and the opportunity to hone the writing skills that would later make him a best-selling author. During his free time aboard ship, he jotted down colorful stories about each of the ports-of-call he visited—stories that would give him inadvertent notoriety back in Germany.

The ship's purser, it turns out, had gotten hold of several of the stories and, unbeknownst to the young doctor, sent them to a newspaper in Berlin, which published them. When Hutschnecker returned to Berlin, there was a check waiting for him from the newspaper. It was the first time, but not the last, that he would achieve a measure of fame as a doctor and a writer.[4]

After returning home to Berlin, Dr. Hutschnecker read *Mein Kampf* and grew alarmed. He became a vocal critic of Hitler, referring to him in public as a *schwein*—German for "pig."[5]

But when Hitler came to power in 1933, the fate of all Jews in Germany and all of Europe was cast into doubt.

In 1936, several of Dr. Hutschnecker's patients whose family members had joined the Schutzstaffel—Hitler's elite and sinister commando forces, also known as the SS—warned him that, as a Jew, he was in terrible danger. It was the year of the Nazi Olympics in Berlin; the year that German troops re-entered the Rhineland; the year that Jews in Germany would lose their right to vote; the year that Jews were banned from all professional jobs in Germany.

Dr. Hutschnecker's brother, Leonard, who would become a world-famous art dealer, had immigrated to the U.S. the previous year, so Dr. Hutschnecker and his wife Florita did what every Jew in Germany did who would have any chance of surviving the coming Holocaust—they left the country, packing up their household belongings under the watchful eye of a member of Hitler's dreaded secret police, the Gestapo.

They sailed for America, arriving at Ellis Island on January 21, 1936, and found an apartment in New York City on East 82nd Street near Central Park and the Metropolitan Museum. The Hutschneckers filed papers for U.S. citizenship, and he applied for a medical license, which was granted on May 23, 1936. He was then a doctor licensed to practice medicine in America—at least for a little while.[6]

CHAPTER 6

The Consultation

I t was just after noon on September 7, 1960, when Dr. Hutschnecker's wife, Florita, working as his receptionist, answered the door to his office. Standing there before her was a short man with a long face, kind eyes, and black, slicked-back hair. He looked a little like George Raft, the actor in so many of the old gangster movies.

"*Guten tag,*" Reinhardt greeted her in German. "*Ich bin* Guenther Reinhardt."

Dr. Hutschnecker had been expecting him, she replied in German, and ushered him into a small waiting room. He took a seat and waited patiently for the doctor, the old-fashioned recording device whirling silently in his coat pocket.

A few minutes later, Dr. Hutschnecker entered the room, but at first Reinhardt mistook him for the doctor's houseboy.

"The physician is a small man, wiry and of slight built," Reinhardt wrote in his 12-page confidential report on their meeting. "His facial features are amazingly Oriental; so much so that when the physician first entered his office, it was the instant reaction of the investigator that this man was a Chinese or Filipino houseman."[1] (In his report, Reinhardt always referred to himself in the third person as "the investigator.")

Short and slender, the 62-year-old doctor did have a certain Asian air, although he was entirely of German and Jewish descent. People used to say he looked like Peter Lorre, the actor in all those old horror films, who wasn't Asian either, but sometimes played one in the movies.

They shook hands and the doctor took Reinhardt into his office, which was lavishly decorated in the German style—heavy wooden furniture and expensive Oriental rugs. Shelves filled with medical textbooks lined the walls. Reinhardt noticed a framed sketch of Albert Einstein on the wall, signed by the great physicist himself, another of Baron de Rothschild, the famous philanthropist and Jewish activist, and several paintings in the "primitive style." But there was no photo of Richard Nixon in the office, as the detective had been led to believe.

The two men talked briefly and the doctor was pleased to learn that Reinhardt, like himself, spoke fluent German. "Most of the conversation was in German," Reinhardt wrote in his confidential report.

When he'd made his appointment to see Dr. Hutschnecker a few weeks earlier, the detective couldn't tell the doctor the real reason for this "consultation," so he invented a clever ruse to gain the doctor's confidence and get him to open up.

"The very nature of the problem ruled out any approach other than that of surreptitious inquiry," he wrote on the first page of his report.

Reinhardt had arranged the meeting on the pretext that he was working for an attorney for a very wealthy and politically prominent Pennsylvanian whose oldest son had recently had his colon removed. The son, Reinhardt explained, had failed to adjust to the new regimen that the operation demanded of him, had become despondent, and suffered from acute depression. But there was no son, no wealthy family, no botched operation. It was all made up.

The young man's family doctor, Reinhardt told Dr. Hutschnecker, "suggested...that he submit himself to treatment by a psychosomatic specialist."

This pleased Dr. Hutschnecker immensely, because he was, in fact, the top psychosomatic specialist in the country, and had written a book about it in 1951 that became a surprise bestseller.

Reinhardt, of course, knew all about the doctor's book.

He told the doctor that his young client was reluctant to visit a psychotherapist, however, because be was worried "that should it become known to the public at large that he is under psychosomatic care, it would cast a stigma upon him which would seriously impair his political future." The pretext was tailor-made for Dr. Hutschnecker because Reinhardt knew that secrecy was a key element of the doctor's relationship with Nixon, and that it would be so with any budding politician.

"Therefore," Reinhardt continued in his lie to Dr. Hutschnecker, his young client's attorneys "suggested to him that he see a psychosomatic specialist in New York where, presumably, there is better medical talent available than in Pittsburgh."

"They obtained your name," he told Hutschnecker, "and instructed me to make a discreet inquiry whether you might consider examining and, if need be, treating the patient without setting up a chart or other records showing the patient's true identity, name and address."

The doctor, Reinhardt wrote, "accepted the pretext story with enthusiasm."

"Dr. Hutschnecker is a man of considerable charm and has a very prepossessing personality," he wrote. "He is quite loquacious. It was obvious that the physician made every effort to impress the investigator, within the limits of professional dignity, with the high plateau of his clientele. He readily agreed to a consultation with the prominent Pennsylvanian and to take him under treatment without making up a chart or any other record relative to his identity."

Reinhardt again stressed that confidentiality was of the utmost importance, and Dr. Hutschnecker told him not to worry. The doctor explained that he specialized in treating psychosomatic illnesses—physical ailments brought on by mental disturbances and stress. But discretion, and keeping his patients' names out of the newspapers, was his real specialty, he said.

"This problem is not new to me," the doctor told the detective. "I am treating the number-one man in our federal government in Washington—or rather, I should say, the number-two man. If you take another step above that you are next to God."

"Do you mean Eisenhower?" Reinhardt asked, playing dumb and fiddling nervously with the wire recorder secreted in his coat pocket to make sure it was working.

"No, the man directly under him," Dr. Hutschnecker replied. "Of course, it is very difficult to hide the fact that I am treating him because when he comes here he generally has two or four Secret Service agents preceding him. They station themselves at strategic points of the building and then comes this man in a big black-hooded State Department limousine. Of course, the whole building is alerted to the fact that a very important person is in the building, but I think that so far nobody actually knows who it is. I also treat him in Washington."

And then Hutschnecker let Reinhardt know right where he kept his most important patient's file. "Those files never get out of my hand," the doctor told him. "I have his file right in my desk."

According to Reinhardt's report, Dr. Hutschnecker then "patted his hand against the left lower drawer of his office desk," indicating the exact location of Richard Nixon's patient file.

Bingo!

This was the gold mine the detective had been looking for. Now all he had to do was mine it. He would get that opportunity a few minutes later.

Reinhardt later wrote that before going into the meeting with Dr. Hutschnecker, he "had made arrangements to have one of his assistants place a call to Dr. Hutschnecker while the investigator and Dr. Hutschnecker were in conference. The pretext for the call was an inquiry about the doctor's house, fees, etc. and the purpose of the call was to give the investigator an opportunity to look around the doctor's office."

Reinhardt noted that when the doctor's phone rang on cue, Hutschnecker's wife answered it and summoned him out of the office to take the call, leaving Reinhardt alone in the room with Nixon's patient file in an unlocked desk drawer.

Or so he says. With Guenther Reinhardt, fact and fiction were often interchangeable.

But whether or not Dr. Hutschnecker actually let Reinhardt know where he kept his most important patient's file, and then left Reinhardt alone in the room with it, one thing is certain: Guenther Reinhardt had now confirmed that Dr. Hutschnecker was Nixon's psychotherapist.

Documents at the Nixon Library, declassified now for the first time, show that with his call to Nora de Toledano, Reinhardt had purposely tipped Nixon off that his secret was out—a move that prevented Nixon from trying to expose Jack Kennedy's most closely guarded medical secret until, in a desperate gamble during the last days of the campaign, Nixon would throw a Hail Mary pass to try to win the election.

CHAPTER 7

Jack and Dick

Jack Kennedy and Dick Nixon couldn't have been more dissimilar in appearance, temperament, and background, but as young men their lives intertwined to a remarkable degree. They would both have dazzling political careers; but as meteoric as Jack's was, Nixon's took off even faster.

They both won their first seats in Congress on the same day, November 5, 1946, and worked together for three years on the House Labor Committee. Nixon, four years Jack's senior, was elected to the Senate in 1952, and Jack made it to the Senate two years later—the same year Nixon was elected vice president of the United States. Both were Irish, although Nixon was a Quaker and Kennedy a Catholic, and both had older brothers—their families' favorites—who died in their twenties.

Nixon and Kennedy had both been navy officers during World War II, receiving their naval training at the very same time, only 25 miles apart in Rhode Island. They ended up being stationed in the Solomon Islands in the South Pacific, at one time only a few hundred miles apart. But Jack had been a bona fide war hero whose exploits as the skipper of a patrol torpedo ("PT") boat were legendary, while Nixon had been a supply officer who saw very little combat, and whose main claim to fame in the navy was that he was a master at the game of poker.

They would both come before the American people in 1960 seeking the presidency, and three years later, on November 22, 1963, they were both in Dallas, their paths crossing for the last time.

Born into one of the wealthiest families in America, Jack

Kennedy went to all the best schools: the London School of Economics, Princeton, and Harvard, which he graduated from in 1940. The most prestigious school in the country, Harvard has graduated eight presidents and hundreds of renowned authors, jurists and captains of industry, but JFK is arguably its most famous alumnus. There's even a school named after him there: the John F. Kennedy School of Government.

Born poor, Nixon went to tiny Whittier College, whose only claim to fame is that he went there. Nicknamed "Gloomy Gus" for his hangdog looks and dour demeanor, Nixon graduated second in his class at Whittier (nobody remembers who graduated first). Although he was painfully shy, he was even more ambitious. This, coupled with his skill as a debater, got him elected president of his freshman class, and in his senior year, student body president.

After Whittier, Nixon received a scholarship to attend Duke University Law School, where he excelled, graduating in 1937. Nixon is easily Duke University's most famous alumnus, and the only Duke graduate ever to become president of the United States, but there isn't a single picture or plaque on the campus to commemorate him. There *was* a portrait of him—one of only two made during Nixon's presidency—that hung for a while in Duke Law's mock courtroom. But after Watergate, it was taken down and sent back to Washington. Nixon loved Duke; he established a scholarship at the law school and asked to have his presidential library housed there, but the regents turned him down.

Jack Kennedy graduated from Harvard in 1940, but unlike most Harvard grads in those pre-Pearl Harbor days, Jack wanted to join the army. War was raging in Europe and in the Far East, and he wanted to get in on the action.

But Jack was thin and sickly. He had to leave Princeton after his first year when he came down with an acute attack of jaundice, and severely injured his back playing football at Harvard, an injury that would plague him for the rest of his life.

He flunked his army physical in the spring of 1941 because of his bad back, but after five months of special exercise, was able to pass a less stringent navy physical. As one of Jack's commanders would later observe, "He's the only man in the navy who's faking good health."[1]

With the help of a friend of his father's, Jack got a plum assignment and was commissioned an ensign in the U.S. Naval Reserves. It was October 10, 1941—two months before Pearl Harbor.

Nixon was a young, newlywed lawyer living in Whittier when the Japanese attacked Pearl Harbor on December 7, 1941. The next month, he went to work in Washington with the Office of Price Administration as a junior lawyer in the tire rationing division. The pay was $3,200 a year.[2]

Nixon's job entitled him to a deferment from the draft, but after eight months of rationing tires, he decided to enlist in the navy. He made the decision to go to war, he wrote in his memoirs, "despite my Quaker background and beliefs," and against the wishes of his devoutly Quaker mother.[3]

Nixon applied for a naval commission, was accepted, and in October 1942 completed his officer training at the Naval Air Station in Quonset Point, Rhode Island.

At the very same time—October of 1942—and just 25 miles to the north along the Rhode Island Sound, Jack Kennedy was training in PT boats at the Motor Torpedo Boat Squadron Training Center in Melville, Rhode Island.

For the first time in their lives, Jack Kennedy and Dick Nixon were almost neighbors. It wouldn't be the last.

Jack Kennedy had been sailing fast boats with his father and older brother, Joe, off Cape Cod since he was a boy. In 1936, at age 19, he sailed his boat, the *Flash II*, to victory at the Nantucket Sound Star Class Championship. Two years later, sailing with his brother Joe for Harvard, he won the MacMillan Cup, the East Coast Collegiate Championship.

So Jack was a natural for PT boats, the fastest warships in the navy, with a top speed of 45 knots. After finishing his PT boat training, he got orders to ship out to the Panama Canal, a vital shipping corridor but a backwater in the war. He requested a transfer and was sent to the Solomon Islands in the South Pacific to fight the Japanese navy.

When Nixon finished *his* training, he was sent to a naval air station in landlocked Iowa, a facility that was still under construction, its unfinished runway ending abruptly in the middle of a cornfield.

Fearing he'd be stuck in that cornfield for the rest of the war, Nixon applied for sea duty and was soon ordered to report to San Francisco for assignment overseas. He packed his bags and took the train back to California with his young wife, Pat, stopping first in Whittier to see his mother and grandmother, who were "deeply troubled" by his decision to fight in the war.[4]

Like Jack Kennedy, Nixon's first overseas assignment in the spring of 1943 brought him to the South Pacific, to the island of New Caledonia, a few hundred miles south of Jack Kennedy in the Solomon Islands. Once again, they were almost neighbors.

Nixon was assigned to a supply station where his unit prepared manifests and flight plans for C-47 cargo planes as they brought supplies in and flew the wounded out.

"We would unload the boxes and crates of supplies," he wrote, "and then carefully carry aboard the stretchers of the critically wounded."[5]

But Nixon wanted to see combat.

"Like many assigned 'down the line,'" Nixon wrote in his memoirs, "I wanted to get where the action was, and I spent a lot of my time trying to get a battle station assignment."[6]

While Nixon was yearning for combat, Lieutenant (junior grade) Jack Kennedy was seeing plenty of it. In a famous incident in August 1943, Kennedy's patrol boat, *PT 109*, was sunk when a Japanese destroyer rammed it while Jack and his crew were patrolling the waters off the Solomon Islands. Two of his shipmates were killed, and though seriously injured himself, Kennedy saved the survivors and swam for help, rescuing his men after a six-day ordeal.[7]

Kennedy received the Navy and Marine Corps Medal and the Purple Heart, and many years later, a hit movie, *PT 109*, was made about his wartime heroics.

A few hundred miles to the south, Lieutenant (junior grade) Richard Nixon was still working as a supply officer on New Caledonia, but in January 1944, after being promoted to lieutenant, his request for reassignment to a battle station finally came through. He was sent to Bougainville in the Solomon Islands, and although it had already been secured by the Marines, it still came under occasional attack by Japanese planes.

"Shortly after I arrived," he later wrote, "the Japanese staged an assault. When it was over, we counted 35 shell holes within a hundred feet of the air raid bunker six of us shared."[8]

Counting bullet holes and measuring how close incoming shells landed is typically not something seasoned combatants do. But still, Nixon had come under fire during the war, so he could rightly say that he had seen combat, even if it was from the relative safety of an air raid bunker.

Most of Lieutenant Nixon's time on Bougainville was spent writing letters to his wife and parents, scrounging provisions for his men and playing poker.

"The only things that really bothered me," Nixon wrote to his parents from Bougainville, "were the lack of sleep and the centipedes."[9]

Nixon, whose men nicknamed him "Nick," became a master of scrounging provisions and supplies, much of it stolen from the supply depot he was assigned to. He acquired hard-to-find Australian beer and hamburger meat, which he served free of charge to transiting bomber crews from a lean-to shanty dubbed "Nick's Hamburger Stand." Through a series of trades of supplies he'd lifted, he also kept himself and his men in relative comfort.

"Some of the stuff, shall we say, was 'liberated,'" said one of his men, "but Nick could swap anything. Just a small trade would set in motion a series of bigger trades that not only had his men well-housed, but kept the hamburger stand operating. If you ever saw Henry Fonda in *Mister Roberts,* you have a pretty good idea of what Nick was like."[10]

Others, however, have suggested that the larcenous *Sgt. Bilko* character would have been a more apt comparison.

Nixon saw limited action again a few months later when he was assigned to support the invasion of Green Island in the Solomon Islands.

"We landed in the bay in a PBY seaplane," he wrote. "The Japanese had already retreated, however, and the only danger came from a few straggling snipers and the ever-present centipedes."[11]

Nixon wasn't a war hero like Jack Kennedy, but he was one of the best poker players in the navy, beating his men and fellow officers out of more than $10,000 by playing cards—a small fortune in those days that he would use to finance his first congressional campaign right after the war.

"In Whittier, any kind of gambling had been anathema to me as a Quaker," Nixon wrote in his memoirs. "The pressures of wartime, and even more oppressive monotony, made it an irresistible diversion. I found playing poker instructive as well as entertaining and profitable."[12]

Some even felt that Nixon, who would later earn the nickname "Tricky Dick" because of his penchant for dirty political tricks, was not above cheating at poker, either.

"Before he deals," JFK would later joke about Nixon, "someone's gonna cut the cards."[13]

With the war behind them, Nixon and Kennedy returned to civilian life, and it wasn't long before they were both running for Congress. They were each elected to the House of Representatives in 1946, and the next year, struck up a friendship when they began serving together on the House Labor Committee. And in 1950, when Nixon was elected to the Senate, he got help from Jack and Joe Kennedy, who gave Nixon a $1,000 cash campaign contribution, stuffed into an envelope that Jack personally delivered to Nixon.

Jack Kennedy won his first Senate seat in 1952, the same year Nixon was chosen as Dwight D. Eisenhower's vice presidential running mate. And when Nixon got the nomination, just a few days after first meeting Arnold Hutschnecker, Jack sent him a handwritten note of congratulations.

"Dear Dick," Kennedy wrote, "I was tremendously pleased that the convention selected you for VP. I was always convinced that you would move ahead to the top—but I never thought it would come this quickly. You were an ideal selection and will bring to the ticket a great deal of strength. Please give my best to your wife and all kinds of good luck to you. Cordially, Jack Kennedy."[14]

Eisenhower and Nixon won the 1952 election in a landslide, easily defeating Adlai Stevenson and his now all-but-forgotten running mate, John Sparkman.

Jack brought his fiancée, Jacqueline Bouvier, to Eisenhower's inaugural ball in January 1953, and when they were married eight months later, Jack invited Nixon to the wedding, but Nixon couldn't make it—he had to play golf with President Eisenhower instead.[15]

When Nixon moved into the vice president's office in January 1953, he and Jack Kennedy were neighbors once again, and would remain so for the next seven years. In those days, the vice president's office was located in the Senate Office Building—or "The SOB," as it was called—and Nixon's office, Room 361, was directly across the hall from Jack's, Room 362. Now they really were next-door neighbors, and they passed each other in the hallway nearly every day.

CHAPTER 8

J. Edgar Hoover Sacks Guenther Reinhardt

With the U.S. entry into World War II, the government once again put Guenther Reinhardt's unique talents to work as an intelligence operative in the U.S. and Latin America.

In the early years of the war, Reinhardt masqueraded as a Communist, infiltrating American Communist organizations and then passing his findings on to the FBI.[1]

In 1942, one of Reinhardt's assignments took him to Mexico, where he claims to have had a one-on-one jailhouse interview with the Soviet agent who in 1940 had assassinated Leon Trotsky, the Russian revolutionary who'd fled to Mexico to escape Stalin's purges.[2] Reinhardt said he got into the Mexican jail to speak to Trotsky's assassin by telling the warden that he was "an America reporter."

According to Reinhardt, the FBI wanted him to determine the nationality of Trotsky's assassin, about whom little was known at the time. He had been arrested under the name Frank Jacson, but the FBI did not know his real name or birthplace. Reinhardt, an expert linguist who prided himself on being able to tell anyone's nationality just by their accent, would give the FBI their answer. In this case, however, it would be the wrong answer.

Visiting Jacson in jail, Reinhardt observed right off that his was no ordinary Mexican prison cell. The prisoner had been provided with hotel-style accommodations, complete with a screened yard, a fully stocked bookshelf, expensive Scotch, a comfortable American bed, a work bench, tools for his hobby (making model airplanes), and tailor-made clothes, including the blue silk Brooks Brothers dressing gown he wore during their interview. From all this, Reinhardt concluded that Jacson's luxurious prison lifestyle was being underwritten by the Soviet government, which would, in fact, greet Jacson as a national hero upon his release 18 years later.

In *Crime Without Punishment*, Reinhardt wrote that, after talking to Jacson for nearly two hours, he knew exactly where Trotsky's assassin was from. "His accent, it was clear to me, placed his 'native' home in a Russian area close to the Balkans. It was the first solid lead toward establishing his actual identity. Later, that clue led to his real name, Turkov, and his real birthplace, Bessarabia, now Russian Romania."

Little was known about Jacson when Reinhardt wrote that account of their meeting, but a great deal has been learned about him since his release from prison in 1960, when he went first to Cuba, and then to Russia, where he was awarded the Hero of the Soviet Union medal, the country's highest honor.

As it turns out, Reinhardt was right about Trotsky's assassin being arrested under the name Frank Jacson, and he was right about the Soviet Union paying for his swank prison accommodations. But he was wrong about just about everything else. We now know that Jacson's real name was Ramón Mercader, not Turkov, and that he was born in Barcelona, Spain, and raised in France, not Russian Romania.

After visiting Jacson in jail, Reinhardt said that he then wrote a 9,000-word story about his interview with Trotsky's assassin and sold it "to a crime magazine" under a phony name. Once again, he was using journalism as a cover for his spy work.

"I used the pseudonym Raymond Haskell for the article," he later wrote, "but made sure that Haskell's actual identity was funneled into Communist channels so that they, too, would pass the interview off as straight reporting."[3]

Whether Reinhardt ever actually visited Jacson in jail is not known. But it wouldn't be the last time he'd write a story filled with inaccuracies and falsehoods. With Guenther Reinhardt, as with so many of his stories, the line between fact and fiction was often a blurry one.

Guenther's special employment with the FBI came to an end, disgracefully, on March 31, 1943, when he was sacked by J. Edgar Hoover himself. Reinhardt was suspected of wiretapping—for a foreign government, no less—President Roosevelt's chief national security advisor, Adolph Berle, the assistant secretary of state. No charges were brought against him, and the incident—which would have been very embarrassing if it ever came to light—was quietly covered up.[4]

Five years later, when Guenther applied for a job with the State Department to work for Voice of America, the foreign radio network that the State Department controlled and operated, he put down his old bosses at the FBI as references. When J. Edgar Hoover learned of this, he ordered one of his men to "informally advise" the State Department that they should not hire Guenther, and to let them know of "the unsatisfactory nature of Reinhardt's services."[5]

During the seven years that he worked for the FBI, Guenther wrote thousands of pages of reports on the various organizations he'd infiltrated, all of which he suspected of being secretly controlled by the Communist Party. His own FBI file, a small part of which has now been unsealed for the first time under the Freedom of Information Act, consists of more than 40,000 pages of official FBI memoranda, notes, and documents. Stacked one page on top of the other, the file would stretch from floor to ceiling—a ceiling 12 feet high.

According to the FBI's own website, only a handful of other people in the Bureau's entire history have amassed larger FBI files: Ethel and Julius Rosenberg, the executed atomic spies (142,000 pages); Ma Barker and her Barker/Karpis Gang (76,159 pages); Nathan Gregory Silvermaster, a suspected—but never indicted— leader of a post-World War II Soviet espionage ring (50,971); and Alger Hiss and Whittaker Chambers (46,213 pages).[6]

In April 1944, Reinhardt, working part-time as a news commentator for the New York radio station WINS, published a story under his own byline in *Coronet*, a popular American magazine, that purported to give its readers his first-hand account of having covered Adolf Hitler's treason trial 20 years earlier.

In the article, Reinhardt claimed that in 1924, while still in college in Germany, he'd landed a job as a cub reporter with his hometown newspaper in Mannheim and was assigned to cover the trial of Adolf Hitler, who in November 1923 had led a small but fanatical band of National Socialists in a failed attempt to overthrow the Bavarian government in what has come to be known as the Beer Hall Putsch.

The article offered its World War II-era readers a colorful picture of a crazed Hitler, alternately brooding and shrieking at the judges from the witness stand.

Describing Hitler, Reinhardt wrote: "The wild-eyed man who sat nervously on the defendant's bench in the Munich courtroom wore a rumpled greenish jacket, baggy pants that didn't quite match and a high, soiled, ill-fitting, stiff collar with tie askew. His hair fell over his left eye and he fingered a greasy and battered felt hat which, being bilious green in hue, supplied the finishing touch to a sartorial nightmare."[7]

The Hitler treason trial was one of the most important trials of the twentieth century, for it gave Hitler a platform that launched the former assistant house painter and little-known firebrand to national prominence.

Young Reinhardt may very well have attended the trial, but it's possible that he didn't. His article contains numerous factual errors and several complete flights of fancy.

"During the trial," Reinhardt wrote, "Hitler's war record was thoroughly examined. Contrary to popular belief, he never achieved the rank of corporal during three years of service in the last war. He started out as a buck private and wound up as a first-class private."[8]

He also wrote that, contrary to popular belief, Hitler, a decorated WWI veteran, was not awarded the Iron Cross during World War

I, but actually "bestowed that decoration on himself around 1927."[9]

Both of these claims, however, are false according to Sir Ian Kershaw, the famed British scholar and author of seven books about Hitler and Nazi Germany whom BBC News has called "the world's leading expert on Adolf Hitler and the Third Reich."

"Hitler was promoted to corporal on November 3, 1914," Kershaw said in an interview for this book. "Hitler was awarded the Iron Cross Second Class on December 2, 1914, and the coveted Iron Cross First Class on August 4, 1918."[10]

Reinhardt also wrote that Hitler "was out on bail during the entire progress of the trial."[11]

This, too, was false.

"Hitler was not 'out on bail' during the trial," Kershaw said. "His sentence allowed for the time he was in custody from his arrest until the end of the trial."[12]

While it is possible that Reinhardt, writing about it for *Coronet* 20 years after the trial, may have simply misremembered Hitler being "out on bail," it is not likely that he was simply mistaken about what he wrote next in his article.

"One night during the trial," Reinhardt wrote, "I was invited to the suburban villa of Baron von Nemes, who was a friend of my family. The estate adjoining his was owned by General Erich Ludendorff [the head of the German army during World War I, and one of Hitler's co-defendants]."

Reinhardt wrote that he and a friend slipped onto the general's property that night and "peeked into the brilliantly-lighted living room. Among those present were Hitler…Ludendorff, and Rudolf Hess."[13]

This, however, was a total fabrication. Because Hitler had not been released on bail during the trial, it would have been impossible for Reinhardt to see him lounging in a neighbor's living room during the trial.

"I knew him pretty well," recalled Werner Michel, his former colleague in occupied Germany, "and became quite skeptical on where truth ended and fiction began."[14]

CHAPTER 9

The Pink Sheet

After the war, Nixon was asked by a group of Orange County businessmen, known as the Committee of 100, to run for Congress. He readily accepted their offer and went on to defeat his Democratic rival, five-term Democratic congressman Jerry Voorhis, the old-fashioned way: by calling him a Communist sympathizer.

In his first debate with Voorhis in 1946, Nixon associated Voorhis with "lip-service Americans" who fronted for "un-American elements, wittingly or otherwise…"[1]

Then, three days before the election, Nixon's headquarters put out a statement accusing Voorhis of "consistently voting with the Moscow-PAC-Henry Wallace line in Congress."[2]

"There were a good many below-the-belt blows" struck during the campaign, recalled Voorhis, who was no match for the nascent Nixon slander machine.[3]

Nixon knew that Voorhis was no Communist, and many years later, confided to a former Voorhis aide that he knew as much all along. But that didn't matter. "The important thing is to win," Nixon told the aide.[4]

Nixon easily won reelection in 1948, and won his first Senate seat in 1950 by running an ugly smear campaign against his hapless Democratic opponent, Congresswoman Helen Gahagan Douglas.

Tall, blond, and beautiful, Helen Gahagan had been a well-known star on Broadway in the 1920s and married Melvyn Douglas, the leading man in one of her plays, in 1931. After their wedding, they drove across the country from New York to Los

Angeles. Those were hard times—the depth of the Great Depression—and as they traveled west, they witnessed the endless caravan of beaten-down old cars piled high with the worldly belongings of the Dust Bowl refugees who were heading in the same direction. It was a startling sight for this daughter of wealth, and it inspired her take a new career path—a life in politics dedicated to helping the poor and downtrodden.

A personal friend of First Lady Eleanor Roosevelt, Gahagan Douglas was a staunch supporter of President Franklin Roosevelt, whom Helen called "the greatest man in the world." In 1944, she became the Democratic National Committeewoman from California, and was elected to Congress that same year, representing California's liberal Fourteenth District, just south of San Francisco. She won reelection in 1946 and '48, and had a famous affair with a congressional colleague, Lyndon Johnson, who in 1960 would be Jack Kennedy's vice presidential running mate.

During the late 1940s, Johnson and Gahagan Douglas attended Washington parties as a couple and often arrived at work at the House Office Building in the same car, from which they emerged walking hand-in-hand.[5]

"Helen Douglas' affair with Lyndon Johnson started just after she got to Washington," said the sister of one of Johnson's earlier mistresses.[6]

"Lyndon would park his car in front of [her] house night after night after night," said a longtime Texas friend of Johnson's. "It was an open scandal in Washington."[7]

In 1950, she decided to run for the U.S. Senate—a seat already held by Democrat Sheridan Downey, who was seeking a third term. Party elders had urged her to wait to run for the Senate in 1952, when a seat held by a Republican would be up for grabs, but Gahagan Douglas didn't want to wait two years. Downey, she said, had neglected veterans and small farmers, and had to be unseated now.

Gahagan Douglas, who had become one of the most sought-after speakers at Democratic gatherings, was well ahead of Downey in the polls when he abruptly withdrew from the primary race and threw his support to a third candidate, Elias Manchester Boddy, the owner and publisher of the *Los Angeles Daily News*. And when Gahagan Douglas defeated him for the nomination, Downey, angry at her for trying to unseat him, did the unthinkable: he publicly endorsed her Republican challenger, Richard Nixon.

During the general election, Nixon outmaneuvered her at every turn. It was the height of the Red Scare and America was at war in Korea, and just the suggestion that someone was "soft on Communism" was enough to destroy a person's reputation. And that's what Nixon did to Gahagan Douglas.

He accused her of being soft on Communism, and his campaign put out a "pink sheet" that strongly implied that she was a Communist sympathizer. In his last radio address before the election, Nixon even went so far as to falsely accuse her of "flatly refusing to tell you which side she is on" in the Korean War.

Her ties to Hollywood didn't help, either. It was the time of the Blacklist, and for many voters, the patriotism of everyone associated with the movie industry was suspect.

Gahagan Douglas fought back, tagging Nixon with the hated nickname that would stick with him for the rest of his life: "Tricky Dick." But she was no match for Nixon, who had far more money to spend on his campaign than she did, including the $1,000 contribution from Jack Kennedy's father.

In his 1978 memoirs, Nixon recounted the surprise visit Jack Kennedy made to his office at the House Office Building that afternoon in the summer of 1950.

"My personal secretary came in and said, 'Congressman Kennedy is here and would like to talk to you,'" Nixon recalled. "Jack Kennedy was ushered in and I motioned him into a chair. He took an envelope from his breast pocket and handed it to me. 'Dick, I know you're in a pretty rough campaign,' he said, 'and my father wanted to help out.'"

The two men talked for a while about Nixon's campaign against Gahagan Douglas, and as Jack rose to leave, he told Nixon, "I obviously can't endorse you, but it isn't going to break my heart if you can turn the Senate's loss into Hollywood's gain."[8]

"After he left," Nixon wrote, "I opened the envelope and found it contained a $1,000 contribution."

An aide later recalled that Nixon was "completely flabbergasted."[9]

In the end, Nixon easily defeated Gahagan Douglas, receiving 59 percent of the vote to her 41 percent, giving him a seat in the U.S. Senate and national stature.

Two years later, Sheridan Downey, the man Nixon had replaced in the Senate and the same man Gahagan Douglas had defeated in the Democratic primary, gave Nixon a little book that would change his life. The book was called *The Will to Live*, written by a doctor whom Nixon would later seek out for help.

CHAPTER 10

The 1956 Democratic National Convention

John F. Kennedy lost the only political race of his life in 1956 when he was narrowly defeated in his bid to become Adlai Stevenson's vice presidential running mate. It was a major setback for him, but politically, it proved to be an astonishing stroke of good luck.

Stevenson, the popular and progressive former governor of Illinois, was something of a tragic figure. As a 12-year-old boy from a wealthy family in Bloomington, he accidentally shot and killed a 16-year-old friend while demonstrating drill techniques with a rifle that he didn't know was loaded. Devastated by the accident, he dedicated his life to public service and "living for two."

Stevenson had already lost one presidential election to Eisenhower back in 1952, when Nixon called him a "traitor," and was fated to lose the 1956 race as well. But he was very popular with the party's liberal base and knew, perhaps better than anyone else in America, just what kind of man Richard Nixon really was. He'd openly opposed Nixon's persecution of Alger Hiss, appearing as a character witness for Hiss at his trial in 1949. And after President Eisenhower suffered a major heart attack in 1955, putting Vice President Nixon one weak heartbeat away from the presidency, Stevenson said, "I recoil at the prospect of Richard Nixon as a guardian of this nation's future."

The 1956 Democratic National Convention got off to an ominous start that sweaty August in Chicago when one of the convention guests keeled over and died of a heart attack after taking part in a rally in support of the candidacy of New York governor Averell Harriman.[1] That same day, a reporter covering the convention for the International News Service had to be rushed from the convention floor to a nearby hospital to undergo emergency abdominal surgery.[2]

That night, August 16, 1956, Jack Kennedy made a rousing and eloquent speech to the convention delegates, placing Stevenson's name into nomination for president—a high honor for the young senator from Massachusetts. That same night, Stevenson was nominated by acclamation.

The next day, as the delegates arrived at the International Amphitheater on Chicago's South Side, they were greeted by the strains of the convention's theme song, "The Yellow Rose of Texas," and by the fragrant aroma of thousands of yellow roses that had been shipped by air to Chicago by a pair of Texas Democrats.[3]

It must have been a welcome relief from the stench of tens of thousands of hogs awaiting slaughter at the sprawling and stinking Union Stock Yard, located just across the street from the convention hall. As poet Carl Sandberg once noted, Chicago still was the "hog butcher for the world."

With Stevenson chosen as their standard-bearer, the delegates now had the unusual task of selecting his running mate. Unlike today, when presidential candidates choose their own running mates, Stevenson had decided to let the convention delegates select the vice presidential candidate without telling them who, if anyone, he preferred. It was an unusual, almost unprecedented, move even in those days of smoke-filled rooms and old-school politics. It was now going to be an open convention.

Estes Kefauver, the senator from Tennessee who had battled Stevenson to a second-place finish in the primaries, had withdrawn from the presidential contest just days before the convention began and was now widely considered the front-runner for the number-two job on the ticket. But Jack Kennedy's youth, vigor, and status as a bona fide war hero made him a strong contender, as well.

And Jack had made quite a splash at the convention. Stevenson had personally picked him to deliver his nominating speech, and Jack had narrated the documentary film about the history of the Democratic Party that was shown during the opening night of the convention. And when Stevenson won the nomination, Jack, the chairman of his state's convention delegation, delivered four-fifths of its votes for Stevenson on the first ballot. Even the *Chicago Sun-Times*, which was widely read on the convention floor, gave its endorsement to Kennedy as Stevenson's running mate.

But there were problems. Jack was Catholic, and no Catholic had ever been elected vice president of the United States—or president, for that matter. Anti-Catholic sentiment was strong in those days, particularly in the South and in the Midwestern farm states. Then, shortly after the start of the convention, rumors began circulating that Jack had contributed money to Richard Nixon's Senate campaign six years earlier. And it was true—at least partly. Jack's father had, after all, made a $1,000 cash contribution to Nixon, and Jack had personally delivered it.

As the rumor began spreading around the convention floor, it threatened to sink Jack's chance of being picked as Stevenson's running mate. For if Kennedy won the VP slot on the Democratic ticket and the story surfaced again later in the general election that Jack had once delivered a $1,000 campaign contribution to Richard Nixon, who would be Jack's vice presidential opponent, it could prove to be an embarrassing and potentially fatal blow to the Stevenson campaign.

This was just the kind of rumor that could sink Jack's candidacy, and there was only one person outside the immediate Kennedy family who knew about it and stood to gain from it—Richard Nixon, who apparently didn't want to face Jack in a vice presidential showdown in 1956. With an eye on the 1960 presidential race four years away, Nixon most likely didn't want to see Jack catapulted onto the national stage, which could make him a viable challenger for the presidency.

Jack would have to do something quick if he had any hope of

suppressing the rumor and staying in the running for a spot on Stevenson's ticket. So he sent his loyal aide, Theodore Sorensen, to tell Stevenson's people that it wasn't Jack who'd made the contribution to Nixon, but Jack's father, Joe. This was more or less the truth, even though Jack had personally hand-delivered it to Nixon himself, a detail Sorensen didn't mention to the Stevenson people.

"Sorensen hurriedly explained that it was the father, not the son, who *may* have contributed," MacGregor Burns wrote in his book about Jack Kennedy.[4]

Sorensen also wrote about the incident in his book, *Kennedy*.

"I encountered and refuted rumors...about a financial contribution he had supposedly made to Nixon..." Sorensen wrote.[5]

All the while, Jack kept campaigning, buttonholing delegates and gathering support for his vice presidential bid. And by the last day of the convention, when the delegates were set to choose a vice presidential candidate, Kennedy was picking up steam in what would become the most dramatic finish of any political convention of the twentieth century.

Tennessee senator Kefauver was Kennedy's main rival, and right off, Jack showed his characteristic class by placing Kefauver's name into nomination for the job Jack coveted. After the first ballot, Jack was ahead with 648 delegate votes, falling just 38 ½ votes short of the total needed to win.

As the second round of voting began, conventioneers marched around, waving their banners and signs in support of their candidates. But then, Senator Albert Gore of Tennessee, who'd finished third in the first round of balloting (and whose son would one day become vice president), withdrew his candidacy in favor of his fellow Tennessean and released his delegates to Kefauver. This started a stampede of delegates to Kefauver, and a few minutes later, Kefauver emerged the victor on the second ballot, with 755 ½ delegate votes to Kennedy's 589.[6] As the *New York Times* reported the next day, Jack had missed winning the nomination "by an eyelash."

Amid the pandemonium, Jack pushed his way to the rostrum and graciously moved that Kefauver be nominated by acclamation.

The crowd went wild, and as they shouted their approval, Jack left the stage as the band swung into the melodic tune of "The Tennessee Waltz."

In such a close race, in which every vote counted, Nixon's dirty trick might just have been the factor that lost Jack the race. But as it turned out, it was the best thing that could have happened to Jack's political career. For, a few months later, Stevenson and Kefauver went on to be soundly defeated by Eisenhower and Nixon in the general election. With Kennedy on his ticket, Stevenson might have picked up Massachusetts and Rhode Island, but they would have surely lost all the same. And Jack's drive for the presidency four years later might have been derailed before it even left the station. For in hindsight, Jack realized that it would have been very unlikely for the Democratic Party to turn to the number-two man on the ticket that had lost to Eisenhower and Nixon in 1956 to be its standard-bearer in the 1960 presidential race against Nixon.

A year after the 1956 convention, Jack expressed this understanding to his mother, Rose, telling her that if his older brother Joe hadn't been killed in the war, he would have also entered politics, but being the "golden boy" that he was, Joe would have traveled the same path but with different results.

"Joe was the star of our family," Jack told his mother. "He did everything better than the rest of us. If he had lived, he would have gone into politics, and he would have been elected to the House and to the Senate, as I was. And, like me, he would have gone for the vice-presidential nomination at the 1956 convention, but unlike me, he wouldn't have been beaten: Joe would have won the nomination. And then he and Stevenson would have been beaten by Eisenhower, and today Joe's political career would have been in shambles."[7]

Perhaps Kennedy owed Nixon's bag of tricks a debt of gratitude.

CHAPTER 11

The Arrest of Dr. Hutschnecker

The long and winding path that brought Richard Nixon—and later, Guenther Reinhardt—to Arnold Hutschnecker's door began on a bitterly cold morning in New York City on December 23, 1943. It was two days before Christmas, and Dr. Hutschnecker and his wife Florita were sipping tea and reading the *New York Times*. The newspaper said that Berlin, where they had lived for so many years, was in flames from raids carried out by British and American bombers. In Poland, SS storm troopers were wiping out the last holdouts in the Warsaw Ghetto.

Jews were being rounded up and killed all over Europe, and Arnold and Florita didn't know what had become of her parents and their many relatives who'd stayed behind in Germany. Most of them, they presumed, were already dead.

If there was any good news, it was that Florita had been granted American citizenship the month before. But for some reason, the doctor's application was being held up.

When the doorbell rang, Dr. Hutschnecker looked at his watch. It was early; his first patient wasn't due for another hour. Florita went to the door, but it wasn't a patient. It was the police—U.S. federal marshals.

Despite the war, Dr. Hutschnecker's Park Avenue medical practice had been thriving, but it all came crashing down on that cold Thursday morning in December. It would be one of the darkest days of Arnold Hutschnecker's life, which is saying a lot for a man who'd barely survived a Russian firing squad.

Dr. Hutschnecker, an ardent pacifist, had narrowly survived the First World War and had escaped the Holocaust and the ravages of World War II, but he could not escape the wreckage of war entirely. The police were there to arrest him for conspiring to help one of his rich, young patients, Gert Hans von Gontard, evade the draft. The next day, Dr. Hutschnecker's name would appear on the front page of the *New York Times* as that of an accused criminal.[1]

Gert von Gontard, handsome and regal with a receding hairline and a permanently arched left eyebrow, had been a patient of Dr. Hutschnecker's since suffering a mental breakdown in 1939.

Born in Germany in 1906 to one of the world's richest families, Gert's American mother was Clara Busch von Gontard, the daughter of Adolphus Busch, co-founder of the Anheuser-Busch brewing empire. Gert's father was Baron Paul von Gontard, a German aristocrat who had at one time been president of the Daimler Mercedes-Benz Corporation.

Gert's father wasn't just a nobleman and businessman. He was also a major arms manufacturer, and as general director of Berlin-Karlsruhe Industriewerke, one of Germany's biggest manufactures of machine guns, he'd helped arm Germany during WWI, then helped re-arm the country after WWI in violation of the Treaty of Versailles.

But young Gert von Gontard was more interested in the arts than in his father's weapons business. In 1930, at the age of 23, he founded and edited an important literary and political magazine in Berlin called *Neue Revue*. Over the next three years, *Neue Revue* would publish many critical articles about the Nazi Party, which was rapidly rising to power in Germany. And when Hitler was named chancellor of Germany on January 30, 1933, young Gert found himself on Hitler's "death list."

Shortly after Hitler came to power, Gert fled to America to join his mother and brother in St. Louis, barely escaping death at the hands of the Nazis.

"I got out by the skin of my teeth," he later recalled.[2]

But a backwater town like St. Louis was no place for an artistic and intellectual young man like Gert von Gontard, who by 1936 had made his way to Hollywood, where he produced several plays by the great German writer Johann Wolfgang von Goethe.

"Gert was a genius," recalled his nephew, Adalbert von Gontard Jr. "Just a brilliant, wonderful man."[3]

By November 1939, Gert, now a U.S. citizen, had moved to New York, where he became a member of the community of expatriate German artists and literary figures. After suffering a nervous breakdown, he began paying regular visits to Dr. Arnold Hutschnecker.

Dismissed by the *New York Times* as a "playboy" and "an active member of café society," Gert fancied himself a writer. In 1940 he published a 324-page book called *In Defense of Love*, a rambling, angry, and amusing rant against psychoanalysis, which he called "psychic cannibalism" and a pseudo-science practiced by "tormentors of the tormented." Psychoanalysts, he scoffed, were nothing more than "pediatricians for adults."[4]

But Gert loved Dr. Hutschnecker, who had helped him so much after his breakdown, and Hutschnecker loved him too.

"I love you, you miserable stinker," Hutschnecker once wrote in a letter to Gert.

Both men shared a low opinion of American culture. "Thank you for restoring my suppressed state of consciousness produced by the emigration atmosphere, daily worries and the provincial— rather little bourgeois—American milieu," Hutschnecker said in a letter to Gert.[5]

In the summer of 1940, with war raging in Europe and Asia, Dr. Hutschnecker enlisted with the Committee on Preparedness, a volunteer group set up to provide medical services in the event of a sneak attack on New York City. As much as he hated war, when Pearl Harbor was attacked, Dr. Hutschnecker tried to enlist with the Surgeon General's Office to serve in the war effort as a military medical officer. His application was rejected, however, because as a German immigrant who was not yet a U.S. citizen, the Naturalization Service still had him listed as an "alien enemy."

"I appealed to the Surgeon General, as well as to the Naturalization Service," Hutschnecker later wrote, "and after long and arduous efforts to serve in the war I was frustrated because I could not become a citizen in time to do so."[6]

In the days and years leading up to America's entry into the war, every able-bodied male between ages 18 and 36 was required to register for the draft. Over the next five years, more than ten million men would be drafted, and another six million would voluntarily enlist.

Gert von Gontard didn't want to be inducted into the military, and he certainly wasn't going to enlist. His longtime secretary noted in her diary that Gert told her "he would never join the army—the army would never see him—he would not be good for the army—the army is for common, ordinary people."[7]

In 1940 and 1941, dodging the draft would become a full-time job for Gert. He had a lot of important and well-placed friends who helped him do it, including John E. Wilson, the chief clerk of his local draft board in Manhattan.

Gert wasn't averse to spending a little money to grease the way. His secretary's diary showed that she'd attended several lavish parties thrown by her boss at fashionable New York restaurants, where Gert had wined and dined members of his draft board.[8]

In April 1940, Gert got a fraudulent deferment from his draft board by claiming that he was involved in "essential war work." But when authorities started looking into his claim, he came up with another scheme—he'd try to get a legitimate deferment by finagling a job with the Federal Bureau of Investigation. But there was a problem: he had a medical condition, a chronic inflammation of the gall bladder which, if disclosed to the FBI, would make him ineligible for employment there, even though it wasn't serious enough to keep him from being drafted. Not surprisingly, the FBI was a lot choosier than the army about who they let in.

So on June 27, 1942, Gert called Dr. Hutschnecker at his Park Avenue apartment and told him that he had to see him right away, and that he had some papers he wanted the doctor to sign.

"I have a medical examination form that I want you to fill out," he told the doctor over the phone, saying that he needed Dr. Hutschnecker to write him up a clean bill of health so he could go to work for the FBI. It was a Sunday, but Dr. Hutschnecker couldn't say no to Gert, whom he considered a friend.

Several years later, Dr. Hutschnecker recalled receiving Gert's urgent call.

"I remember distinctly it was a Sunday when Mr. von Gontard called me and he told me it was rather urgent, he wanted to see me," Dr. Hutschnecker told the New York State Medical Board during a hearing to consider the revocation of his medical license for having helped Gert evade the draft. "He came down that afternoon and showed me this form and he told me that he had a possibility to get into the FBI and that he had to attach a statement of his physical condition."

Dr. Hutschnecker performed a routine examination, taking Gert's blood pressure, weighing him, and checking his mouth, lungs, and kidney function. He wrote the results on Gert's FBI application form.

"After I was through with the examination," Dr. Hutschnecker recalled, "I sat down to check off various questions, and when we came to question number five, which reads 'gastro-intestinal,' I told him that I had to answer 'gall bladder history,' and he begged me not to and a discussion developed."[9]

"If you begin marking down all my previous ailments," Gert pleaded with the doctor, "that thing will be thrown out before it will ever get where I want to have it and this is some kind of work which appeals to me, which my heart would be in and which I would really like to do."[10]

Hutschnecker, however, balked at falsifying the civil service form.

"I did not want to do it," Hutschnecker later said.

But von Gontard persisted.

"Weren't you the one who always told me when I have regular

work and do some work which I would like to do that would improve my state of health?" Gert argued. "And weren't you always after me to do something for the war effort?"

"Yes," Hutschnecker replied sheepishly.

"Now here is my chance and now you want to spoil it for me," von Gontard whined. "I have done all the things that you wanted me to do—I quit drinking completely."[11]

Yes, the doctor thought, Gert had quit drinking, and he'd cut down on his smoking too, and his gall bladder was much improved. He spoke German and English fluently, and might be of some help to the government. Maybe working for the FBI was just what he and the FBI needed.

"I thought that he had all the gifts and abilities for such a job, so I really did not consider anything wrong," Dr. Hutschnecker later recalled. "I thought that it would interfere with him if I would not permit him, if I would be the one standing in his way to get this job; and then I signed it…He stayed with me for about two hours discussing and arguing and I only learned later the importance and significance of it. I know I shouldn't have done it and at that moment did not see any harm to anyone."[12]

Dr. Hutschnecker signed the papers, but it was all for naught. Gert didn't get into the FBI anyway. So six months later, on December 30, 1942, Gert talked Dr. Hutschnecker into writing a letter to his draft board advising them that Gert had been under his professional care for a chronic inflammation of the gall bladder since 1939.

A year later, on December 22, 1943, Dr. Hutschnecker was arrested, along with Gert and several others who had helped Gert dodge the draft, including the the chief clerk of the local draft board. They were all indicted on January 10, 1944—von Gontard on federal charges of having evaded induction under the Selective Service Act, and Dr. Hutschnecker and the others for aiding and abetting him. If convicted, they each faced up to five years in prison and fines of $10,000 each. But for Dr. Hutschnecker, there were two additional penalties looming: if convicted, he would lose his medical license, and he would never be able to become a U.S. citizen.

Things turned out even worse, however, for 58-year-old John E. Wilson, the disgraced chief clerk of the local draft board who'd been wined and dined by Gert in one of his earlier schemes to dodge the draft. Suspended from his job after his arrest, Wilson came back to his office unannounced a week after his indictment and leapt to his death from his high-rise window.[13]

Gert and Dr. Hutschnecker would both stand trial. For Dr. Hutschnecker, it would prove a harrowing and humiliating ordeal that would nearly ruin his career.

CHAPTER 12

Nixon's Mother

Richard Nixon strode from the steaming bathroom, singing. Barefoot, dressed only in a bathrobe, his black hair still wet from the shower, he stopped, looked at his old friend and psychotherapist, and smiled.

It was 1959. Nixon was vice president of the United States, and in a few months he would announce his candidacy for the presidency. High above Manhattan in his suite at the Waldorf Astoria, Richard Nixon was on top of the world.

Standing there in his bathrobe, smiling broadly, Nixon had never appeared happier to Dr. Hutschnecker, who had been summoned to the Waldorf for a "working breakfast"—their code word for "treatment."

When Nixon called, Hutschnecker said later, "He'd never say, 'I have a problem.' He'd say, 'Could we have breakfast?' And I'd go. He needed me. It was what we call a transference—a trust. He came to me when he had decisions to make. Or when something was pending, and it troubled him."[1]

As Nixon stood there in his bathrobe and bare feet, Dr. Hutschnecker was reminded that Nixon, too, had once been a shy, studious little boy who yearned for love and acceptance.[2]

Richard Nixon was born in the tiny town of Yorba Linda during the Freeze of 1913, an unusually severe cold spell that killed most of the avocado and citrus trees in Southern California.

The roads in Yorba Linda wouldn't be paved until three years after Nixon was born, and during the rainy season, the dirt roads became bogs of mud. Horse-drawn wagons often got stuck in mud so deep that the horses would have to be unhitched and the wagons abandoned until the roads dried out, then dug out with picks and shovels.

Yorba Linda was a town of 700 Quaker families, with a population of 2,500. The original property deeds, granted more than a decade before Prohibition, contained a clause that prevented the sale of alcohol in liquor stores or saloons. The town's social life—hikes, snow trips, beach parties, and the like—all revolved around the Religious Society of Friends, whose members are known to the public as Quakers, and among themselves as Friends.

The second-oldest of five sons, Richard Nixon said he was born at home in a lovely little clapboard house built by his father.

"I was born in a house my father built," are the first words in his memoirs.[3]

But even that is a lie.

In 1959, the City of Yorba Linda designated the house built by Nixon's father a historical landmark. Hundreds of townspeople came to the ceremony, which included the unveiling of a bronze plaque on a big stone slab placed near the front porch. The plaque read: "The birthplace of Richard Milhouse Nixon, who, through devotion to his country, rose to become Vice President of the United States, 1952–1960."

But Nixon's mother, Hannah, set the record straight. Speaking to the crowd that came to pay tribute to her son that day in 1959, Hannah said: "He was born in a hospital, but we lived here until Richard was seven."[4]

Nixon's father had built the house on a knoll under a pepper tree, right next to a ditch that irrigated most of the orange and lemon groves in the area. The ditch even had a name. It was called the Anaheim Union Ditch.

Like nearly everyone else in Yorba Linda, Nixon's mother was a devout Quaker who wanted him to grow up to be a preacher.

"I would have been a good one," he later laughed.[5]

Plain and matronly even when she was young, Hannah instructed her boys in the Quaker ways of non-violence. When the world was torn by war a year after Richard was born, she prayed for peace every night and every day. Her teachings were so strong that many years later, and without any sense of irony, Richard Nixon would come to see himself as "the Peace President."

Richard was just a little boy when he was nearly killed while riding with his mother and brother Donald in a horse-drawn wagon on the rutty road that ran beside the Anaheim Union Ditch.

"Dick was standing up in the buckboard," recalled William Barton, one of Nixon's childhood friends, "and one day when she was coming in from town, the horse kind of shied, made a quick move, and jerked the buggy so that Dick lost his balance and fell out. The wheel ran over him and it practically scalped his head. They had to take him to the hospital in Anaheim to get it sewed up."[6]

His father, Frank Nixon, was a lemon farmer with a sour disposition when Richard was born, but his nine-acre grove eventually failed, mainly because it was on the wrong side of the ditch where the land was poor.

"It didn't happen to be very good soil," a neighbor recalled.

Frank uprooted his family in 1922 and moved a few miles down the road to Whittier. There, he opened a gas station, grocery store, and, later, a little diner. Hannah made pies and sold them in the store.

Friends of the Nixons recall Frank as a strict, argumentative, and fast-talking hothead, but "a good Christian" nonetheless, though not as devout as Hannah.

"Frank Nixon, was just as strict as he could be," recalled Gerald Shaw, a Nixon family friend. "Oh, man, he was strict!"[7]

Not surprisingly, young Richard—bookish and shy—took after his mother, who was the calm force that held the family together.

"She was really a strong hand," recalled William Barton. "She was very capable, and not excitable in any way; a very even-handed and even-tempered person. She was the kind who would balance the wheel of the whole family. She was really the one that kept the family close together."[8]

"She was one of the finest persons I have ever known," said Charles Ball, Hannah's pastor in Whittier. "The Bible meant much to her, and she sought to live by its principles and precepts. She was one of the finest Christian ladies that you could have known. She was just the kind of person who lived the Christianity she professed."[9]

Her faith would be a great comfort to her when two of her sons died young.

When Richard was twelve, his brother, Arthur, died of tuberculosis at the age of seven. Two years later, his oldest brother, Harold—the light of the Nixon family—contracted the dreaded disease. When Harold's condition worsened in the spring of 1928, Hannah took him to Prescott, Arizona, where the weather would be better for his health. To support herself and her sick son, she took in four other boys who had been stricken by tuberculosis, all of whom would die in her care.

Richard, who was 15 when his mother and brother left for Arizona, stayed behind in Whittier with his father and brother, Donald. In the summer, he would visit his mother and oldest brother in Prescott, where he landed a job as a barker for a Wheel of Fortune at the Frontier Days Rodeo.[10]

Harold died in his mother's arms at the age of twenty-three on March 7, 1933. It was Hannah's forty-eighth birthday.

"When Harold died," Nixon later said, "it was sort of the end of everything. And I remember from that time on, March 7, which we'd always remember her birthday, she would never let us celebrate it. That time on, she always went out to the Rose Hill Cemetery, and she put flowers on the graves."[11]

"Nobody will ever write a book, probably, about my mother," Nixon said in his farewell address at the White House on the last day of his presidency. "Well, I guess all of you would say this about your mother—my mother was a saint. And I think of her—two boys dying of tuberculosis, nursing four others in order that she could take care of my older brother for three years in Arizona, and seeing each of them die, and when they died, it was like one of her own. Yes, she will have no books written about her. But she was a saint."[12]

Hannah Nixon lived to see Nixon elected to Congress, to the U.S. Senate, and then vice president of the United States. But throughout her life, she never said the words he wanted most to hear—"I love you"—words she considered sacred.[13]

Emotionally deprived as a child, Nixon grew into a man who regarded love and affection with aversion.[14]

Devoted to his pacifist mother, but quick to anger like his volatile father, Nixon, for much of his life, managed to keep the darker aspects of his personality under control and out of view. But Dr. Hutschnecker believed that when Hannah died in 1967, the year before her oldest surviving son would be elected president of the United States, the dark half of Nixon's character took over.[15]

CHAPTER 13

Occupied Germany

After the war, Reinhardt left his wife, Helen, in Greenwich Village again and headed back to Germany. It is not known who took care of her in his absence. By that time, they had been married seven years, and she had become an invalid who was hopelessly insane.

"She is bed-ridden and completely paralyzed, and at times incoherent," he wrote, describing her illness as "sleeping sickness"—a crippling form of encephalitis that swept the world in the 1920s.[1]

Reinhardt worked for a few months in 1946 as a foreign correspondent for the International News Service, then landed a job as a civilian reports officer in the Public Safety Branch of the U.S. military government in Frankfurt.

"It was during this period that Reinhardt was involved in hunting down six Hungarian SS guards responsible for murdering downed American airmen and securing the evidence for their conviction," wrote Ian Sayer and Douglas Botting in *Nazi Gold*.[2]

At first, Reinhardt got glowing reports for his work in occupied Germany. According to a confidential report on Reinhardt compiled by the office of the army's inspector general, "Mr. Reinhardt was employed in the command on 7 September 1946, primarily to serve as press representative for the Deputy G-2 USFET [U.S. Forces, European Theater]. He appeared at that time to be unusually intelligent and energetic, at first displaying a great capacity for work, a prodigious memory, and a marked ability to gather information."[3]

Reinhardt, however, soon began behaving erratically and making unauthorized contacts with officials of the State Department and the military government, to whom he misstated his position and the scope of his authority. Before long, he was fired.

"It was necessary to relieve him of his assignments on 4 May 1947," the army inspector general's report stated, "because of a displayed lack of tact and common sense, plus a peculiar persistence in breaches of security involving discussions of classified military matters with unauthorized persons."

The very next day, however, he was hired to work for the Counterintelligence Corps "because of his linguistic ability, education, FBI experience, and knowledge of Germany."[4]

His new boss was Colonel Dale Garvey, commander of the 970th Counterintelligence Corps Detachment, Region IV, which oversaw all intelligence work in southern Germany, from Munich all the way down to the Austrian border.

Colonel Garvey liked Reinhardt's work in Frankfurt so much that when he moved his headquarters down to Lake Starnberg in southern Bavaria, he took Reinhardt with him.

In those wild days, Germany had become the front line in a new war—the Cold War between the United States and Stalin's Soviet Union. Communist spies were trying to find out what the Americans were up to, and there were literally thousands of high-ranking former Nazis on the loose. Southern Germany was a particular hotbed of espionage and counterintelligence.

Reinhardt made a good impression when Colonel Garvey introduced him to the CIC men already stationed at Lake Starnberg, whose mission was to keep track of counter-subversive elements in the area.

"Mr. Reinhardt is a superb analyst," Colonel Garvey told his men. "He knows a lot about the Nazis and the Communists."[5]

"We were all impressed with him at first," recalled Werner Michel, a young lieutenant in the Counterintelligence Corps who would go on to serve as inspector general for intelligence for the secretary of defense.[6]

The other men liked Reinhardt too—at least, they did at first.

They even gave him a nickname, "Bucky." But over the next few months, stationed at the alpine lake where many years earlier the King of Bavaria had gone mad and killed himself, Guenther Reinhardt's strange life began to spiral out of control.

CHAPTER 14

JFK and "The New Nixon"

In August, at the height of the 1960 presidential campaign, a newspaper cartoon portrayed the two rivals peeking warily at each other from behind their half-opened office doors on the third floor of the Senate Office Building. An accompanying story said, "Currently, they are on a 'Hi, Dick,' and 'How are you, Jack?' basis."[1]

Kennedy sent the cartoon to Nixon and asked him to autograph it, which Nixon did and returned it to Jack with an uncharacteristically funny note: "To my friend & neighbor Jack Kennedy, with best wishes for almost everything!"[2]

Through the years they remained on friendly terms, and during the 1960 campaign, though they were rivals, maintained a cordial relationship and gracious correspondence.

When Nixon was hospitalized for two weeks during the '60 campaign with a badly infected left knee, Jack sent him a friendly "get well" telegram.

"I am extremely sorry to hear of the necessity of your being hospitalized for treatment of your knee," Jack telegrammed Nixon at the Walter Reed Army Hospital in Washington, D.C. "I hope your stay in the hospital will be of short duration and that you will make a speedy and effective recovery. I look forward to seeing you on the campaign trail. With every good wish I am sincerely, John F. Kennedy."[3]

After receiving Jack's telegram, Nixon wrote back: "It was

thoughtful of you to wire me as you did. I hope you have no similar accident. Much against my will, I am trying to do what the doctor orders. I hope to be back on the campaign trail before too long. Sincerely, Dick Nixon."[4]

Nixon had won election to the House in '46, the Senate in '50, and the vice presidency in '52 by personally hurling wild, unsubstantiated and slanderous allegations at his political opponents. He had become a master of the smear, the false accusation, the underhanded jab, and the dirty trick, calling every one of his opponents a crook or a Communist dupe. And the 1950s were a perfect time for that. It was the decade of the witch-hunt, the blacklist, and guilt by association. It was the McCarthy Era.

But 1960 was the dawning of a new decade. The mood in the country was changing and Dick Nixon knew he'd have to change with it. So in 1960, he would try something different: instead of directly accusing Jack Kennedy of being a crook or a Communist, as he would have done in the old days, Nixon came up with the idea of having somebody else—one of his surrogates—do it for him, which would allow Nixon to rise above the fray and say it wasn't true. That way, the smear would still be out there in the minds of the voting public, but Nixon could pretend he had nothing to do with it, that he was the "good guy"—the "new Nixon."

That's what happened in March of 1960, the day before the New Hampshire primary. Nixon had one of his surrogates, New Hampshire governor Wesley Powell, the chairman of Nixon's New Hampshire campaign committee, put out a statement to the Associated Press and United Press International accusing Jack Kennedy of being "soft on Communism."

Senator Kennedy, Powell told reporters, had "straddled the Communist issue" and had a "soft, straddling record in his approach to the Communist menace."[5]

It was, of course, untrue. Jack Kennedy was a "cold warrior" of the old school who had taken just as hard a line on the Soviet Union as any other mainstream American politician, Democrat or Republican.

But the lie was out there, printed in newspapers all across the country. And now Nixon put on his white hat and came riding to Kennedy's defense, looking like he'd had nothing to do with putting Governor Powell up to it.

That same day, Nixon had his press secretary, Herb Klein, put out a statement vouching for Kennedy's patriotism. "The vice president has known and worked with Senator Kennedy since they served together on the House Labor Committee in 1947," the statement said. "While they have differed on some issues, they have always been in complete agreement in their unalterable opposition to Communism at home and abroad."[6]

It was vintage Dick Nixon, and a nice twist on his old politics of accusation. And Nixon didn't even have the class to defend Jack in person. He let his spokesman do it.

But Jack wasn't fooled, and over the course of the campaign, he lashed out repeatedly at Nixon. And as Election Day drew nearer, his barbs became more pointed.

In April, Kennedy gave a campaign speech in Indiana accusing Nixon of having been "carefully pre-selected by his party's entrenched interests, pre-digested for the American people's consumption, and pre-packaged for sale to the American voter."[7]

In June, he told a crowd in Boston that Americans should not show "the face of Richard Nixon to the world as the face of the United States."[8]

In August, speaking at a Democratic rally in Alexandria, Virginia, he mocked Nixon's foreign policy experience, saying that "Mr. Nixon is experienced in policies of weakness, retreat, and defeat."[9]

In October, Kennedy ridiculed the very notion of a "new Nixon."

"Mr. Nixon's record of public actions is so changeable and contradictory that his political philosophy defies definition," Kennedy said. "With all this talk about an old Nixon and a new Nixon, it should be remembered that there was no old Lincoln or a new Lincoln, no old Wilson or new Wilson, no old FDR or new FDR. I cannot believe that the American people in these difficult times will choose a man with this fuzzy image of his own political philosophy."[10]

The day before the election at Boston Garden, Kennedy compared Nixon to a trained circus animal.

"I run against a candidate," he told a wildly cheering crowd, "who reminds me of the symbol of his party: the circus elephant, with his head full of ivory, a long memory and no vision, and you have seen elephants being led around the circus ring. They grab the tail of the elephant in front of them."[11]

Nixon fought back, but his attacks, less personal and more political, lacked Jack's poetic touch. Accepting his party's nomination in July, Nixon accused Kennedy of being "rash and impulsive" for suggesting that the U.S. should have "apologized" for flying U-2 spy plane missions over the Soviet Union.[12] In October, he called Kennedy's assertion that the U.S. should encourage an anti-Castro uprising in Cuba "dangerously irresponsible,"[13] and belittled Jack's ideas about dealing with Red China as "wooly thinking."[14]

During a swing through Texas in the last days of the campaign, Nixon predicted that the Democrats would try to steal the state's electoral votes, but vowed to win the election anyway. The Democrats, he said, could "vote every tombstone in Texas, but we are still going to lick 'em." And at a campaign stop in Fort Worth, he accused Kennedy of changing his views so often that it was hard to tell which side of an issue he was on. "I say we can't have a 'jumping Jack' as president of the United States," Nixon told the roaring crowd.[15]

But behind the scenes, their tactics were even nastier than their words, as both sides waged a secret war to destroy the other.

CHAPTER 15

Addison's Disease

L ooking fit and healthy, Jack Kennedy announced his candidacy for the presidency on January 2, 1960. It was the first momentous event of the sixties.

"In the past 40 months, I have toured every state in the Union and I have talked to Democrats in all walks of life," he told reporters assembled in the Senate Caucus Room. "My candidacy is therefore based on the conviction that I can win both the nomination and the election."[1]

But his health, and rumors that he had Addison's disease—a serious and sometimes fatal illness of the adrenal system—almost kept him from winning either.

The first hint that Addison's disease was going to play a role in Kennedy's run for the White House came just three days later, when syndicated columnist Drew Pearson sent his legman, Jack Anderson (later a famous columnist himself), to follow up on a tip that Kennedy had Addison's disease.

Anderson cornered Kennedy in a Senate hallway on January 5 and asked him point-blank if he had the disease.

Kennedy recalled the encounter for his guests later that night, during a dinner party at his fashionable brick-fronted row house on N Street in Georgetown. It came up after one of his guests, trusted friend and future *Washington Post* editor Ben Bradlee, mentioned that Kennedy had looked terrible when he first ran for Congress back in 1946.

"You looked like the wrath of God," Bradlee laughed. "You weighed 120 and you were bright green!"

"That's why my father thought that I was not equipped for political life," Kennedy replied, puffing on a cigar.

"Did you run for Congress with that greenness?" Bradlee asked.

"Oh, yeah," Kennedy laughed, adding that the "greenness" was caused by the anti-malarial drug Atabrine and "some adrenal insufficiency."

"Was it Addison's, or was it…that damned disease?" Bradlee stammered.

"Addison's disease," Kennedy replied matter-of-factly. "They say I have it. Jack Anderson asked me today if I had it."

"Who?" Bradlee asked, not recognizing the name.

"Drew Pearson's man," Kennedy replied. "[I told him,] 'No. God, a guy with Addison's disease looks sort of brown and everything.'"

One of the common symptoms of Addison's disease is a discoloration and bronzing of the skin. But when Jack Anderson asked if that's why he was so tanned, Kennedy told his guests that he'd replied, "Christ, that's the sun."[2]

Everyone at the dinner table laughed. But Jack Kennedy's Addison's disease was no laughing matter.

The first hint that Addison's disease might play a *deciding* role in the 1960 election came a few months later, when someone broke into the office of Kennedy's endocrinologist and rifled through the files looking for his medical records. On the same day, thieves tried unsuccessfully to break into the office of one of his other doctors. Kennedy knew that if they found what they were looking for and handed it over to reporters who weren't too particular about how their sources got their information, his presidential campaign could be over before he even got the nomination.

That Jack Kennedy had a history of health problems was no secret. He'd nearly died of scarlet fever when he was a kid and had a bad back that he'd injured playing football at Harvard, and famously re-injured during World War II. He'd already been given the last rites of the Catholic Church three times and lived to read about it in the newspapers: first in 1947, the year after he was first elected to Congress, when he fell seriously ill while touring England; then in 1951, the year before he was elected to the Senate, when he came down with a terrible fever while visiting Japan; and finally in 1954, when an infection ravaged his body following a botched back operation in the U.S.

As Kennedy lay near death in 1954, Vice President Nixon went to visit him in the hospital and learned that he might die. When Nixon got back to his office, across the hall from Kennedy's in the Senate Office Building, he broke down in tears.[3]

Kennedy was first diagnosed with Addison's disease in 1946, the year he looked so "green," just a few months before he made his first run for Congress. Four-time Pulitzer Prize-winning journalist Arthur Krock recalled being told at that time by Kennedy's father that Jack had Addison's disease and was probably dying. Joe Kennedy, Krock recalled, "wept sitting in the chair opposite me in the office" as he talked about Jack's condition.[4]

That diagnosis was confirmed a year later when Kennedy fell gravely ill while visiting England. He was weak, nauseous, and vomiting, and his blood pressure was startlingly low. The London physician who examined him diagnosed his condition as Addison's disease and told one of Kennedy's friends that Jack "hasn't got a year to live."[5]

He survived, but for the rest of his life he would have to have regular injections of cortisone or other medications to keep the disease in check.[6]

Addison's disease had often been a fatal illness until cortisone was discovered in the 1930s and doctors began treating Addison's patients with it in the 1940s. (The man who discovered cortisone would later win the Nobel Prize for medicine.) The adrenal glands, which sit atop both kidneys, produce several key hormones, including adrenaline and cortisol. People with Addison's disease don't produce enough cortisol, which helps the immune system fight infections, regulates the metabolism of proteins, carbohydrates, and fats, balances the effects of insulin in breaking down sugar, and helps maintain blood pressure.

Addison's disease was one of the main reasons Kennedy was always getting so sick, but for years he and his doctors publicly denied that he had Addison's disease.

In 1959 Kennedy told an aide, "No one who has the real Addison's disease should run for the presidency, but I do not have it."[7]

During the 1960 fight for the Democratic nomination, Jack got one of his doctors, Janet Travell, to issue a signed statement that said, "Senator Kennedy does not have Addison's disease."

At a press conference held right after he was elected president, Kennedy told reporters, "I have never had Addison's disease. I have been through a long campaign and my health is very good today."[8]

We now know that Jack Kennedy did, in fact, have Addison's disease. Numerous articles and books written about Kennedy since his death have recognized this. An article posted on the John F. Kennedy Presidential Library's official website titled "JFK and Addison's Disease" states: "We know now that Kennedy's Addison's disclaimer was untrue."[9]

In 1966, six years after she had claimed Kennedy did not have Addison's disease, Dr. Travell was asked again if he did in fact have the disease. "The term 'Addison's disease' has been extended at the present time to include all degrees of adrenal insufficiency and all causes of adrenal insufficiency," Travell replied. "So I would have to say yes to your question."[10]

In his unpublished memoirs, Dr. Hutschnecker wrote: "In 1960, the general public did not know that Kennedy was suffering from Addison's disease. Most people simply thought Kennedy was suffering from a 'back ailment,' the result of an injury from WWII."

Had it been revealed that Jack had Addison's disease, Hutschnecker wrote, "this information could have literally swayed an election."[11]

Richard Nixon knew. According to Dr. Hutschnecker, Nixon had told him about it back in 1954, when Nixon visited Kennedy in the hospital after his botched back operation.[12]

But Nixon, who never missed an opportunity to exploit an opponent's weakness, couldn't divulge Kennedy's health secret during the 1960 campaign without risking exposure of his own. That would have to wait until the last days of the race, when Nixon gambled it would be too late for Kennedy to retaliate.

CHAPTER 16

Nixon Starts a Rumor in Bed

Five days after Guenther Reinhardt showed up at Dr. Hutschnecker's door, Richard Nixon put out a press statement saying that he had "no recollection" of Jack Kennedy or his father having contributed money to his Senate race in California 10 years earlier.

It was, of course, a lie; Nixon *knew* that Jack had personally handed him a $1,000 cash contribution from his father, Joe Kennedy, back in 1950—he even had his secretary write a memo about it a few months earlier. But on this day, as in so many days in the future, a lie would serve his purposes better than the truth.

Nixon had started the "rumor" of Jack's 1950 campaign contribution while laid up in bed in Walter Reed Army Hospital with a badly infected left knee, but he'd been preparing this trap for months—since back in March of 1960, when Jack had emerged as the frontrunner in the race to win the Democratic presidential nomination. And now that the Kennedy camp had pulled a dirty trick on him by sending a private detective around to snoop on his psychotherapist, it was time to spring it.

It might not be much, but it was the best he could do from a hospital bed with his left leg suspended by pulleys to drian the pus from his infected knee.

He had his surrogates start the "rumor" by letting a few friendly reporters back in California know, off the record, that Jack had supported him 10 years earlier during his Senate race against

Helen Gahagan Douglas, the popular and liberal Democrat and former Hollywood actress. Hopefully, it would prove embarrassing enough to Jack to cost him a few votes among the Democratic Party's liberal base in California, which in the 1960 presidential election was shaping up to be a tight race for the state's 32 electoral votes. Voters everywhere—but particularly angry and liberal ones in California—might wonder why they should vote for a guy who had helped Nixon defeat Gahagan Douglas, one of their all-time favorite liberal candidates, saddling them with the hated Richard Nixon as their United States senator, and putting Nixon back into the national spotlight.

And the rumor was true. In 1950, Jack had indeed come to Nixon's office and handed him a $1,000 cash contribution on behalf of his father, Joe Kennedy. Why he did it remains a mystery. Perhaps Gahagan Douglas was too liberal for Joe Kennedy; perhaps it was because she was a woman; or perhaps Joe Kennedy had given campaign contributions to both candidates so that whoever won would owe him a favor.

Whatever Joe's motive, 10 years later, Nixon now had to find a way of planting the rumor in the press without it appearing that he'd been its source. For if it came out that he'd started the rumor, voters might see him as an underhanded cad who'd stabbed a friend in the back by using his generosity against him just to get elected.

So in March, as Nixon was preparing to take on Kennedy in the 1960 campaign, he asked Rose Mary Woods to write up a memo about the day Jack Kennedy visited his office and gave him the money.

Woods called Dorothy "Dottie" Kabis, who had worked in Nixon's congressional office back in 1950, to get the details right. After talking to Dottie, whom President Nixon would later appoint treasurer of the United States, Woods wrote a memo to Nixon, saying, "Dottie's recollection is that Jack K. brought in $1,000 cash. She said he dropped in—as he used to do—and then after he had left you buzzed her and told her about it. She says it must have been after the primary because she was out in California all during the primary, so she would say that it was in June, July, or August [1950]."[1]

As he was setting his trap ten years later, Nixon knew that a dirty little trick like this could have a major impact on a tight political race. In fact, he'd already used the same trick on Jack once before, when he'd floated the same rumor at the 1956 Democratic National Convention, when Kennedy had come within an "eyelash" of being named Adlai Stevenson's running mate—a race that would have pitted Jack against Dick Nixon for the vice presidency. Fortunately for Jack, he'd narrowly lost his bid to be Stevenson's running mate. Now, four years later, Nixon was pulling the same stunt again.

Not wanting to be seen as the source of the rumor, Nixon did the one thing that would distance himself from it: he denied that it had ever happened, even though he knew that it had.

In early September 1960, several California newspapers carried stories alleging that the Kennedys had contributed to Nixon's Senate race back in 1950. The news reports offered no proof, however, and only cited unnamed sources.

Nixon addressed the stories on September 12, 1960—three days after he got out of the hospital—when he had his press secretary, Herb Klein, put out a statement.

"There have been many news reports regarding contributions by the senator and his father to this campaign at that time," Nixon said in his statement. "The vice president does not recall a contribution of this kind. It therefore seems unlikely this happened."[2]

Then, in a Machiavellian stroke, he went on to embellish the lie and to make the rumor about the Kennedys' campaign contribution seem possible, all the while distancing himself from it.

"He cannot answer the question categorically, however," Klein said in his press statement, "because there are many campaign committees in a state such as California and it is impossible to check the records of each."[3]

In other words, it could be true, but Nixon just couldn't verify it.

This was classic Nixon. He may not have had class, as Jack Kennedy would later observe, but he sure had balls.

Two months later, when all the votes were counted in California, Nixon won his home state by the slimmest majority—one-half of one percent—his closest margin of victory in any state. His little stunt, launched from a hospital bed in Washington, may have helped him carry California, which would become absolutely essential to maintaining his lifelong belief that Kennedy had cheated him out of the 1960 election.

If he had lost California—his home state—he couldn't have clung so fiercely to the image he had of himself as a winner whose victory had been stolen, a corrupting fantasy that in the years to come would allow him to commit any number of political crimes to gain and hold on to power.

As Arnold Hutschnecker would later observe, Nixon had become "trapped" by "a ferocious overdrive to win at all costs."[4]

CHAPTER 17

The Trial of Dr. Hutschnecker

The trial of Arnold Hutschnecker and the other defendants in the Gert von Gontard draft evasion case began on May 2, 1944, in federal court in New York City. Over the next five weeks, more than 40 witnesses were called, over 200 exhibits entered, and some 3,000 pages of testimony taken. Of the four surviving defendants, only Dr. Hutschnecker and a New York City detective who was also accused of helping Gert evade the draft tesified in their own behalf. Both insisted they were innocent.

When handing the case to the jury—ten men and two women—Judge Murray Hulbert instructed them that their primary duty was to determine whether the actions of the defendants had been "forthright and in good faith" or "part of a conspiracy to make false statements, counsel, aid, and abet von Gontard in evading the draft."[1]

The case went to the jury at noon on June 12, 1944, just six days after D-Day, the Allied invasion of Normandy. It was not a good time to be a draft dodger.

After deliberating for less than 12 hours, the jury returned to the courtroom that same night with a verdict. Dr. Hutschnecker and the other defendants were all present when the foreman, George Suraud, read the verdict: not guilty on all charges.[2]

It was a tremendous relief for Dr. Hutschnecker, who cried and hugged his lawyer, Louis P. Neustein.

Von Gontard smiled his aristocratic smile and shook hands

with everyone, even the reporters who had skewered him in the papers every day.

Ironically, von Gontard's efforts to stay out of the military during wartime, which had brought shame on three of his co-defendants and caused the suicide of another, were not successful anyway. On August 18, 1944, he was inducted into the U.S. Army—just six days short of his 38th birthday, when he would have been too old to be drafted.

Before being sent to Camp Upton on Long Island for basic training, Gert told reporters that he was "very happy to be in the army."[3]

Over the next year he served honorably and with distinction. After the war, he returned to New York to resume his life of philanthropy and the arts.

Dr. Hutschnecker, now free of the charges that had hung over him for the past six months, vigorously resumed his Park Avenue medical practice. But his troubles were far from over.

CHAPTER 18

Guenther Reinhardt and the Lost Mountain of Gold

Working out of the Counterintelligence Corps' headquarters at Lake Starnberg in 1946, Guenther Reinhardt uncovered a plot that would rock the army. Three U.S. Army colonels, he'd learned, had teamed up with a cabal of high-ranking former Nazis and were smuggling massive amounts of gold out of Germany.

Or so he said.

"There *were* people involved in smuggling and black-marketeering," said Reinhardt's former CIC colleague, Werner Michel. "It was a very unstable time in Germany, and some very unstable people were involved. But I must tell you, at that time, there was very little evidence of a Nazi underground. There were a number of incidents of this type where Bucky [Reinhardt] came up with information that we weren't able to evaluate. So much of his information was fabricated, or you couldn't confirm it."[1]

In the spring of 1945, as Nazi Germany was on the verge of defeat, Hitler ordered the vast stockpile of gold and currency he'd looted from national banks all over Europe to be removed from the German Reichsbank and loaded onto trains and transported south.[2]

The final destination of the Nazi treasure was allegedly the bottom of an alpine lake in Mittenwald, not far from the Austrian border and the picturesque Lake Starnberg.

After the war, the American and Russian occupation forces

started hearing rumors about the missing gold hoard and began a secret scramble to locate this vast mountain of bullion, estimated to be worth more than $5 billion at the time—over $100 billion in today's dollars. The biggest treaure hunt in world history was on.

The hunt for Hitler's gold was taking place not far from where Reinhardt was stationed at Lake Starnberg, and it wouldn't be long before he'd join in. His hunt, however, would be for the hunters.

Reinhardt had originally been assigned by his CIC commander to help locate fugitive Nazis and Russian spies. "Disloyalty and foreign agents became very much my business," he later wrote.[3]

Germany after the war was "a grim Wonderland—a maze-house of Red mirrors and deadly sleight of hand," Reinhardt wrote in *Crime Without Punishment*. "From the top to the bottom of the structure of America's occupation of Germany, Soviet agents worked and wielded power. Shoring up their infiltration were powerful pressures from 'friends' in America. The Soviet agents in Germany killed, spied, stole, and subverted. Their crimes stretched across all the zones of occupation. Their punishments scarcely were noticeable."[4]

It wasn't long before Reinhardt threw himself instead into a crusade against the cabal of former Nazis and U.S. Army colonels that he believed had discovered the treasure of Hitler's gold—a fact he doesn't even mention in *Crime Without Punishment*. A speed-typist, he feverishly pounded out daily reports on his findings, which consisted largely of rumors and wild, unsubstantiated accusations.

"Guenther Reinhardt pursued subversion of American interests in Germany, whether from within or without, with the demonic energy and fanatical single-mindedness of a man possessed," wrote Sayer and Botting in *Nazi Gold*.[5]

But there never was any proof that any U.S. Army officers had been involved with former Nazis in a plot to steal the mountain of lost Nazi gold, which to this day has never been recovered—at least, not officially.

Reinhardt, Michel, and several other CIC men shared a large

villa near Lake Starnberg, where in 1886, Ludwig II, the deposed King of Bavaria, killed himself by jumping into the lake's frigid blue waters. The king's attending physician also drowned trying to save him.

Reinhardt was also drowning in sea of depression, but no one jumped in to save him. He was unhappily married at the time, but he had met a woman in Germany, an attractive, dark-haired American civilian named Nora who was working for the army's information control division at Lake Starnberg. Before long, she moved in with Reinhardt at the large house by the lake.

"He lived in the same villa, House Pirna, with me and his girlfriend, and she was as unstable as he was," Michel said. "They would have terrible fights, and then they would passionately make up and everything would be fine. I think she shared some of his traits. She was very uneven. His wife lived back on Christopher Street in Greenwich Village. She was an invalid. He mentioned that, in one of his more lucid moments—and there weren't that many—that she was completely paralyzed and immobile."[6]

Michel recalled one night, when they were sitting by the lake, that Reinhardt suddenly went out on the dock, pulled out his revolver, and started shooting out at the water. "He thought there were Nazis out there," Michel said. "He had these delusions. He was brilliant but he would break down and start crying right in front of people, and a few minutes later he would be completely elated about something."[7]

Other times, Michel said, "Bucky would stop vehicles on the road to our villa and question them and pull out his weapon and yell at them, 'You're a Nazi!' He was always doing things like that."[8]

"He was a fantastic chap," recalled another friend, British journalist Tom Agoston, who worked with Reinhardt in Germany after the war at the International News Service. "But he was unbalanced."

One night, in Frankfurt, Guenther called Agoston at 2:00 AM.

"I just want to say goodbye," Guenther told his friend.

"Well, what's happening?" Agoston asked, still half-asleep. "Are you going home?"

"No," Reinhardt said flatly. "I'm going to commit suicide."

"For God's sake, where are you?" Agoston asked, now wide awake. "Don't be a bloody fool."

Agoston got dressed and drove over to Guenther's flat. He rang the bell, and Guenther came to the door, wearing a white tropical uniform.

"What's this?" Agoston asked.

"I'm in the Coast Guard," Guenther replied matter-of-factly.

He invited Agoston in. Right away, Agoston noticed three pistols sitting on Guenther's desk.

"I'm going to blow my brains out," Guenther said, looking at the guns.

But he didn't do it. He let his friend talk him out of it, and then went to bed.

"I had to stop him," Agoston recalled.[9]

The next day, it was as if nothing had happened.

On another occasion, Guenther wangled an invitation to speak on Armed Forces Radio in Munich. While being interviewed, he blurted out information about an active case the CIC was working, which compromised the investigation. On that same trip to Munich, Reinhardt met a group of U.S. senators—including senator and future vice president Alben Barkley—who were on a fact-finding tour of occupied Germany. Reinhardt told them some wild stories about what was going on there.[10]

"He was a nut with a lot of contacts in Washington," recalled Paul Bruehl, a civilian CIC case officer and former colleague of Reinhardt's at Lake Starnberg. "He was amazing in that way. The contacts he had were real, there's no question about that. He always threatened people with his contacts in Washington. He'd tell you that he could make trouble for you if he didn't get his way. He was so messed up he should have never been in counterintelligence. He was interesting but you couldn't believe three-quarters of what he said."[11]

All this was finally too much for the CIC men at Lake Starnberg, who eventually went to Colonel Garvey and asked him to send Reinhardt to a psychiatrist, or send him home.

"Two of us went and told Colonel Garvey, 'We can't just stand by and watch the various incidents Reinhardt is involved in,'" Michel recalled. "'We think he has an unstable personality.'"[12]

"What do you want me to do?" asked the colonel, who still liked Reinhardt.

"Get him examined by a psychiatrist," Michel replied.

The colonel thought about it for a moment. "This is very serious, you know," he said solemnly. But he knew it had to be done.

So the colonel called Reinhardt into his office and read off the litany of incidents he'd been involved in. "You can be examined or you can be fired," he told Reinhardt.

Reinhardt reluctantly consented to a psychiatric exam, and it didn't take the examining physician long to determine that his employment with the Counterintelligence Corps should be terminated immediately.

"Don't do this to me," Reinhardt begged the colonel, crying real tears. "You're destroying me if you send me home like this."

"Okay," the colonel said. "If you resign, I will consider the matter closed."[13]

So Reinhardt resigned, packed his bags, and went back to America, taking his girlfriend with him. But he would get his revenge.

CHAPTER 19

The Rat Pack

Frank Sinatra did everything he could to help Jack Kennedy get elected president in 1960. He hit the campaign trail for Jack, raised money for him, and even recorded a song. Sung to the tune of Sinatra's hit song, "High Hopes," it became the campaign's theme song:

> Everyone is voting for Jack
> 'Cause he's got what all the rest lack
> Everyone wants to back—Jack
> Jack is on the right track.
> 'Cause he's got high hopes
> He's got high hopes.

Sinatra sang the song at campaign rallies for Jack all across the country. On September 7—at the very same time Guenther Reinhardt was visiting Dr. Hutschnecker in Manhattan—he sang it at a fundraiser for Jack at the Beverly Hills home of actress Janet Leigh.

"The Hollywood wing of the Democratic Party, starring Frank Sinatra and Janet Leigh, swung into the presidential campaign today in behalf of Senator John F. Kennedy," the *New York Times* reported the next day.

Leigh, the wife of actor Tony Curtis, had opened her home to host the event for a group called Key Women for Kennedy. Five hundred female campaign workers had been expected to attend, but nearly 2,000 showed up—so many that the Curtis's next-door neighbors obligingly tore down the fence separating the two estates to accommodate the overflow crowd.

Ever the gracious hostess, Leigh gave no indication that she was worried about the hundreds of women trampling her lawn and wandering about in her home.

"This is how I am working for Senator Kennedy," she told a reporter.

Joining Leigh to greet the guests were Ted Kennedy, Jack's brother; Peter Lawford, Jack's brother-in-law; Mrs. Edmund G. Brown, the wife of the California governor; and Mrs. Stanley Mosk, the wife of the state's attorney general. But Sinatra was the main attraction, and the main event. The throng was so large that he had to sing twice—once for the ladies standing and seated around Janet Leigh's swimming pool, and a second time for the throng jammed into the neighbor's backyard.

When Jack was elected president, he showed his appreciation by having Sinatra and Lawford produce his inaugural gala.

"I know we're all indebted to a great friend—Frank Sinatra," Kennedy said at his inaugural gala. "After he has ceased to sing, he is going to be standing up and speaking for the Democratic Party… And I want him and my sister Pat's husband, Peter Lawford, to know that we're all indebted to them, and we're proud to have them with us."[1]

But Jack was indebted to Sinatra for more than just singing at campaign stops and fundraisers.

During the primary races, Jack's father reportedly called Sinatra and asked him to get his friends in the Chicago Mob to help turn out the labor vote in West Virginia.

Legendary *60 Minutes* producer Don Hewitt recalled the arrangement in a 2002 oral history interview for the Kennedy Library: "Tina Sinatra told me, and then she said it on our air, that Joe Kennedy called her father and said, 'We need help in West Virginia. We've got to get the labor vote because it's going to Hubert Humphrey.' And Frank Sinatra went to [Chicago Mafia boss] Sam Giancana and the Mob and got the votes that won West Virginia. I think also Illinois, but I know West Virginia."[2]

Sinatra's behind-the-scenes work to help Jack get the nomination was the repayment of a favor Frank owed Joe Kennedy.

In 1957, Sinatra had signed a three-year contract with the ABC Television network to star in a one-hour variety show, named, appropriately enough, *The Frank Sinatra Show*. Frank got $3 million up front for the show, plus a share of the profits. "This guarantees me $7 million," Sinatra told reporters.[3]

But the show was a complete failure. Panned by the critics, the show was also a flop with viewers. After the first season, Frank wanted out of the deal, saying he was too busy with movie commitments. ABC canceled the show, but let Frank keep the money.

The Internal Revenue Service, however, was not so generous. They wanted their share of his $7 million.

"ABC let him off the hook, but the IRS nailed him," recalled Milt Ebbins, who was the manager for Peter Lawford, Sinatra's "brother" in the famed Rat Pack. "The penalties and interest were stacking up, and one day Frank told me, 'There isn't a building high enough to jump off.' So Peter Lawford went to Joe Kennedy and asked him if he could help Frank. Joe Kennedy settled the whole thing for $60,000 and saved Frank's ass."[4]

Still feeling that he owed Joe Kennedy, Sinatra performed yet another vital behind-the-scenes task to help get Jack elected: he was the middleman between Guenther Reinhardt and the Kennedy campaign.

There had been rumors circulating about Nixon seeing a "shrink," dating as far back as 1955, when Guenther's old pal and mentor, Walter Winchell, first revealed it in his column in the *New York Daily Mirror*. Winchell hadn't learned the doctor's name, but by 1960, Guenther Reinhardt had. Reinhardt's confidential report suggests that he learned Dr. Hutschnecker's name from a mutual friend, a prominent New York attorney named Louis P. Neustein.

As a private detective, Guenther had conducted numerous investigations for dozens of New York lawyers, and Neustein was one of his clients. In his confidential memo, Guenther described Neustein as "a very close personal friend" he'd worked for on several cases.

Neustein had been one of Dr. Hutschnecker's best friends since 1944, when he defended the doctor in the sensational criminal case that nearly landed Hutschnecker in federal prison. Hutschnecker, who believed he owed his life to Neustein, even kept an autographed photo of the lawyer in his office. Neustein knew all about Dr. Hutschnecker's treatment of Richard Nixon, too, and cheerfully told Guenther all about it.

The pieces of the puzzle began to come together for Reinhardt in 1957, when Nixon tried to get President Eisenhower to become a patient of Dr. Hutschnecker's. Eisenhower had just undergone surgery for ileitis, a chronic inflammation of the intestinal tract, and shortly thereafter, suffered a minor stroke. As president, of course, he had access to the best doctors in the country. But Nixon urged him to see Dr. Hutschnecker, even though two years earlier Nixon had ignored his own advisors' warnings to stop seeing the psychotherapist because of the risks attendant to a politician seeing a "shrink."[5]

Perhaps Nixon really felt that Dr. Hutschnecker could help Ike. Or maybe it was just a cynical ploy to provide himself with cover in the event that his own association with the doctor ever came to light. For if it was okay for the president to see a psychotherapist, why not the vice president?

"By 1957, Nixon had enough trust in me to want Eisenhower to come as a patient after his operation for ileitis," Dr. Hutschnecker later recalled, never suspecting what may have been Nixon's real motive.[6]

Nixon gave Eisenhower a signed copy of Hutschnecker's book, *The Will to Live*, and the president sent the doctor a kind thank you note. But Ike didn't want anything to do with seeing a psychotherapist, much less one who'd been treating Nixon.

"Although Eisenhower would acknowledge, in a letter, receiving my book, we never met," Hutschnecker wrote.[7]

If Nixon's motives were more calculating and cynical than sincere and heartfelt (and they usually were), it wouldn't be the last time he'd try to dupe Eisenhower into one of his schemes involving doctors.

Dr. Hutschnecker had no idea that any of this was going on behind the scenes. But he was thrilled to get a signed letter from President Eisenhower—so much so that he proudly showed it to a few friends, including one of his very best friends, attorney Louis Neustein, who in turn mentioned it to Guenther Reinhardt.

In his confidential report, Guenther wrote that on the morning after his consultation with Dr. Hutschnecker in September 1960, he put in a phone call to Neustein on the pretext of wanting to talk to him about "another matter," but what he really wanted to talk about was Dr. Hutschnecker and Richard Nixon.

Neustein got right on the phone and told Guenther that he'd just come from seeing Dr. Hutschnecker, whom he called "Hutch," and that the doctor had mentioned Guenther's visit the previous day, and that Guenther might be referring a new client to Dr. Hutschnecker. This seemed to please Neustein, who then reminded Guenther that he'd "defended Dr. Hutschnecker in his trial in the Gert Von Gontard matter," the 1944 draft evasion case that nearly landed Hutschnecker in jail, and that they had subsequently become "very close personal friends."[8]

Of course, Guenther already knew all about that. They'd talked about it before, and while poking around in Hutschnecker's office, Guenther had noticed the lawyer's framed picture hanging on the wall.

Neustein then mentioned that he and members of his family had been treated by Hutschnecker, adding that the doctor was "an extremely fine and reliable man and a good friend."[9]

Reinhardt, still keeping up the ruse that he'd gone to see Dr. Hutschnecker about treating the son of a wealthy Pittsburgh family, told Neustein that the only reason he'd gone to see the doctor was "to find out whether he could keep the identity of a prominent patient a secret."

"Well, he is treating Richard Nixon," Neustein told him, "and you don't read about that in the papers."[10]

Then Neustein told Guenther that "as long as Mr. Nixon did not consider it a stigma to be treated by a psychosomatic specialist, [Reinhardt's client] should have no compunction about the same treatment."[11]

Reinhardt led him on a little more, asking how he could be so sure Nixon was one of the doctor's patients.

"Well, I have met Richard Nixon in Dr. Hutschnecker's office," Neustein replied, adding that the doctor had told him that he sometimes traveled to Washington to treat Nixon, and that "whenever Nixon is in New York, he generally calls on Dr. Hutschnecker."[12]

Reinhardt noted in his 12-page confidential report that Neustein "also said he had seen a letter which President Eisenhower had written to Hutch, thanking him for a copy of his latest book, *The Will to Live*"—a seemingly insignificant but verifiable detail that proved, if nothing else, that Reinhardt was not making up the conversation with the attorney.[13]

Trying to draw the lawyer into talking more about Nixon, Guenther asked him if the doctor treated the vice president for a serious medical condition.

"No," Neustein replied. "He is very often under heavy pressure and this has an influence upon his body chemistry, as it would have in the case of any normal person."

After getting off the phone with Neustein, Guenther wrote that he planned to "confirm the visits of Mr. N. at Dr. Hutschnecker's office in approximately two weeks by a surreptitious inquiry among the building personnel at 829 Park Avenue."

Then, at the end of his report, he wrote, "Except for this phase, the investigation has been suspended."[14]

After visiting Dr. Hutschnecker that September, just before the 1960 election, Guenther wrote up a 12-page confidential report on the relationship between Nixon and Hutschnecker and gave it to Frank Sinatra, who then handed it over to Joe Kennedy.*

---

*Joe Kennedy's personal papers are housed at the John F. Kennedy Library and Museum in Boston, Massachusetts. To view the Joseph P. Kennedy

In her biography of Sinatra, author Kitty Kelley noted that an aide to Bobby Kennedy, Jack's brother and campaign manager, told her Sinatra had "personally employed" a private detective to spy on Dr. Hutschnecker during the 1960 campaign.[15]

In all likelihood, Guenther had initially reached out to Joe Kennedy, the man with the deepest pockets, to let him know that he'd discovered Richard Nixon's most closely guarded secret, and Joe then got Sinatra to act as the intermediary—to pay Guenther for his work and pick up the report.

Joe Kennedy then sent three copies of Reinhardt's report to his son-in-law, Peter Lawford. Those copies were found in 2005, in Lawford's voluminous files—files that Lawford had given to Milt Ebbins, his business partner and longtime personal manager, back in the 1970s. The copies of Reinhardt's report were found sealed in a gray envelope addressed to Joe Kennedy with Lawford's return address, marked "personal and confidential" and "to be opened only by Joseph Kennedy." Why Joe Kennedy sent the copies of Reinhardt's report to his son-in-law remains a mystery, but it may have

---

Papers Collection, researchers must apply to the library's donor committee. The author of this book did so on August 6, 2008, stating that the purpose of the request was to review Joseph Kennedy's correspondence from 1960 to see if there was any mention of a private detective named Guenther Reinhardt.

A few weeks later, on November 3, 2008, the author received a letter on the library's stationery stating that the author's request to review Joe Kennedy's papers had been denied.

The Presidential Records Act of 1978 governs the official records of presidents and vice presidents, and changed the legal ownership of the official records of presidents from private to public. The Presidential Records Act also allows for public access to presidential records through the Freedom of Information Act beginning five years after the end of a president's administration—but only for those records created by presidents or received by presidential libraries after January 20, 1981. The presidential records of John F. Kennedy—and all presidents before Ronald Reagan—are not subject to the Freedom of Information Act, and can be hidden from public view for as long as the curators choose.

been to circulate them among some of the gossip columnists Lawford knew on the West Coast. Lawford was supposed to have sent the copies back to Joe Kennedy, but he never did. Instead, they sat in Lawford's files, collecting dust for nearly 50 years.[16]

Reinhardt may also have given Joe Kennedy something else he picked up while spying on Dr. Hutschnecker—Nixon's stolen psychiatric file.

CHAPTER 20

Kennedy's Father

Joseph P. Kennedy, the patriarch of the Kennedy clan, was driven by ambition and an unbridled lust for power. A Harvard graduate, Class of 1912, he became, at the age of 26, the nation's youngest bank president—a job he got because his father, a wealthy saloonkeeper, businessman, and Boston politician, was a major shareholder in the bank.

Joe Kennedy made his first million dollars by the time he was 30, and made millions more in Hollywood as the head of RKO Pictures, where he had a famous affair with silent movie star Gloria Swanson.

But it was back in New York one day in the fall of 1929 that he saved the family fortune, which was heavily invested in stocks. During the stock market boom of the 1920s, Joe Kennedy had amassed a vast fortune through insider trading and stock manipulation that would be illegal today.

According to Kennedy family lore, Joe got out of the stock market just before the Crash of 1929, thanks to a tip from an elderly black man who shined his shoes every day. It was a story that Joe Kennedy often told to his children, and to his son-in-law, actor Peter Lawford, who later told it to his manager, Milt Ebbins.

"Lawford told it to me at one of the dinners that Joe had," Ebbins said with a laugh.

"Joe Kennedy had a shoeshine guy who shined his shoes every day," Ebbins recalled. "And one day, right before the stock market crash of 1929, the shoeshine guy was shining his shoes. I think his name was Joe, too. And Joe Kennedy said, 'So, Joe, what do you hear?'[1]

"'Sell everything,' Old Joe whispered, looking up from polishing Kennedy's shoes."

Joe Kennedy was taken aback. Old Joe was a favorite among Wall Street brokers, including Wall Street tycoon J. P. Morgan, and Joe Kennedy had been tipping him a dollar every day for tidbits of conversations he'd overheard while shining their shoes. His information was always good, but this would turn out to be the most important tip of Joe Kennedy's life.

"What do you mean, sell everything?" he asked Joe.

"I was shining Mr. Morgan's shoes this morning—J. P. Morgan," Old Joe said as he went back to shining Kennedy's shoes, "and there were guys in the room with him, and they were talking and talking, and they were saying, 'We gotta sell! We gotta sell everything! We gotta sell! We gotta sell!' That's it, sell, sell, sell. And Mr. Morgan said, 'Okay, sell everything.'"

"They didn't think he could speak English," Ebbins said. "He just sat there shining their shoes, and he never looked up, and he never said hello or anything. He just shined their shoes, got his money and left. And J. P. Morgan tipped him a quarter. A shine was a dime in those days, and Morgan always tipped him a quarter. And every day that he'd shine the shoes of these executives, he'd report what he heard to Joe Kennedy, who always tipped him a buck.

"So Joe Kennedy sold everything—every fucking stock that he had, and that's where he made a hundred million dollars."

When the stock market crashed in October 1929, the nation was soon plunged into the Great Depression. But Joe Kennedy was left one of the richest men in the country—all because of the advice of a shoeshine man.

When Prohibition ended in 1933, Joe Kennedy made millions more when his company, Somerset Importers, became the exclusive importer of Gordon's Dry Gin and Dewar's Scotch Whisky. Some say that Joe Kennedy made even more millions importing booze *during* Prohibition.

In 1932, Joe Kennedy raised large sums of money for the election of Franklin Roosevelt, whom Joe had known since World War

I, when Roosevelt was assistant secretary of the navy and Joe was assistant general manager of Bethlehem Steel, a large navy contractor. And when Roosevelt became president in 1933, he repaid Joe by giving him a job. Ironically, the job was chairman of the newly created U.S. Securities and Exchange Commission, which was supposed to ensure that the stock market was free of the kind of insider trading and stock manipulation that Joe had practiced so skillfully.

Joe Kennedy loved money, but he loved power more, and he was constantly seeking higher office. He raised more money for Roosevelt's reelection in 1936, and in 1938 Roosevelt named him U.S. Ambassador to Great Britain, making him the first Irish Catholic to ever hold the post. But when war came to Europe in 1939, Joe Kennedy was clearly not the right man to be Roosevelt's representative to America's staunch but beleaguered ally. As German troops marched across Europe, Joe Kennedy argued that the U.S. should not get involved in the war, and even opposed giving England military equipment to defend itself. And in early November 1940, with the epic Battle of Britain still being waged in the skies over England, Ambassador Kennedy, during a brief visit in Boston, gave an ill-advised interview to reporters from his hometown newspaper, the *Boston Globe*.

"Democracy is finished in England," he told the reporters. "It may be here [in the U.S.]"

The defeatist comment caused a firestorm of outrage in America and Britain, and Joe was immediately sacked. His political career was over and any hopes he'd had of becoming the first Irish Catholic president of the United States were finished, too.

But Joe Kennedy's ambition remained, so he would channel it into his sons. Joseph P. Kennedy Jr., the oldest of Joe's nine children and Jack's senior by two years, was the obvious first choice. Handsome, charming, and brilliant, Joe Jr. was a true golden boy, the shining star of the Kennedy clan.

But Joe Jr. didn't make it through the war. A decorated navy pilot, he was killed in a daring bomber raid on a German rocket installation in occupied France on August 12, 1944.

Joe Jr.'s death was a devastating blow to the Kennedy family. But life would have to go on, and there were three more sons for Joe Sr. to pour his ambitions into.

Jack Kennedy didn't see any more action after he heroically rescued his men when the Japanese destroyer cut their PT boat in half. He was assigned to another boat, but he came down with malaria, and his injured back was getting worse. He'd returned to the U.S. in January 1944, and in May entered the Naval Hospital at Chelsea, Massachusetts, for further treatment of his back injury. He was released from all active duty in March 1945, just a few months before the war ended.

When Jack returned home, Joe Kennedy immediately set about mapping his political future.

"It was like being drafted," Jack told columnist Bob Considine. "My father wanted his eldest son in politics. 'Wanted' isn't the right word. He demanded it."[2]

"I got Jack into politics," Joe Sr. bragged. "I was the one. I told him Joe was dead and that therefore it was his responsibility to run for Congress. He didn't want to, he felt he didn't have the ability… But I told him he had to."[3]

Dr. Hutschnecker never met Jack Kennedy's father, but that didn't stop him from analyzing him. Joe Kennedy, Dr. Hutschnecker wrote, was "a hard-driving, power-hungry, ruthlessly determined, and overly aggressive father, psychologically classified as a hostile-aggressive type, [who] had trained his son for leadership with almost the precision of a scientist adept in Pavlovian methods of conditioning."

Dr. Hutschnecker also saw a parallel between Frederick the Great of Prussia and Jack Kennedy, both of whom, he said, "had ruthless fathers who had carefully mapped out the careers of their sons, preparing them for their destined future; one with Europe's best-trained Prussian army and money, and the other with a mass of political power and money."

Dr. Hutschnecker recalled that one of his patients, an attractive young woman, had once been a dinner companion of Joe Kennedy's.

"I wanted power," Joe had told her. "I thought money would give me power and so I made money, only to discover that it was politics, not money, that really gave a man power. So I went into politics."

Not being able to rise above the position of Ambassador to Great Britain, Joe Kennedy, Dr. Hutschnecker believed, "was living out his ambition by molding his son for the highest symbol of power, the presidency of the United States."[4]

But one thing Dr. Hutschnecker didn't recognize was that Joe Kennedy loved his children even more than money, even more than power, and would do anything to make them happy.

Joe Kennedy bankrolled Jack's first congressional race in 1946, his Senate run in 1952, and his presidential campaign in 1960. And there's considerable evidence to suggest that Joe didn't balk at buying a few votes in the right places when he had to. Jack even joked about it one night in 1958 during a speech at the Gridiron Club, Washington's oldest and most prestigious journalists' organization. Jack hadn't announced his candidacy for the presidency yet, but nearly every reporter attending the black-tie dinner knew he was going to run.

"I have just received the following wire from my generous Daddy," Jack joked. "'Dear Jack: Don't buy a single vote more than is necessary—I'll be damned if I'll pay for a landslide.'"[5]

But Joe Kennedy would do even more than that. He would bankroll Guenther Reinhardt, hold Nixon at bay, and save the presidency for his oldest surviving son.

CHAPTER 21

The Medical Board vs. Dr. Arnold Hutschnecker

Four months after his trial ended, new charges were brought against Dr. Hutschnecker by the New York State Medical Board, which accused him of "fraud and deceit in the practice of medicine" in the Gert von Gontard matter.[1]

The medical board couldn't put him in jail, but as far as Dr. Hutschnecker was concerned, they could do something almost as bad—they could take away his license to practice medicine. To make matters worse, the U.S. Naturalization Service had put his citizenship application on hold pending the outcome of this new investigation.

The board accused Dr. Hutschnecker of filing a false medical certificate with the U.S. Civil Service Commission by stating that von Gontard had been in good enough health to work for the FBI, and then turning around six months later and telling the draft board that he was not well enough to serve in the military.[2]

Hearings on the charges were held on November 9 and 16, 1944, before a subcommittee of the Medical Grievance Committee. Dr. Hutschnecker admitted that he'd told the FBI one thing and the draft board another, but denied any intent to decieve or defraud, saying he'd signed the two conflicting medical certificates "in good faith and in the interests of his patient's health," which he now deeply regretted.[3]

The hearing committee, however, found him guilty and voted to suspend his license for one year.

After a series of appeals to the medical board and the state courts, Dr. Hutschnecker's medical license was suspended on December 31, 1945. He was no longer a doctor—the only profession he'd ever known. It was not going to be a happy New Year.

Nearly bankrupt by the costs of the trial and appeals, Hutschnecker closed his office, referred his patients to another doctor, and left town, moving with his wife to a friend's home in Connecticut and borrowing money from friends just to get by. Hutschnecker's father, David, was becoming increasingly ill from the effects of prostrate cancer, and his cousin, who had survived the war and two years at the infamous Auschwitz concentration camp, was now penniless and in dire need of his help.

Florita's parents, Arnold's cousin wrote, "had unfortunately been sent to Auschwitz in January 1943. What happened to them, you can very well imagine."[4]

But without a source of income, Hutschnecker had no way of helping his family. On June 20, 1946, more than six months into the one-year suspension of his medical license, Hutschnecker's citizenship papers finally came through. He wasn't a doctor anymore, but at least he was finally an American. But family and financial problems were mounting, so a few days later he filed papers with the medical board, pleading with them to give him back his license.

"Upon the suspension of my license to practice," he told the medical board, "I sublet the apartment at 829 Park Avenue, which served as both my office and my home, and left the city, going to the home of a friend in Connecticut. The surrender of the office and apartment was made necessary by the fact that since my practice was suspended, my source of livelihood ceased, and I was without funds or income…The order of suspension has now been in effect for a little over six months, and the hardship which this suspension has worked upon me has been most severe."[5]

His father was dying of prostate cancer, his destitute cousin in Germany needed help, and he was without any source of income to help them.

"I have been living entirely upon the bounty of my friends," he told the medical board, pleading for an early reinstatement of his license. "My training and education has been such that I am not equipped to perform any other work except that of my profession, the practice of medicine, to which I have devoted my life."[6]

The medical board, however, showed him no mercy; he would have to wait another six months before getting his license back to practice medicine. In the meantime, having no other skills, Hutschnecker fell back upon the only other thing he could do. At his friend's home in Connecticut, he started writing.

"There I spent my entire time in the writing of a manuscript, and in the study and research necessary in that writing," he told the medical board. "Since my suspension I have engaged in no employment, no profession, and no business of any kind whatsoever. I have been sustained during my suspension period only by the firm belief that the research work to which I have devoted myself and the manuscript embracing it, will become a valuable contribution to the progress of medicine."[7]

The manuscript he was working on would become a little book titled *The Will to Live*. Published in 1951, it became one of the first best-selling self-help books of its kind. In the summer of 1952, Richard Nixon read the book and reached out to Dr. Hutschnecker for help.

CHAPTER 22

"You Can't Trust the Bastards"

V ice President Richard Nixon breezed through the 1960 primaries and on July 28 was nominated for president at the Republican National Convention in Chicago where, 100 years earlier, the Republican Party's first convention had nominated Abraham Lincoln. But Nixon, a virulent anti-Semite and racist, was no Abraham Lincoln.

Allegations that Nixon was anti-Semitic would first surface two weeks later, in a little Jewish newspaper in Southern California.

Nixon had come of age in an America rife with anti-Semitism. Many country clubs remained restricted to non-Jews well into the 1960s, and property deeds all across the country contained restrictive covenants that did not allow buyers to sell their homes to "Negroes or Jews." Many top universities even had quotas on how many Jews could attend as students or teach as professors.

Although the Quakers had no such tradition, growing up in this environment, Nixon's anti-Semitism blossomed in the late 1940s, when he began his crusade against Alger Hiss, whom Nixon and former Communist Whittaker Chambers famously accused of being a Communist spy.

"The only two non-Jews in the Communist conspiracy were Chambers and Hiss," Nixon would say many years later on the now-infamous White House tapes. "Every other one was a Jew."[1]

It wasn't until August of 1960 that rumors of Nixon's anti-Semitism were first made public.

"The curtain had no more than run down on the Republican National Convention in Chicago when there commenced a series of inquires to this newspaper," wrote Joseph Jonah Cummins, the editor and publisher of the *B'nai B'rith Messenger*, a weekly Jewish newspaper in Los Angeles, in a front page editorial on August 12, 1960.[2]

"Is it true that Richard Nixon is an anti-Semite?" asked one of the callers.

"When a Jewish newspaper is flooded with over a hundred such inquiries, it is indicative that the character assassins are getting an early start," Cummins wrote, trying to assure his readers that Nixon was not anti-Semitic.

About an hour before he wrote his editorial, Cummins received a phone call from an old friend, Birdie Stodel, a respected leader of the local Jewish community, who had the same question.

"I attended a meeting of women last night at which about 50 women were present and one woman stated that she had documented proof that Richard Nixon is an anti-Semite," Stodel told Cummins. "I answered that 'that is ridiculous,' but she was so persistent that I thought I'd call you. She made a strong impression on many of the women present."

Cummins advised Stodel that she "should telephone that lovely lady and tell her that she is doing our people a disservice by thus slandering Mr. Nixon."

"There is no element of anti-Semitism in this campaign," he wrote in his editorial. "Yet, with so much slander against Richard Nixon, we feel it our solemn duty to state, unequivocally, that no man in public life in America is more devoid of anti-Semitism than Richard Nixon."[3]

Six days later, on August 18, the little newspaper's attempt to refute rumors that Nixon was anti-Semitic made it all the way to the U.S. Senate when Republican Jacob Javits, the only Jewish member of the Senate, took to the Senate floor to denounce claims that Nixon was an anti-Semite.

Calling the allegations "scurrilous and vicious rumors," Javits said: "The campaign to charge Vice President Nixon with anti-Semitism is a vicious canard about which there is not and never has been the slightest shred of truth."

The next day, August 19—three weeks before Guenther Reinhardt showed up at Dr. Hutschnecker's Park Avenue office for his consultation—the *New York Times* carried a story on page 10 about Javits' denial.

"The New York Republican took the floor to call attention to an editorial in the *B'nai B'rith Messenger*," the *Times* said in its article. "The editorial rejected such charges against Mr. Nixon and appealed for a halt to all religious bias in the election."

"The effort to inject a religious issue in this presidential campaign," Javits declared, "should be regarded by every American as an affront to his citizenship."[4]

In fact, Nixon really was an anti-Semite and would become widely known as one of the most anti-Semitic presidents in modern American history. As revealed many years later in Nixon's secret White House tapes, he was almost pathological in his disdain for and distrust of Jews.

"The Jews are all over the government," Nixon complained to his chief of staff, H. R. "Bob" Haldeman, on one of the tapes recorded in 1971, adding that Washington "is full of Jews" and asserting, "Most Jews are disloyal."[5]

On the tapes, Nixon can be heard saying that this doesn't apply to his top Jewish aides, such as national security adviser Henry Kissinger, his White House counsel, Leonard Garment, or speechwriter, William Safire. "But, Bob," he told Haldeman, "generally speaking, you can't trust the bastards. They turn on you. Am I wrong or right?"[6]

Haldeman agreed wholeheartedly that he was right.

And more than thirty years before the identity of *Washington Post* reporter Bob Woodward's famous source, Deep Throat, was revealed to the world, Haldeman told President Nixon that it was FBI assistant director Mark Felt. And Nixon's first question was about Felt's religion.

"Is he a Catholic?" Nixon asked. Haldeman replied, errone-ously, that he thought Felt was Jewish. "Christ," Nixon blurted out. "They put a Jew in there?"[7]

Nixon was at it again on February 1, 1972, when evangelist Billy Graham came to the White House for a prayer breakfast. Afterwards, Nixon, Haldeman, and Graham met privately in the Oval Office, and the conversation eventually turned to one of their favorite subjects: how the Jews were destroying the country.

After chatting about Nixon's upcoming reelection campaign, Graham noted that he had been invited to have lunch with the edi-tors of *Time* magazine.

"You meet with all their editors, you better take your Jewish beanie," laughed Haldeman, always the anti-Semitic enabler.

Taking his cue from Haldeman, Graham launched into a rant about how the Jews had gained a "stranglehold" on the media that "has got to be broken or the country's going down the drain."

"You believe that?" Nixon asked.

"Yes, sir," Graham replied.

"Oh boy, so do I," Nixon said. "I can't ever say that, but I be-lieve it."

Graham added that he had Jewish friends in the media who "swarm around me and are friendly to me," but confided that "they don't know how I really feel about what they're doing to this country."

"You must not let them know," Nixon replied conspiratorially.[8]

A few months earlier, President Nixon got the chance to put his anti-Semitic talk into action when he ordered a harassment campaign against Jewish contributors to Democratic candidates, ordering Haldeman to tell the Internal Revenue Service to have them all investigated.

"Now here's the point, Bob," he told Haldeman, "please get me the names of the Jews. You know, the big Jewish contributors to the Democrats. Could we please investigate some of the cocksuckers?"[9]

The only obstacle to his plan, he told Haldeman the next day, was that "the IRS is full of Jews, Bob."[10]

The fact that Nixon's own psychologist was Jewish didn't prevent him from disparaging Jewish physiatrists. On May 26, 1971, after reading the morning's news summary in the Oval Office, Nixon turned to Haldeman and said: "Every one of the bastards that are out for legalizing marijuana is Jewish. What the Christ is the matter with the Jews, Bob? What is the matter with them? I suppose it's because most of them are psychiatrists, you know. There's so many. All the greatest psychiatrists are Jewish."[11]

The White House tapes also reveal that Nixon was a blatant racist. "I have the greatest affection for them," he said condescendingly about African Americans during an Oval Office conversation with Haldeman recorded in 1971, "but I know they're not going to make it for 500 years. They aren't. You know it, too. The Mexicans are a different cup of tea. They have a heritage. At the present time they steal, they're dishonest, but they do have some concept of family life. They don't live like a bunch of dogs, which the Negroes do live like."[12]

On January 23, 1973—the day after the Supreme Court decriminalized abortion in Roe v. Wade—Nixon made a racist observation about the occasional need for abortions.

"There are times when abortions are necessary," he told White House Chief Counsel Chuck Colson. "I know that. Suppose you have a black and a white, or a rape."[13]

During the 1960 presidential campaign, Nixon's running mate, former senator and U.N. Ambassador Henry Cabot Lodge Jr., pledged that a Nixon administration would put an end to the scourge of segregation—a promise that Nixon had no intention of keeping.

Less than a month before Election Day, Lodge and Kennedy spoke on the same day about civil rights issues to the National Council of Women in New York City. Kennedy spoke at great length about assisting African nations, many of which had just gained their independence from colonial masters. He also spoke briefly and broadly on the subject of racism in America, calling for "the elimination of discrimination against Negroes in the United States."[14]

Lodge told the progressive women's organization that racial discrimination in the U.S. should be ended, not just because it would aid the country's fight against Communism, but also "because we want to do it and because it is a national purpose."[15]

A story about the two speakers' comments was printed on page 26 of the *New York Times*. But a speech Lodge made later that day would make the front page of the *Times*.

Campaigning at a street rally in Harlem, Lodge described civil rights as "the central issue of our times," and said that "if elected, we will be guided by the following: there should be a Negro in the cabinet; there should be greater use of Negroes in the Foreign Service from the rank of ambassador down; we will exercise the good offices of the White House and the full powers of the federal government to end segregation in the public schools, end segregation in public eating places, [and] end segregation and discrimination in other public facilities; we will vigorously enforce existing law and, if necessary, seek legislation to guarantee the right to vote."[16]

All this, he proclaimed, "is offered as a pledge—and as a pledge that will be redeemed beginning in January 1961 if you elect Richard Nixon president."

Nixon, who apparently had no idea that his running mate was going to make such a sweeping pronouncement about civil rights, was aghast, as were many Southern white congressmen and governors. So Nixon made him take it back.

Speaking to reporters the next day during a campaign swing through the South, Lodge sheepishly withdrew his promise.

"I cannot pledge anything," he said, noting that his pledge about a black person being named to Nixon's cabinet had been an expression of what he thought *should* be done, and was not necessarily a Republican Party commitment.[17]

Lodge, a political moderate, had been an odd choice for the number-two man on the ticket from the beginning. Generally, a presidential candidate looks for a vice presidential running mate who can win his home state, which the presidential candidate might not otherwise carry, as LBJ would carry Texas for Jack Kennedy. But Lodge had no hope of carrying his own home state, Massachusetts, where he'd already been beaten by Jack Kennedy once before.

Lodge, like JFK, had been a genuine World War II hero. A highly decorated army officer, he'd single-handedly captured a four-man German patrol. And like Jack, Lodge was a Harvard grad from a patrician and politically powerful Boston family.

Lodge had played a key role in persuading Dwight Eisenhower to run for the presidency in 1952, and then had managed Ike's victorious campaign. But by spending so much time on Eisenhower's campaign, he'd neglected his own, and narrowly lost his Senate seat to a young congressman named John F. Kennedy. Ironically, Lodge's father had defeated Jack's grandfather, John F. Fitzgerald, for the same Senate seat in 1916, and Jack's brother, Ted, defeated Lodge's son, George C. Lodge, for the same seat in 1962.

During the 1960 campaign, not only did Lodge *not* help Nixon carry Massachusetts—Kennedy won the state by more than 20 percentage points—but his promise to bring African Americans into the Nixon administration certainly cost Nixon the votes of some segregationists in the South, many of whom voted instead for write-in candidate Harry Byrd, the racist governor of Virginia. This contributed to Nixon's narrow defeat in the general election.

Many years later, in a conversation picked up on the White House tapes, Nixon revealed what he really thought about African Americans, and that he never had any intention of putting one of them in his cabinet.

On November 19, 1972, two weeks after he was reelected president, one of Nixon's advisors suggested that he name Walter Washington, the first black mayor of Washington, D.C., as U.N. Ambassador, replacing George H. W. Bush, who Nixon wanted back in Washington to help him manage the growing Watergate scandal.

"Why put a black in there?" Nixon asked incredulously. "Why do it? Why?"[18]

"I wouldn't do it," answered Charles Colson, Nixon's chief counsel. "Mr. President, you were just elected with one of the biggest landslides in history, but with no better participation from the blacks…Who the hell cares about the blacks?"

Nixon agreed. "You know," he told Colson, "basically, we don't owe the blacks a damn thing anyway."

Nixon didn't mention Dr. Hutschnecker in his memoirs, and Dr. Hutschnecker didn't mention Nixon's racist and anti-Semitic rants in his unpublished book about Nixon, even though many of the White House tapes had been made public and were widely reported on before his book was written. Perhaps the fact that he'd received Nixon's permission to write the book prevented him from telling the whole awful truth about a man who had become his friend.

The issue of Nixon's anti-Semitism never again surfaced in the 1960 campaign, but in such a close election, it can be fairly said that the Jewish vote put JFK over the top. In New York, for example, Jack won the state by only 384,000 votes, or by about five percent of the total votes cast. But heavily Jewish precincts in the state gave Jack more than 800,000 votes—easily his margin of victory.[19]

Kennedy, who had also won a large majority of the Jewish vote in Illinois and New Jersey, where his margins of victory over Nixon were even thinner, recognized that the Jewish vote had put him over the top.

In the spring of 1961, only a few months after his inauguration, President Kennedy met briefly in Manhattan with Israeli Prime Minister David Ben-Gurion. During their meeting, Kennedy took Ben-Gurion aside and quietly told him, "You know, I was elected by the Jews of New York. I would like to do something for them."[20]

Like Dr. Hutschnecker, Guenther Reinhardt was also Jewish, and the only thing the private detective hated more than Communists were anti-Semites. Perhaps, three weeks before visiting Dr. Hutschnecker for his "consultation," Guenther had read the *New York Times'* account of Nixon's alleged anti-Semitism. Or perhaps he'd picked up a whiff of it at the Bohemian Grove, where he and

Nixon had been members, or while working briefly alongside Nixon in 1948 at the House Un-American Activities Committee. If he had, it would have made Guenther a lifelong and implacable foe of Nixon's. For, unlike Dr. Hutschnecker, Guenther was not a man who forgave easily—or at all.

CHAPTER 23

The Return of Guenther Reinhardt

Run out of occupied Germany by the army, Guenther Reinhardt was back in New York City in November 1948, living with his invalid wife Helen, whom he kept locked in a room in their apartment on Christopher Street in the West Village. His girlfriend, Nora, had come back to New York with him. Reinhardt wanted to marry her, but he couldn't get a divorce—or so he says. Once again, he was down on his luck.

"In anticipation of going to Germany," he wrote to an old friend upon his return to America, "I had given up other work—a nice teaching job, lucrative magazine articles, good lecture work, etc. Nora has had a pretty rough time too. But I finally got her the job she always wanted and she is very happy working for one of the finest fashion places in NY. She also goes to college and is doing remarkably well in her studies."[1]

He and Nora, Reinhardt told his friend, couldn't get married because of his domestic situation. "As you know," he wrote, "my wife has been a hopeless invalid for 10 years. For the past year and a half she has also become mentally incompetent, and more than 80 cents out of every dollar I earn goes for her care and upkeep. NY law does not permit any divorce in such situations as she is not insane in the legal sense of the word: inasmuch as she is completely paralyzed she does not conform to the legal requirement of insanity that she 'could be a menace to others or herself.'"[2]

Broke and depressed, Reinhardt still managed to stir up trouble. Not long after his return from Germany, Reinhardt went to Camp Holabird in Baltimore, the headquarters of the Counterintelligence Corps, and tried to get in to see the general in command. But Colonel Garvey had already let the general know that Reinhardt was to be considered *persona non grata*, and the general refused to see him.

Reinhardt didn't give up. He had some important contacts in Washington, and he was determined to have his charges heard, and if possible, to make a buck in the process.

"In some ways he was a genius," one of his former CIC colleagues said with a laugh. "He was able to exploit these relationships."[3]

Reinhardt went to the U.S. Senate to talk to some of the senators he'd met on their tour of occupied Germany, and told them his story about corruption in the occupied zone and the theft of Hitler's gold.

This time, Guenther struck gold himself—at least for a little while. One of the Senate committees hired him as a special investigator, and before long, the army changed course and decided to conduct a full investigation of his allegations.

"They sent a team to Germany and we were all interviewed," recalled Werner Michel, Guenther's former colleague in the CIC. "We were all outraged. But within a few days, the army investigators realized that most of Bucky's allegations were cut from whole cloth and had no basis in reality."[4]

Reinhardt was let go by the Senate committee. "Then he went to the House and was hired by the House Un-American Activities Committee," Michel recalled. "But the same thing happened. Nothing came of his allegations and they got rid of him, too."[5]

It was during this stint, working for HUAC in 1948, that Reinhardt first crossed paths with one of the committee's junior members—a young, first-term congressman from California named Richard Nixon.

CHAPTER 24

The Break-In

Young, handsome, and charismatic, John F. Kennedy dazzled the country during the 1960 Democratic primaries, knocking Minnesota senator Hubert Humphrey out of the race with impressive wins in Wisconsin and, with the help of Frank Sinatra and the Mob, West Virginia. He then beat perennial presidential candidate Adlai Stevenson and a field of "favorite sons" with huge wins in Illinois, Indiana, Pennsylvania, Oregon, Nebraska, and Massachusetts.

Positioning himself as a centrist, Kennedy easily defeated two of the party's more liberal elder statesmen: Oregon senator Wayne Morse, who later gained fame for his staunch opposition to the war in Vietnam, and Stuart Symington, the Missouri senator who, unlike Kennedy, refused to speak during the campaign to segregated audiences in the South.

By early June, the primaries were over and the nomination was almost his. But Jack Kennedy was worried. Someone had tried to steal his medical records, and he had a pretty good idea who was behind it.

They'd broken into the Manhattan offices of Dr. Eugene Cohen, Jack's endocrinologist, and turned the place upside down. The lock on the door was busted, filing cabinet drawers were left hanging half-open, and patient files lay strewn across the floor. On that same day, the thieves tried unsuccessfully to break into the offices of Dr. Janet Travell, Jack's pain doctor; the door had been jimmied with a crowbar, but they hadn't been able to bust the lock.

Over the years, Jack had seen dozens of doctors, but in the

summer of 1960, his two primary physicians were Travell, who treated his bad back, and Cohen, who treated him for his Addison's disease. Dr. Travell, the top pain specialist in the country, had pioneered the diagnosis and treatment of myofascial pain, the chronic back condition that had plagued JFK since his college days.

Travell, a kind, caring woman who looked something like former First Lady Eleanor Roosevelt's younger, slightly prettier sister, was born on December 17, 1901, in her parents' home in a fashionable section of lower New York City. Inspired to study medicine by her father, who was also a doctor, she graduated from Wellesley College in 1922, received her medical degree from Cornell University Medical College in 1926, and interned at the Cornell Medical Division of the New York Hospital, where she was the only female doctor on staff.[1]

When Senator Jack Kennedy first came to see Travell at her Manhattan offices in May 1955, he arrived on crutches and in so much pain that he could barely climb the three or four steps from the street to her door.

Kennedy had nearly died seven months earlier when a postoperative infection from the botched operation on his lower back left him in a coma. He survived that ordeal, of course, and while recuperating wrote his Pulitzer Prize-winning book, *Profiles in Courage.*

Travell began treating Kennedy by injecting low doses of the anesthetic procaine into the lumbar muscles in his lower back. But Travell also discovered that Kennedy's left leg was shorter than his right, so she had lifts made for the heels of all his left shoes to balance the stress on his back. It was Travell who recommended that Kennedy sit, whenever possible, in a rocking chair to ease the pressure on his back. The rocking chair would come to symbolize the Kennedy presidency.

Travell's treatments were so successful, Bobby Kennedy wrote during the first year of his brother's presidency, that if not for her, Jack "would not presently be president of the United States."[2]

That's not all Travell did for Jack Kennedy. When someone

broke into Dr. Cohen's office and attempted to break into Travell's own office shortly before the 1960 Democratic Convention, Jack asked her to go around to as many hospitals as she could where he'd been a patient and secure his medical records. For the next few days, she dropped everything and did just that.

In 1966, during an oral history interview with JFK advisor and speechwriter Ted Sorensen, Dr. Travell described those frantic days.

"I recall at one time that your office was broken into and some records taken," Sorensen reminded her. "Was [Kennedy] concerned that might have been aimed at him?"

"Oh, yes," she replied. "He didn't know it, but his records were not in the office. Dr. Eugene Cohen's office was ransacked about the same time and his patients' records were thrown all over. They were obviously looking for patients' records and they didn't find anything. They didn't even get into my office. They just sliced the door and they tried to break the lock. They did not actually get inside my office. They wouldn't have found anything."

Sorensen pressed on. "The fact that there was an attempt made on both your office and Dr. Cohen's office at the same time, though, would lead to the hypothesis that they were after…"

"…His records," Travell said, finishing Sorensen's sentence. "I went around where he had been a patient in New York Hospital, in Boston and Palm Beach, wherever he had been, approached the superintendent or somebody on the staff whom I know. All of his records were put under safekeeping and under lock and key instead of in an open office file. I tracked down almost everything that was available. I think that this was very important. I'm not sure but what [sic] Dr. Cohen's office was broken into twice."[3]

But there was no way to be sure that Travell had gotten everything, and that she had gotten to them before someone else had microfilmed Jack's medical files. In the wrong hands, those files could destroy Jack's chance of ever becoming president.

Sorensen and Travell never discussed who they thought was behind the break-ins and attempted break-in, but the most likely and obvious suspect was Richard Nixon. Not only would Nixon stand to gain the most from such a crime, but history and Nixon's famous White House tapes tell us that, after becoming president in 1969, politically motivated break-ins would become a signature of his administration. The men President Nixon put in charge of the "White House Plumbers" not only staged the Watergate burglary that led to his downfall, but also broke into the doctor's office of a hated political enemy and stole his psychiatric file.

Still another reason to suspect Nixon was a story related by Dr. Hutschnecker in his unpublished manuscript about his years of treating Nixon for psychosomatic disorders. On September 25, 1972, just five weeks before the election and three months after the Watergate break-in, Nixon's secretary, Rose Mary Woods, called Dr. Hutschnecker to tell him that the president wanted to send over Andrew Hutch, a Secret Service agent, to pick up all of Nixon's medical records for safekeeping until after the election.

"I considered this to be an invasion of my privacy and I was angry, to say the least," Dr. Hutschnecker wrote, "but in the end, I reluctantly agreed to it. I understood the pressure Nixon was under and the panic that had generated the request to take my files."[4]

Hutschnecker realized Nixon was worried that the doctor's notes on their sessions could be a political liability if they fell into the wrong hands, and wanted to safeguard them against theft.

The Secret Service agent came to Hutschnecker's offices on Park Avenue, collected all of his files on Nixon, and then quickly departed. It was all very cordial and professional, but Hutschnecker later wrote that the incident reminded him of the Gestapo watching over him as he packed up his household to leave for America 36 years earlier.[5]

Perhaps Nixon's concern about the security of his own medical records was a recognition of the fact that stealing opponents' medical records had just become a part of the game of politics—and an expression of the "guilty knowledge" that he had once done the same to Jack Kennedy in 1960.

Or perhaps someone else broke into Kennedy's doctors' offices.

JFK biographer Robert Dallek believes that Nixon was probably behind the 1960 break-ins, and said so in a 2002 *Vanity Fair* article.

"It appears that Richard Nixon may have tried at one point to gain access to Kennedy's medical history," Dallek wrote. "Although the thieves remain unidentified, it is reasonable to speculate that they were Nixon operatives."[6]

One of Nixon's top aides during the 1960 campaign flatly denies this, however.

"It couldn't have happened," said Herb Klein, who was Nixon's 1960 campaign press secretary. "Anything that would have been close to [a break-in] would have been discussed with me, and it wasn't," Klein said. "We would never have gotten into that sort of thing."[7]

In his article, Dallek wrote that the break-ins happened in "the fall of 1960," but we now know that they actually occurred several months earlier. That's an important detail, because if the break-ins had occurred in the fall, it would have been *after* Kennedy had received the Democratic Party's nomination at its convention in July and had already begun the campaign for the general election against Nixon, who would have stood to gain the most from a disclosure of Jack's medical records.

No police records exist today as to the exact date of the 1960 break-ins, but we now know that they occurred *before* the Democratic Convention in July. On June 11, 1960—three weeks before the start of the convention—Dr. Travell and Dr. Cohen wrote a statement saying that Jack's "adrenal glands do function," and advised Jack to sue anyone who said otherwise, even if they "have had access to old medical records"—a clear reference to records that may have been stolen in break-ins that had already occurred.[8]

Before the start of the Democratic Convention, there was one other politician who might have had a reason to want to steal Kennedy's medical records—a politician who wanted the Democratic nomination for himself. Like Nixon, this politician had a long history of doing anything it took to win, and on the eve of the Democratic Convention, would have two of his subordinates call a press conference and tell reporters that Kennedy had Addison's disease.

That politician was Lyndon Baines Johnson, who would later become Jack's running mate in the 1960 election. Like Nixon, Johnson had the means, motive, and opportunity to stage such a crime.

There was, of course, one other person who was not above stealing medical files or gaining unauthorized entry into a doctor's office, who must be considered a suspect in the 1960 break-ins at the offices of Jack Kennedy's doctors: Guenther Reinhardt. Not only did the private detective get into Nixon's psychotherapist's office in September of 1960 under false pretenses and then may have even stolen Nixon's medical file, but he also would be arrested three years later for stealing classified state documents. Guenther also lived within walking distance of Janet Travell's office in Chelsea.

Today, no one knows for sure, but it's certainly possible that Nixon's campaign hired Reinhardt to break into Kennedy's doctor's office in June, and that after getting paid, Reinhardt went to Joe Kennedy, who then hired the private detective to break into Dr. Hutschnecker's office three months later. There's nothing Guenther liked more than getting paid by both sides.

No matter who was behind the 1960 break-ins at JFK's doctors' offices, Jack Kennedy had every reason to believe that it was Nixon. And Jack's powerful and protective father had every reason to want to prevent Nixon from using stolen medical files against Jack by getting his hands on Richard Nixon's own medical files.

CHAPTER 25

Stampeding the Herd

A swaggering bully, Lyndon Baines Johnson was a veteran practitioner of the art of winning elections by any means necessary. And in the summer of 1960, the powerful and cunning Senate majority leader was preparing to open his own bag of tricks to steal the Democratic Party's presidential nomination from his rival, John F. Kennedy.

Johnson had fixed his first election at Southwest Texas State Teachers College in 1929, taking over his school's student government by engineering a scheme that allowed young LBJ and his supporters to vote more than once.[1]

The dirty tricks didn't stop there. LBJ won his first U.S. Senate seat in 1948 after winning his party's nomination by the narrowest of margins in the infamous "Box 13" incident, one of the dirtiest tricks in American political history. Back in those days, Texas was a solidly Democratic state, and winning the Democratic Party's nomination for a U.S. Senate seat virtually assured the nominee's victory in the general election. In the Democratic primary that year, Johnson, then a U.S. congressman, was opposed in the Senate race by former Texas governor Coke Stevens, an infamous racist and white supremacist. It was a bitter contest, and after all the ballots were counted, Stevens squeaked out a narrow victory, defeating Johnson by only 87 votes out of nearly one million ballots cast. But days after the last ballots had been tabulated, a ballot box from Precinct 13 in the little south Texas town of Alice, in Jim Wells County, mysteriously showed up. That ballot box contained 203 ballots—202 for LBJ and one vote for Stevens. And the town's voters, many of whom it was later learned had been dead for years, had, impossibly, each cast their ballots in alphabetical order.[2] The stuffed ballot box gave LBJ the victory, and the ironic nickname "Landslide Lyndon."

A famous photograph later turned up showing the ballot box from Precinct 13 sitting unopened on the hood of a car surrounded by several of Johnson's grinning supporters.

By comparison, the power play Johnson was going to make on John Kennedy at the Democratic Convention in Los Angeles that summer of 1960 was going to be downright honest.

Johnson hadn't officially entered any of the 1960 primaries, although he did receive a few write-in votes—less than one-third of one percent of all the ballots cast. But in those days there were only 13 state primaries, and party bosses still controlled large blocks of convention delegates. If Jack Kennedy could be made to look like damaged goods, a lot of his delegates might come running Johnson's way. And that was LBJ's plan—to stampede the herd.

Johnson was going to announce his candidacy for president at the convention, and though he had only picked up a handful of delegate votes at state conventions, he'd picked up something that would prove even more important—a juicy piece of information about Jack Kennedy's health that might throw the convention into a panic. If Kennedy was seen as unelectable in the upcoming general election against Richard Nixon, the delegates might decide to drop Kennedy and look for a new, healthier candidate.

Right away, before the convention was even gaveled to order, Johnson started spreading doubt about Kennedy's health, calling Jack a "little scrawny fellow with rickets."

"Have you ever seen his ankles?" Johnson asked a reporter from the *Chicago Daily News* on the eve of the convention, tracing a tiny circle in the air with his finger. "They're about so 'round."[3]

But he'd leave the real dirty work to his subordinates. As the delegates began arriving in Los Angeles, two of Johnson's longtime aides—John Connally, LBJ's campaign manager and future governor of Texas, and India Edwards, co-chairwoman of the Citizens for Johnson National Committee—began hatching the plot that just might deliver the nomination for their boss.

The Democratic National Convention was being held that sweltering summer of 1960 in the Los Angeles Memorial Sports Arena, whose opening a year earlier, ironically, had been presided over by Vice President Richard Nixon.

"The Dodgers might take it all this year!" Nixon told a roaring crowd at the dedication ceremonies on July 4, 1959.[4]

Nixon was right. The Dodgers, who'd moved to Los Angeles from Brooklyn the previous year, would go on to win the World Series in October 1959, defeating the Chicago White Sox four games to two.

Nixon was equally prescient in his speech about the political hurricane that a year later would blow through the very building he was dedicating that day.

After talking briefly about the major sporting events that would one day be held at the arena, Nixon joked with the crowd. "There are other events to be held here, of which I am aware," he said with a wink. "The 1960 Democratic Convention will be held here and it may turn out to be the battle of the century."

Nixon was right about that, too. Exactly one year later in that same arena, a week before the start of the Democratic National Convention and the day before Lyndon Johnson formally announced his candidacy, LBJ's top campaign aides held a press conference that they hoped would sink Jack Kennedy's candidacy.

Johnson's aides, John Connally and India Edwards, had called their press conference, ostensibly, to tout the physical fitness of their candidate, but it was really a trap. They knew full well that reporters would inquire, as they always did, about Johnson's health, and that would give them the opening they needed in order to raise questions about Kennedy's health, and to reveal for the first time publicly that JFK had Addison's disease.

Five years earlier, on July 2, 1955, not long after he was first elected majority leader of the Senate, Lyndon Johnson, who was then only 46 years old, suffered a massive heart attack while visiting the Virginia estate of his longtime friend and benefactor, George Brown, co-founder of the giant Texas-based Brown & Root construction firm and military contractor. (Seven years later, an even bigger company, Halliburton Energy Services, would acquire Brown & Root.)

George Brown, who had been the principal source of campaign funds for Johnson's initial run for Congress in 1937, and who had been a major donor to Johnson's campaigns ever since, called an ambulance and had Johnson rushed to a hospital, where he remained in intensive care for more than a month. After his release in August 1955, LBJ recuperated at his ranch in Texas, and didn't return to his duties in the Senate until December. He had been sidelined for five months.

The story of Johnson's heart attack made national headlines. "Lyndon Johnson Ill; Out for this Session," read one in the *New York Times.* Over the years, whenever he held a press conference, some reporter would usually ask him about his health. If he announced that he was running for president, those questions would surely come up again. That's what LBJ was counting on.

"They were always bringing that up," India Edwards said years later. "And no matter how many times you said that he was perfectly sound, they were still bringing it up."[5]

So the night before the big press conference, Johnson had Connally, his campaign manager, give Edwards the idea of turning the tables on Kennedy in order to reveal *his* most closely-kept medical secret, one that could give the nomination to Johnson.

Taking a page out of Nixon's dirty playbook, Johnson would let Connally and Edwards work out the details, and let Edwards take the fall.

Edwards met Connally that night in his hotel room to discuss it.

"Don't you think it's time that we said something about Kennedy's health?" he asked her, no hint of conspiracy in his voice.

"Yes, I do," she replied. And she really did. She didn't think JFK should get a free pass on his health problems while LBJ always had to answer the same stupid questions.

They knew this was going to cause a big uproar, so they talked for a while about which one of them should drop the bomb. Finally, just as LBJ and Connally had hoped, Edwards volunteered.

"John, let me do it," she said, "because I have no career ahead of me, and you have. You're a young man. It will cause a terrible stink. It won't matter to me."[6]

And she was right about his bright future. Connally, who had helped Johnson engineer the "Box 13" incident back in 1948, would be named secretary of the navy in 1961; elected governor of Texas in 1962, and would be wounded by the same bullet that first struck President Kennedy on that terrible day in Dallas in November 1963.

Edwards, a lifelong Democrat, had been around politics long enough to know that, after the stunt they were going to pull, her future in politics would probably be over. And she was right about that, too.

Edwards had gotten into politics in 1944. Up until then, she'd been a journalist, working for more than 20 years at the *Chicago Tribune*, first as a reporter, then as the society editor, and finally as the women's editor. She left the paper to marry her third husband, a State Department official, and moved to Washington in 1942. Then, in 1943, her life was shattered when her only son was killed during the war at age 19. He had just been commissioned a lieutenant in the Army Air Corps, and was a bombardier instructor at Wendover Field in Utah, where the crew of the *Enola Gay*, the plane that dropped the atom bomb on Hiroshima, would later train. He was flying in close formation on a training mission in December 1943 when his plane touched wings with another bomber and both planes crashed in the Utah desert. All 25 men aboard both planes were killed.

India Edwards went into mourning and didn't come out of her grief until one day the next June when she was listening to radio coverage of the 1944 Republican Convention. Ultraconservative congresswoman Clare Boothe Luce, the wife of the publisher of *Time* and *Life* magazines, was speaking to the Republican delegates in Chicago.

"Clare Boothe Luce made a speech," Edwards recalled, still angry about it many years later, "in which she presumed to speak for the boys who had been killed to say that if they could come back they would say to vote against Roosevelt because he was responsible for their deaths."[7]

Clare Boothe Luce had long been an outspoken critic of President Franklin Roosevelt, but this was too much. Outraged, Edwards went down to the Democratic headquarters at the Mayflower Hotel the next day and volunteered to work for Roosevelt's reelection. Over the next decade, she would hold increasingly important positions in the Democratic Party. She was named associate director of the Women's Division of the Democratic National Committee in 1947, executive director of the Women's Division in 1948, and in 1950 became vice chairman of the Democratic National Committee, making her the highest-ranking female in the Democratic Party. In 1960, she went to work for Lyndon Johnson, trying to get him the Democratic nomination for president.

On the day of their press conference, Connally was standing beside Edwards when one of the reporters asked about Johnson's health.

"And so, sure enough," she recalled, "somebody in the press conference did say something about Johnson, you know, not being able to be president because of his heart attack. So I said, 'Well, what about Jack Kennedy's health? He's not what I would call a picture of the greatest health in the world. He has, as I understand it, Addison's disease, and has to have cortisone all the time or else he goes into a coma.'"[8]

Edwards kept talking as the reporters scribbled madly in their notebooks. "Doctors have told me he would not be alive if it were not for cortisone," she said, noting that she'd heard this from "several doctors," although none who had actually examined or treated Kennedy.[9]

She told the reporters that she was making this known because she objected to the Kennedy campaign's "muscle-flexing in boasting about [JFK's] youth."

Edwards had been told by a man she trusted—she never would say who—that he'd been present at the home of a governor when Jack Kennedy paid a visit there and fell into a coma because he'd forgotten to bring along his cortisone.

"They had to get a state trooper up in the middle of the night," she recalled many years later. "And this kind of story was all over the place; that he had this adrenaline deficiency. Everybody knew that he had been a very ill man aside from the fact that he had been injured in the war, and I had talked to a couple of doctors about it…I was the one who did it, but John [Connally] knew I was going to do it. It was John Connally's decision as well as mine…and the lid was off."[10]

The revelation sent shockwaves through the Kennedy campaign.

"It was as though a bomb went off," recalled Clark Clifford, a longtime Kennedy family attorney and advisor who would later become Secretary of Defense.[11]

This was just the scenario that Kennedy had feared the most: a last-minute disclosure about his health that would knock him out of the race. And Jack knew that there was only one thing to do. He'd have to lie, and get his doctors to lie, too. Anything less would mean losing the nomination—and the presidency.

CHAPTER 26

Denial

Ensconced at the Biltmore Hotel in downtown Los Angeles, where the Kennedy campaign had its headquarters, an outraged Bobby Kennedy, Jack's brother and campaign manager, issued a flat denial of India Edwards's charge.

Kennedy, he dissembled, "does not now, nor has he ever had, an ailment described classically as Addison's disease, which is a tuberculose destruction of the adrenal gland. Any statement to the contrary is malicious and false."[1]

Furious at LBJ for engineering this potentially fatal pre-convention stunt, Bobby accused Johnson of trying to throw the election to Nixon.

"Evidently," he told reporters, "there are those within the Democratic Party who would prefer that if they cannot win the nomination themselves, they want the Democrat who does win to lose in November."[2]

Bobby then hurriedly tracked down Bobby Baker, one of Johnson's top advisors, and heatedly warned him to stop this attack on his brother or face the wrath of the Kennedys. Bobby Kennedy, Baker later recalled, "grew so red in the face I thought he might have a stroke."

"You've got your nerve," Bobby snapped at him. "John Connally and India Edwards lied in saying my brother is dying of Addison's disease. You Johnson people are running a stinking damned campaign, and you're gonna get yours when the time comes!"[3]

But Jack Kennedy was not going to let Lyndon Johnson's dirty trick stop him now—not on the eve of the Democratic Convention.

Somehow, he'd have to get his doctors to do what they had, until now, refused to do—lie for him.

A month earlier and not long after the break-ins at his doctors' offices, Jack Kennedy, fearful that his health might become a campaign issue, told his trusted advisor, Ted Sorensen, to call his doctors and get them to sign a certificate saying he didn't have Addison's disease.

Dr. Eugene Cohen was in charge of the treatment of Jack's Addison's disease, but he didn't want to sign a false certificate. He could lose his reputation and his medical license, which are everything to a good doctor. Jack's pain doctor, Janet Travell, pleaded with Dr. Cohen to do this one thing for Jack, but she couldn't get him to budge.

"He did not wish to sign Senator Kennedy's health certificate, if one may call it that, that we gave him in June 1960," Travell recalled in her oral history interview with Sorensen. "Dr. Cohen and I were both going on vacation. [Sorensen] called me in my office on 16th Street and said this might come up and since we were going away, would we prepare something. I made the draft. I called Dr. Cohen."[4]

It was a Friday afternoon in June when Dr. Travell arrived at Cohen's office in Manhattan. She showed Cohen the draft she'd written, but he balked.

"You know I don't like publicity," he told her. "I don't want to get mixed up in this."

"Well, now, Gene," she said. "He's a patient of yours. If he was president of a bank and wanted a health certificate, would you give him one?"

"Oh, yes," Cohen replied.

"Do you have an obligation to him or not?" she pressed.

"Why, yes," he replied, still not convinced.

"Who else is going to sign his health certificate?" she asked.

"Oh, all right," he said, finally relenting.

The two doctors looked over the draft she'd written and agreed to meet again the next morning, a Saturday, at Dr. Travell's office at New York Hospital. That setting, Travell recalled, "would be quiet and no secretaries on duty."[5]

On Saturday, they met at her office and bickered for several more hours about the wording of the certificate.

"We spent three or four hours on it," Travell told Sorensen. "I typed it out. Gene Cohen said he would sign it provided that it should not be released with his name—with our names on it."

By the end of the day, all she could get Dr. Cohen to sign off on was a timidly worded statement about Jack's health that said: "... the fact that your adrenal glands do function has been confirmed by a leading endocrinologist outside of New York City. We have documented evidence of this."

In their statement, they also suggested that Jack "could forewarn anyone who makes a statement to the contrary that he will be open to suit, even though he may have had access to old hospital records"—a clear reference to the break-ins at their offices.[6]

Dr. Cohen, however, insisted that his name not be mentioned in connection with this deception.

"Again, we understand that our names will not be used publicly," they wrote as a postscript to their letter.

Below is a copy of the letter that Travell and Cohen wrote and sent to JFK that day.

Janet G. Travell
Nine West 16th Street
New York, New York
WA 9-2648

June 11, 1960

Senator John F. Kennedy
Senate Office Building
Washington, D.C.

Dear Senator Kennedy:
Enclosed is the statement concerning your health which Dr. Cohen and I jointly are happy to send you. I have included a signed copy for your files.

As an addendum to this statement, we wish to point out that the fact that your adrenal glands do function has been confirmed by a leading endocrinologist outside of New York City. We have documented evidence of this.

Under the circumstances, you could forewarn anyone who makes a statement to the contrary that he will be open to suit, even though he may have had access to old hospital records which do not apply to the present situation or have been proven to be in error.

With very best wishes,
Janet Travell, M.D.
Eugene J. Cohen, M.D.

PS—Again, we understand that our names will not be used publicly.

Jack Kennedy knew that this timid letter wasn't going to fool anyone, but it would have to do for now. The convention was still three weeks away.

A few days later, Dr. Travell met with Jack and tried to give him the private, unlisted phone number where she could be reached in case of an emergency while she was vacationing in the Massachusetts countryside. She wrote the number on a piece of paper and put it in his coat pocket.

"Don't give it to me, I'll only lose it," he complained petulantly. "I can't ever keep a piece of paper like that."

"Well," she told him, "just remember the town I'm in and that I'm not listed and you can't find me, and hang on to the piece of paper."[7]

Sure enough, Jack lost the piece of paper, but two weeks later, on the Fourth of July—a week before the convention was to begin—Dr. Travell received a phone call from Jack at her vacation retreat.

"How'd you locate me?" she asked him.

"Oh, we called the sheriff," Jack said, reminding her that she'd told him the name of the town where she'd be vacationing. "The sheriff knows everybody in town."[8]

They both laughed, and then Jack got down to business. He told her he needed a stronger letter from her and Dr. Cohen—one with their names on it that Jack could use publicly to refute claims that he had Addison's disease. Johnson's aides had just dropped their bombshell that day; the convention was a week away and Jack needed something that would stop all this talk about his health.

After hanging up with Jack, Travell got on the phone with Cohen, who was also on vacation. But after several more hours of negotiating, all she could get him to sign was another weakly worded statement. The next day, Dr. Travell called Jack back and read him the new letter she'd gotten Dr. Cohen to sign off on.

"In the past," she and Cohen wrote in their July 5, 1960, letter to Kennedy, "you were treated for adrenal insufficiency which developed following extraordinary stress and malaria during the war period. You have not taken cortisone or hydrocortisone in several years, but on our advice have continued to take by mouth small doses of other cortico steroids even though the last ACTH (Adrenocorticotropic hormone) stimulation test for adrenal function was normal. Adrenal insufficiency no longer presents any threat to a person who is fully rehabilitated on such simple oral therapy."

Jack was not happy. What good would all that lukewarm, medical mumbo-jumbo do in a dogfight with Lyndon Johnson on the floor of the convention? Jack needed something signed by a doctor saying he didn't have Addison's disease, and he needed it now.

Dr. Travell called Dr. Cohen back, but he still wouldn't budge. It was up to her now. She was going to have to risk losing her license and her reputation if she was going to help Jack this time.

On July 10, Jack and Bobby were photographed by *Life* photographer Hank Walker sitting in a hotel suite at the Biltmore Hotel, the headquarters of the Kennedy campaign during the convention.

It is the most famous image of the campaign, and one of the most famous pictures ever taken of JFK. It shows the two brothers, heads bowed deep in thought, silhouetted against a hotel window sunset. No one alive today knows what they were discussing, but it is very possible that they were talking about how to handle the question of Jack's Addison's disease, which at that moment was threatening to sink the campaign.

The next day, Dr. Travell came through for them.

Though not a specialist in Addison's disease, Janet Travell had the one qualification that mattered most: she was loyal to Jack and, in an almost motherly way, would do practically anything to protect him.

On July 11, the day the convention started, she wrote out a categorical statement that said, "Senator Kennedy does not have Addison's disease," and transmitted it to Bobby Kennedy, who was waiting for it in Los Angeles, where he was busy fending off more questions about his brother's health—and fuming about Johnson's treachery.

Just in case the thieves *had* managed to steal some of Jack's medical records before she could secure them all, Travell noted in her letter to Bobby that "old hospital records no longer apply to the present situation."

Below is a copy of the actual letter that Travell wrote on July 11, 1960.

Janet G. Travell, M.D.
9 West 16th Street
New York, N.Y.
Watkins 9-2648

Mr. Robert F. Kennedy
Kennedy Headquarters
Hotel Biltmore
Los Angeles, California

Dear Mr. Kennedy;

The matter of Senator Kennedy's health should be a dead issue, but in case any further questions arise, you might wish to be guided by the following facts concerning his adrenal function.

1. Senator Kennedy does not have Addison's disease.
2. He was treated for adrenal insufficiency that developed following extraordinary stress and malaria during the war period.
3. In recent years, the function of his adrenal glands has shown excellent recovery and now approaches normal.
4. Old hospital records no longer apply to the present situation.
5. Prophylactically, Senator Kennedy takes a small dose of steroid by mouth, which his physicians expect eventually to discontinue.
6. No limitations of any kind are placed on his activities.

Sincerely yours,
Janet Travell, M.D.

This was just what Jack needed, and it saved the day. Dr. Travell's letter satisfied the reporters and calmed the delegates, and two days later, on July 13, 1960, Jack won the Democratic Party's nomination on the first ballot. Jack then picked Lyndon Johnson to be his running mate. Or rather, he followed his father's recommendation and picked Johnson. Old man Joe Kennedy knew his son would need Texas to win the general election against Nixon, so Johnson was the obvious choice. And besides, with Johnson on the ticket, he'd have to be quiet about Jack's Addison's disease, and wouldn't be secretly scheming to help Nixon win the election so that Johnson would be first in line for the Democratic Party's nomination in 1964.

But Johnson's selection as Jack's running mate didn't sit well with Bobby Kennedy, who despised Johnson for nearly destroying his brother's chance at the presidency. Because of this, Bobby would hold a grudge against LBJ for the rest of his life.

Jack forgave Lyndon, and he never forgot Dr. Travell for helping him, either. A few months later, as one of his first appointments, President Kennedy would make her the first female to ever hold the position of personal physician to the president of the United States.

Jack even forgave John Connally, who had stood beside India Edwards the day she announced that Jack had Addison's disease. When Jack became president, he named Connally, at Johnson's request, to be the secretary of the navy.

The only person who didn't get anything out of it was India Edwards. Her career in politics was over.

Joe Kennedy couldn't have been more proud of his son that last night at the Sports Arena in Los Angeles as Teno Roncalio, the chairman of the Wyoming Democratic Party, called out the delegate votes that put JFK over the top for the nomination.

"Mr. Chairman...Mr. Chairman..." Roncalio called out above the din of the convention. "Wyoming's vote will make a majority for Senator Kennedy. Mr. Chairman...Mr. Chairman. Wyoming votes...We have 15 votes...There are 15 votes from Wyoming for Kennedy."[*9]

---

*Ted White got this wrong in his Pulitzer Prize-winning book, *The Making of the President: 1960*. On page 169, White wrote that Tracy S. McCraken, Wyoming's national committeeman, called out the 15 Wyoming votes that put JFK over the top. But according to the official minutes of the 1960 Democratic National Convention, it was Teno Roncalio, the chairman of the Wyoming Democratic Party. White apparently picked this up from *Time* magazine's coverage of the convention, which on July 25, 1960, erroneously attributed the call of Wyoming's votes to McCraken. At least White spelled McCraken's name correctly, which was more than the *Time* magazine article did.

Outside the cavernous Sports Arena, a sinister yellow smog was rolling in from the freeway. And inside the convention hall, the cheering had barely died down before Jack would have to start worrying about how to handle Nixon if *he* raised the question of Jack's health.

Fortunately for Jack, Guenther Reinhardt would take care of that.

CHAPTER 27

"Fightin' Joe" McCarthy

In 1950, while still working as an investigator for Hollywood 10 attorney Bartley Crum, Reinhardt began freelancing for another crusading liberal—Drew Pearson, the famed columnist and radio commentator whose reporting two years earlier had sent J. Parnell Thomas, the corrupt chairman of the House Un-American Activities Committee, to jail for fraud and income tax evasion.

Pearson had been breaking big stories in his syndicated column, "Washington Merry-Go-Round," since 1931, and on his weekly radio show, *Drew Pearson Comments*, heard on NBC stations around the country. One of the most famous journalists in America, he was, in a sense, the *60 Minutes* of his day, employing a cadre of researchers and investigators to help him get his scoops. Guenther Reinhardt was one of his legmen.

Guenther started working for Pearson in June 1950, and over the following year wrote up 36 confidential reports for Pearson.

Throughout most of 1950, Pearson had been engaged in running feuds with two of the most powerful and vitriolic spokesmen of the American far right. One of them was Senator Joseph Mc-Carthy, the demented U.S. senator from Wisconsin who earlier that year had begun his unscrupulous crusade against anyone he suspected of being a Communist or a Communist sympathizer, thus launching the era of "McCarthyism."

Pearson started digging into the senator's past and soon began uncovering one piece of shady business after another, including the fact that McCarthy had failed to pay taxes on $45,000 of income during the war, and that he'd received a $10,000 kickback from the Lustron Corporation, a postwar builder of prefabricated housing.

Pearson also raised serious questions about McCarthy's use of questionable tactics in his pursuit of Communists in high places, and in so doing, becoming the first nationally syndicated columnist to take on McCarthy a full four years before legendary TV journalist Edward R. Murrow came out against McCarthy in 1954.

Pearson, who had come to see McCarthy as a dangerous demagogue, mocked and criticized his greed and red-baiting antics nearly every day in his column. And Guenther Reinhardt helped supply some of the fodder.

But Guenther's main job was to dig up dirt on another of Pearson's enemies—his archrival, right-wing columnist and radio personality Westbrook Pegler, a union-bashing, anti-Semitic hatemonger.

"We should all honor strike breakers," Pegler wrote in 1950. "The union movement was a saboteur, a slacker and a gross profiteer in World War II."

Pegler didn't think much of American voters either, calling them "a dumb, selfish electorate whose only thought was to sock it to the rich."

President Harry Truman, Pegler wrote, was a "guttersnipe" who "ought to be sent to prison."

But he saved some of his nuttiest barbs for President Franklin Roosevelt, who he called a "feeble-minded *führer*," writing that it was "regrettable" that an assassin who'd tried to shoot Roosevelt in 1933 but missed and killed the mayor of Chicago instead had "hit the wrong man."

Pearson and Pegler had been involved in an ugly and very public dispute for years, frequently exchanging accusations and insults in their columns. In 1946, Pearson filed a libel suit against him after Pegler called him a "miscalled newscaster specializing in falsehoods." Pearson withdrew the suit after they reached a gentlemen's agreement not to call each other names, but filed a second suit in 1950 when Pegler accused him of being a "lying blackguard."

In his suit, Pearson charged that Pegler's continued assault was part of a "wrongful, unlawful, and malicious scheme...to disgrace the plaintiff, hold him up to ridicule and contempt, cause him to be ostracized and, in general, to minimize his importance and effect as a columnist, writer, and radio commentator, and thereby in some measure to cast discredit upon the cause of liberalism in the United States of America."[1]

Guenther's assignment was to go through Pegler's columns and document some of the most outrageous lies Pegler had told, and the crackpot positions he'd taken, so that Pearson could use them against him in court.

On December 12, 1950, Guenther sent a confidential four-page report of his findings to Pearson's friend and attorney, Jack L. Kraus II.

Guenther, who was working for Pearson on the sly, didn't want anyone to know what he was up to; Pearson had powerful enemies and working for him could be dangerous. Pearson's top investigator, David Kerr, had already been hauled before the dreaded House Un-American Activities Committee after it was revealed that he had once worked for *The Daily Worker*. Guenther didn't want any trouble from the same un-American committee that he himself had once worked for, so he used Kraus as an intermediary.

To help him in his undercover work on the Pegler case, Kraus had written Guenther a letter of introduction, which stated: "The bearer of this letter, Mr. Guenther Reinhardt, is conducting some highly confidential investigations in the libel matter concerning [Westbrook Pegler]."[2]

Tragically, Kraus killed himself four years later by jumping off a 300-foot cliff overlooking the Hudson River.

"He was broke," recalls his daughter, Patricia Ann Selig. "He had no money."

It's not clear whether Guenther informed on him or not.

For Guenther, finding dirt on Pegler was easy money. Pegler made outrageous statements on a daily basis, and in his report, Guenther cited dates and columns in which Pegler "supported and advocated lynching," "defended the Ku Klux Klan," and "insinuated strongly that N.Y. Jews…organized and revived the Klan."

Guenther delivered the report—which he numbered "Report #17"—to Pearson's attorney, and for good measure threw in a separate five-page account, "Report #18," documenting Pegler's ties to a Georgia "Jew- and Negro-hater," and to a group of neo-Nazi, "brown-shirted storm troopers" in South America.

Later that night—the night before his 53rd birthday—Pearson and his wife Luvie drove to the exclusive Sulgrave Club off Dupont Circle in northwest Washington, D.C., to attend a dinner honoring former Pennsylvania governor James Duff, who just last month had been elected to the Senate. All of Washington was going to be there, including Richard Nixon, the newly elected U.S. Senator from California whom Pearson skewered regularly in his columns.

It was cold, almost freezing, when they arrived just after 8:00 PM. They checked their hats and coats at the cloakroom and started making their way up the stairs to the ballroom when, to their dismay, they ran into Joe McCarthy, who greeted them with phony effusiveness. He was obviously drunk.

Smiling broadly and speaking loudly about what a happy surprise it was to see him at the party, Joe patted Drew on the back, then leaned in close and whispered in a low, menacing voice, "I am going to make a speech about you on the Senate floor tomorrow, Drew, and I am going to really tear you to pieces."[3]

Then McCarthy straightened up, and with more mock jocularity announced, "I am going to get you a drink!"

As Joe staggered off to the bar, Pearson and his wife exchanged a knowing look, as if to say they certainly wouldn't have come if they'd known *he* was going to be here. What an unhappy birthday surprise.

Drew and Luvie made their way to the ballroom, but a few minutes later, McCarthy caught up with them. He sidled up to them with a big grin and a drink in each hand, spilling most of one as he approached.

Joe handed Drew the half-empty glass, and resumed his menacing monologue, acting friendly one minute, threatening the next.

"I am certainly sorry to meet your wife here," McCarthy said, laughing for everyone to hear. "I am going to feel awfully guilty tomorrow."

Then, under his breath, he snarled, "I am going to tear you to pieces. I am going to murder you."

McCarthy then wheeled around, raised his glass as if to make a toast, and said in a loud voice for all the other guests to hear, "Well, I certainly am sorry Drew is here. This is a terrible thing because I am going to make a speech about him tomorrow."

Too shocked to reply, Pearson turned away and started up a conversation with Louisiana senator Russell Long, and then, as if a bell had rung ending round one, someone announced from across the room that dinner was being served.

McCarthy kept up his harangue all through the meal. Drew was seated at the far end of the table, but Luvie was sitting just across the table from McCarthy and heard every word he said— that Pearson was a Communist, that Joe was going to prove he was a Communist, and that when he got through with him, Luvie would divorce him.

Twice during dinner, McCarthy got up and went over to taunt Drew some more, telling him that he was going to destroy him the next day and that there was nothing Pearson could do about it, because comments made from the Senate floor are exempt from slander suits.

The band struck up a tune, and Pearson got up and walked away from McCarthy, taking his wife for a spin on the dance floor. When the song was over, Drew returned to his seat. McCarthy was gone, but not for long. He came back, pulled up a chair, and started badgering Pearson some more.

"I don't know why the newspapers in Wisconsin carry you up there," he told Pearson in a calm, matter-of-fact voice. "You have hurt me some up there, but I am going to hurt you more. I am really going to put you out of business. I am going to ruin you."

Once again, Pearson got up and walked away from his drunken nemesis and went to dance with his wife. But when he returned to the table, McCarthy came back, too, and started in on him again.

Finally fed up, Pearson turned to McCarthy and in a mild, taunting tone, asked, "Joe, how is your income tax case coming along? When are they going to put you in jail?"

McCarthy's face, already red from the booze, turned a brighter shade of scarlet.

"You take that back!" he screamed, jumping to his feet and nearly knocking over his chair as he grabbed Pearson by the back of the neck. "You are going to leave this place just as soon as you can! You will get out of here! Don't let me see you around here! You go on and get out!"

A hush fell over the room as everyone turned to see McCarthy, a burly ex-Marine whose nickname was "Fightin' Joe," towering over the diminutive reporter.

Pearson, a Quaker and a pacifist who was 12 years McCarthy's senior, started to get up to confront the much larger man, but a congressman's wife spoke up. "Don't be a fool," she said. "Sit down. He's been drinking. Don't embarrass your hostess."

"Don't do it," pleaded 80-year-old former congressman William Stiles Bennet, reaching out an arthritic hand to keep Pearson in his seat.

Pearson sat back down, and after a few more awkward moments, McCarthy took his big hand off Pearson's neck, turned, and walked away as if nothing had happened.

It was nearly ten o'clock, and Pearson had just endured two of the worst hours of his life. But, mercifully, the party was over.

Drew went down to the cloakroom to get his and his wife's coats and hats. As he was fishing in his pocket to get a tip for the hat check attendant, McCarthy came up to him from behind and grabbed him, pinned his arms to his side, swung him around and, in one swift motion, kneed him in the groin.

"Keep your hands out of your pockets," McCarthy ordered drunkenly. "No firearms. No guns."

Dazed by the blow, Pearson struggled to get his arms loose, and McCarthy kneed him again.

"Take that back about my income taxes," he slurred. "Take that back!"

Hearing the commotion in the cloakroom, 37-year-old Richard Nixon, the newly elected senator from California, rushed in and tried to separate the men.

"Let a Quaker stop this fight!" Nixon proclaimed, stiff and awkward as ever.

But McCarthy wouldn't back off. He slapped Pearson, still doubled over from the second knee to the groin, as hard as he could across the face. It sounded like a car door slamming, and Pearson fell to the floor.

"That one is for you, Dick," McCarthy scowled.

Grabbing McCarthy's arm, Nixon said, "Come on, Joe, it's time for you to go home."

"No!" McCarthy bellowed, pulling away sullenly. "Not until he goes first. I am not going to turn my back on that son of a bitch."

While Nixon distracted McCarthy, Pearson got up off the floor and stumbled outside, where his shocked wife was waiting for him at their car. They drove home in the freezing cold. In a few hours, it would be his birthday.

Back at the Sulgrave Club, Nixon half-carried McCarthy outside and the two senators spent the next half hour looking for McCarthy's car. He was so drunk, he couldn't remember where he'd parked it.

Nixon would later tell a friend that he'd never seen a man slapped that hard.

"If I hadn't pulled McCarthy away," Nixon said, "he might have killed Pearson."[4]

Three days later, McCarthy kept his promise and crucified Pearson on the Senate floor.

"Drew Pearson," McCarthy roared, "is a Moscow-directed character assassin…the sugar-coated voice of Russia."[5]

Of course, it was a lie. Pearson, though a pacifist, was strongly anti-Communist and very pro-American. But he was also anti-fascist, and Joe McCarthy was a fascist.

Drew Pearson, McCarthy howled in the Senate, "is a degenerate liar" with a "twisted, perverted mentality." But the person McCarthy was more accurately describing, of course, was himself.

Then "Fightin' Joe" went in for the kill, using the Senate floor as a killing floor. He called on the newspapers that published Pearson's columns, and the radio stations that broadcasted his show, to fire him—to "still this voice of international Communism," and for "every loyal American" to boycott the product of his radio show's sponsor, which in this case was men's hats.

The Adam Hats Company was a big sponsor of radio shows. It had even sponsored Guenther Reinhardt's news commentary show a few years earlier, which was carried on WINS Radio in New York City. Guenther even appeared in print ads for the company.

"For seasonable, reasonable headgear," he was quoted in the ad, "I prefer Adam Hats."

Guenther never made more than $100 a week from his radio show, if that much. But Adam Hats, which sponsored Pearson's show, paid Drew a whopping $5,000 a week, which was a fortune in those days.

But Joe McCarthy was going to fix that.

"It should be remembered," he sneered on the Senate floor, "that anyone who buys an Adam Hat, any store that stocks an Adam Hat, anyone who buys from a store that stocks an Adam Hat, is unknowingly and innocently contributing to the cause of international Communism by keeping that Communist spokesman on the air."

With that, Joe McCarthy doffed a gray Adam Hats fedora and marched off the Senate floor.[6]

A few days later, the Adam Hats Company withdrew its sponsorship from Pearson's show.

Responding to McCarthy's allegations, Pearson issued a statement saying that his record in fighting Communism was well-known to everyone but "the headline-happy senator from Wisconsin." Then he filed a $5.1 million suit against McCarthy for slander and assault and battery, citing as evidence the beating he'd received, and the lies McCarthy had told about him, at the Sulgrave Club.

The case dragged on for years, but Pearson, feeling vindicated, dropped the suit when the Senate censured McCarthy in 1954 for his "inexcusable" and "reprehensible" disregard for the rights of innocent people he'd accused of being Communists. Broken and disgraced, McCarthy died three years later at the age of 48 from acute hepatitis brought on by years of alcoholism.

Pearson's career and reputation only flourished. He'd lost Adam Hats as the sponsor of his radio show, but picked up others and remained on the air for two more years. And during the early days of television, he got his own weekly current events TV show—*The Drew Pearson Show*, which ran Sunday nights on ABC in 1952, and on Wednesday nights on the now-defunct DuMont Television Network in 1953.

Not long after Joe McCarthy beat him up in the cloakroom of the Sulgrave Club, and then tried to kill him on the floor of the United States Senate, Pearson was cast in a Hollywood science fiction movie that would go on to become a classic—*The Day the Earth Stood Still*. It was a small, uncredited role, but it was the perfect part for Pearson: he played a reporter, the only journalist among the panicky Washington press corps to urge calm in response to the arrival of an alien visitor and his giant robot, Gort. Ironically, Pearson had landed his first movie role in 1945 when he was hired to narrate RKO's *Betrayal from the East*, a wartime saga based on Alan Hynd's nonfiction book of the same name. Hynd devoted a whole chapter to how Guenther Reinhardt predicted a Japanese attack and tried to alert government officials to it just two weeks before the Japanese attack on Pearl Harbor.

Pearson's journalism career would thrive as well. Over the years, he would continue to break big stories, accompanying President Kennedy to Colombia and Venezuela in 1962, and later revealing that JFK's brother, Attorney General Robert F. Kennedy, had authorized FBI wiretapping of Martin Luther King, Jr.

He was an early supporter of the civil rights movement and

an early opponent of the war in Vietnam, and in 1968, with a tip from Guenther Reinhardt, he became the first reporter to reveal that Richard Nixon had been seeing a psychologist named Arnold Hutschnecker.

CHAPTER 28

Crime Without Punishment

F ive days after Richard Nixon was elected Vice President of the United States in November 1952, Guenther Reinhardt's new book, *Crime Without Punishment*, received a scathing but honest review in the *New York Times*.

The book, claiming to be an "authoritative exposé" of Soviet agents in America and of their sometimes unwitting American accomplices, was a 322-page screed against enemies real and imagined. And in those days of McCarthyism and Hooverism, when merely being accused could mean a visit from the FBI, Guenther's book was as reckless as it was undocumented.

"Only a few of the cases selected by the author," the *Times* review noted, "are both credible and authenticated. Most of the others seem implausible and conjectural."[1]

The book, a masterpiece of guilt-by-association, alleged that Soviet agents and their dupes had infiltrated all walks of American life—from Hollywood to the State Department, from charitable organizations to the U.S. armed forces. And anyone associated with those groups was suspect.

Pointing out that Reinhardt's book was full of "slandering by innuendo" (which it was), the *Times* review suggested that "those engaged in the fight against subversion must always keep two objectives in mind: the ferreting out of the subversives and the protection of the loyal. Accusations not backed by evidence, questioning of loyalty of representative groups of citizens and presentation of speculation as sensational fact do not help either objective."[2]

Hundreds of people were identified in the book as being subversives or the dupes of subversives. And many of them were completely innocent.

One of Guenther's many victims of guilt-by-innuendo was Dolores Del Rio, the sultry Mexican-born movie star whom Marlene Dietrich once dubbed "the most beautiful woman in Hollywood," and whom Orson Welles called "the most exciting woman I've ever met."

Guenther had met her at a cocktail party during one of his spy missions in Mexico and determined that she was a Communist sympathizer—referring to her in his book as "an attractive dupe."[3]

Not long after the publication of his book, Del Rio, who lived in Mexico and worked in Hollywood, wanted to come to Los Angeles to make another movie, but her visa application was denied by the U.S. State Department.

Gossip columnist Hedda Hopper explained why in one of her columns.

"If you're wondering why Dolores Del Rio didn't get a visa to come to Hollywood for a picture," she wrote, "you might find the answer in Guenther Reinhardt's book *Crime Without Punishment*, chapter titled 'The Little Comintern,' pages 92–94. Reinhardt was formerly with the FBI."[4]

Dolores Del Rio, who was completely innocent of any subversive activity, wouldn't work in Hollywood for another three years.

Another of Guenther's victims was none other than the *Times'* reviewer of his book—a freelance book reviewer named John H. Lichtblau.

After the review was published, Guenther called Lichtblau at his apartment in Manhattan and asked him if they could get together. Guenther was friendly and didn't seem at all upset by John's review.

As it turned out, they had a lot in common. Both were Jewish immigrants; Guenther had come to America from Germany in 1925, eight years before Hitler came to power, and John had come over at the age of eighteen as a refugee from Austria, by way of England, in September 1939, only a few days after the Nazi invasion of Poland and the start of World War II.

They'd both lost relatives in the war, and now they were almost neighbors, living not far apart in New York City. And they'd both served with the U.S. Counterintelligence Corps (CIC) in Germany after the war tracking down fugitive Nazis. They hadn't known each other over in occupied Germany, but the ranks of former CIC men was a fairly small club, and they'd have a lot to talk about. So Guenther invited Lichtblau for a drink.

"He called me and wanted to get together," Lichtblau recalled many years later. "That's how I got to know him. We met four or five times. He was very friendly, very pleasant."[5]

Lichtblau and his wife Charlotte even had dinner at Guenther's house on Christopher Street in the Village a couple of times.

"We had chili con carne one time," Charlotte recalled 56 years later, "and I never liked it after that."

And she didn't like Guenther, either.

"He called many, many times," she said. "I knew he was looking for information on my husband. I knew that he was up to something."[6]

But John Lichtblau was more trusting. The two men swapped stories about their days in the Counterintelligence Corps. Lichtblau, a former CIC warrant officer stationed in northern Bavaria, had been part of the team that captured Colonel Otto Skorzeny, the leader of the Schutzstaffel—the dreaded SS. Guenther had been a civilian employee of the CIC after the war in southern Bavaria, and often bragged—whether it was true or not—that he'd helped capture six Hungarian SS guards who'd murdered downed American airmen, and that he'd then secured the evidence for their conviction at the Nuremberg War Crime Trials.[7]

John Lichtblau even delivered several witnesses to the Nuremberg Trials, and Guenther claimed—whether it was true or not—that he'd been an interpreter at the trials.[8]

But mostly, Guenther wanted John to talk about his current

job at the U.S. Department of Labor.

Lichtblau knew a lot about Nazi Germany and wrote 18 book reviews on the subject for the *New York Times* in the 1950s. But his real job, the one that paid the bills, was as an economist at the U.S. Labor Department specializing in international labor relations. Guenther wanted to know all about it.

Only later would Lichtblau learn what Guenther was really up to.

"He pretended to be my friend so that he could get information to hurt me," he recalled. "He tried to trick me into saying things that he could use against me."

Not long after their last get-together in early 1953, FBI agents showed up at Lichtblau's office at the Labor Department in Washington, D.C.

"There was an FBI investigation," he recalled 56 years later, still hurt that his loyalty had been questioned. "This was the time of the great hunt against Communists. I was accused of being a Communist sympathizer. It was Guenther. There is no question about it. He tried to be friendly with me so that he could get information about me. Then he denounced me. I was asked some questions that came directly from him."

Lichtblau was suspended from his job at the Labor Department while the FBI investigated the charges.

"It was terrible," Charlotte Lichtblau recalled. "We had to move out of Washington and I had to go back to work. There was a seven-hour hearing. John had to testify and I had to testify."

Months after the ordeal began, John Lichtblau was finally cleared of all of Reinhardt's spurious charges, and was reinstated with back pay. He went back to work at the Labor Department for several more months and later enjoyed a long and successful career as an economist in the energy industry. For 16 years he was research director, executive director, and then chairman of the Petroleum Industry Research Foundation, and for nearly 30 years until his retirement in 2006 he was the senior executive of the PIRA Energy Group, a think tank that researches and publishes reports on economic and policy aspects of the world energy industry. He was also a member of the National Petroleum Council from 1968 to 2002, and over the years, Lichtblau has been quoted in more than a thousand newspaper and magazine articles about the oil industry, including nearly 300 in the *New York Times* alone.

But he is still resentful about what Guenther did to him.

"He wanted to take revenge for my review of his book," Lichtblau said. "He was very devious."

Indeed, he was.

CHAPTER 29

Civil Rights

On July 10, 1960, Dr. Martin Luther King Jr. led a march on the Sports Arena, where the Democratic Convention would begin the next day. Dr. King and 2,500 African-American protesters marched single file all the way from the Shrine Auditorium on Jefferson Boulevard to the Sports Arena in Exposition Park, chanting and carrying signs that urged the candidates to "Quit Stalling on Civil Rights." The line of protesters stretched nearly a mile.[1]

The demonstrators circled the Sports Arena and then marched back to the Shrine, where some 5,000 more protesters were waiting to greet them and the candidates who had been invited to speak there that day.

Kennedy had accepted their invitation. So had Missouri senator Stuart Symington, the great liberal and favorite of the civil rights movement who had been the only presidential candidate that year to refuse to speak before segregated audiences in the South. The other leading candidates, Lyndon Johnson and Adlai Stevenson, only sent representatives—a move that did not go over very well with the protesters.

Speaking about civil rights on the eve of the Democratic Convention was a risky move for Kennedy. Racial tensions were running high in America, and he needed the votes of white Southern delegates at the convention to win the nomination.

That year, black students had launched a wave of sit-ins at segregated lunch counters all across the South, and many Southerners were looking for a candidate who would hold back the rising tide of the civil rights movement. In the 1960s, the Democratic Party was the party of segregation in the South—the party of George Wallace, Lester Maddox, Strom Thurmond, Orval Faubus, and James Eastland. Kennedy would need the votes of white Southerners, not only to win the nomination, but to win the election in November, as well.

Kennedy was still working on his speech when his car pulled up at the Shrine. Before he could get out, reporters and photographers surrounded the car. Jack looked over his speech one more time, got out, and made his way into the auditorium, where he would share a stage for the first time with Martin Luther King.

Kennedy had first met Dr. King just two weeks earlier, on June 23, 1960, at JFK's apartment in New York. They had eaten breakfast and talked about civil right for about an hour and a half.

"I was very impressed by the forthright and honest manner in which he discussed the civil rights matter," King wrote to his old friend, former Connecticut governor Chester Bowles, the day after his meeting with Kennedy. "I have no doubt that he would do the right thing on this issue if he were elected president."[2]

Bowles, a longtime civil rights champion, was a staunch supporter of both King and Kennedy. JFK had picked him to be his chief foreign policy advisor, but more importantly, Bowles was the chairman of the Democratic Party's platform committee, which would be drawing up the party's position on civil rights.

"It may interest you to know," King told Bowles the day after he met JFK, "that I had very little enthusiasm for Mr. Kennedy when he first announced his candidacy. When I discovered, however, that he had asked you to serve as his foreign advisor my mind immediately changed. I said to myself, 'If Chester Bowles is Mr. Kennedy's advisor, he must be thinking right on the major issues.'"

Many in the crowd that day at the Shrine Auditorium didn't share Dr. King's enthusiasm and were skeptical of Kennedy's commitment to civil rights. When Kennedy took his seat onstage, he was greeted by a smattering of applause and a lot of boos. Describing JFK's entrance, a headline in the *Los Angeles Sentinel*, L.A.'s leading African-American newspaper, read: "7,000 Boo."

The booing didn't sit well with Clarence Mitchell, the head of the Washington bureau of the National Association for the Advancement of Colored People. Mitchell leapt to the stage and admonished the crowd.

"This is not the NAACP way," he chastised. "We do not boo our invited guests."[3]

The booing stopped, and JFK walked slowly across the stage to the podium. Looking out over the crowd, Kennedy then delivered one of the most important speeches of the campaign, promising that, if elected, he would use "the moral authority of the White House" to "secure to every American equal access to all parts of our public life—to the voting booth, to the schoolroom, to jobs, to housing, to all public facilities, including lunch counters."

"Our job," he told the audience, "is to turn the American vision of a society in which no man has to suffer discrimination based on race into a living reality everywhere in our land.

"I hope my own views are clear. I want our party to speak out with courage and candor on every issue—and that includes civil rights. I want no compromise of basic principles—no evasion of basic controversies—and no second-class citizenship for any American anywhere in this country."[4]

It was a speech that would become the blueprint for Kennedy's civil rights policy in the years ahead. That policy would lead to the landmark 1964 Civil Rights Act, which abolished segregation in all public places, and to the Voting Rights Act of 1965, which provided for fair access to the voting booth for all Americans.

When Kennedy finished speaking that day at the Shrine, there were no more boos, only cheers and applause. JFK had won the day, as well as the hearts and votes of many of the protesters.

After Kennedy spoke, Dr. King brought the crowd to its feet with a refrain that three years later would echo through the ages in his "I Have A Dream" speech.

"We have a determination to be free in this day and age," King told the cheering crowd. "We want to be free everywhere, free at last, free at last!"

The next day, July 11, the 1960 Democratic National Convention got underway at the Los Angeles Sports Arena. Banging his gavel on the podium promptly at 5:00, the Democratic National Committee chairman, Paul Butler, called the convention to order.

After the invocation, everyone stood as the color guard presented the flag—the first with 50 stars ever presented at a national political convention (Hawaii had been admitted to the Union the previous August). Then Butler introduced some of the celebrities who were packed into the crowded hall as guests of the convention. Three of the five "Rat Pack" members were there: Frank Sinatra, Sammy Davis Jr., and Peter Lawford, JFK's brother-in-law. Tony Curtis and his wife, Janet Leigh, were there, and so were Nat King Cole, Shirley MacLaine, Lee Marvin, Edward G. Robinson, Hope Lange, Lloyd Bridges, and horror film star Vincent Price.

As their names were called out, each celebrity received a rousing welcome—all except Sammy Davis, who was booed loudly by many of the white Southern delegates. Nearly everyone in the arena knew why they were booing: not because Davis was black, but because he had recently become engaged to a white woman, Swedish actress May Britt, whom he would later marry.

A headline in a *New York Times* story the next day read, "Delegates Boo Negro."

After Davis left the rostrum, a reporter, noting that Nat King Cole had not been booed when *he* was introduced, asked Davis why he thought so many of the white Southern delegates had booed him.

"You know as well as I know why they booed," Davis replied.[5]

In 1960, 17 Southern states—all the former slave states, plus Oklahoma—still enforced anti-miscegenation laws, which prohibited marriage between whites and African Americans. The Supreme Court didn't strike down those laws until 1967.

After the booing subsided, Frank Sinatra sang "The Star-Spangled Banner" under a lone spotlight shining down from the rafters.

The next day—the second day of the convention—would prove to be one of the most momentous in the history of American political conventions. It was on that day, with civil rights protesters keeping up their daily vigil outside the arena, that the Democratic Party set itself firmly on the path to ending segregation and championing the cause of civil rights.

The main business of the day was the ratification of the Democratic platform—the blueprint, goals, and agenda of the party and its presidential nominee.

The platform committee had drafted a lengthy document setting out the party's position on a whole range of issues: from defense to the economy, from farm policy to health care, and from jobs to housing. There was general unanimity among the delegates in each of these areas, but one issue threatened to divide the party and leave it mortally wounded going into the general election against Nixon: civil rights.

The platform committee, at JFK's direction, had addressed the issue head-on. Reading the committee's report to the convention, Chester Bowles, the committee's chairman—also Kennedy's man and Martin Luther King's friend—unveiled the specific steps that would be taken under a Democratic administration to fight discrimination in all walks of life.

"The time has come," Bowles read from the report, "to assure equal access for all Americans to all areas of community life, including voting booths, schoolrooms, jobs, housing, and public facilities."[6]

Bowles had to wait for the roar of applause to die down before continuing.

"The Democratic administration, which takes office next January, will therefore use the full powers provided in the Civil Rights Act of 1957 and 1960 to secure for all Americans the right to vote," he said, met again by a tremendous round of applause.

"We will support whatever action is necessary to eliminate literacy tests and the payment of poll taxes as requirements for voting," he continued. "A new Democratic administration will also use its full powers, legal and moral, to ensure the beginning of good faith compliance with the constitutional requirement that racial discrimination be ended in public education."

The convention hall rocked with cheers of approval, but not everyone was applauding. Most of the delegates from the Southern states sat quietly in their seats, fuming.

The Southern members of the platform committee had adamantly opposed the report, arguing in their own minority report that there were already enough laws on the books to address issues of civil rights and voting rights.

One speaker after another from the Southern delegations came to the podium to urge the delegates to throw out the civil rights plank of the platform.

One of those speakers, to his great shame, was North Carolina senator Sam Ervin, who 13 years later would become a hero to a generation of Americans when he chaired the Senate Watergate Committee that exposed the crimes of the Nixon Administration.

"As members of the Committee on Platform and Resolutions," Ervin said in his melodious Southern accent, "we move to strike out the portions of the platform relating to civil rights."[7]

The civil rights portion of the platform, he said, "is absolutely incompatible with the basic principle of American law." If enacted, he said, it "would destroy the system of government under which the America we have known and have loved has flourished and guaranteed freedom to all men." He added that these proposals would also make it very difficult for a Democratic presidential candidate to carry the South.

Several Southern governors spoke out against the civil rights plank as well, but the most telling comment would come the next day when Mississippi governor Ross Barnett's name would be placed into nomination for the presidency. During his nominating speech, Mississippi delegate Tom B. Brady said that Governor Barnett "stoutly maintains that to deprive 50 million white citizens of the South of their civil rights, of their right of freedom of choice, cannot be justified by giving vote-bringing civil rights to 18 million Negroes."[8]

In the end, when the convention chairman called for a voice vote on whether or not to strike the civil rights plank from the party's platform, the vast majority of delegates shouting, "No!" easily drowned out the Southerners shouting, "Aye."

Watching the vote on TV in his private suite at the Biltmore, Jack Kennedy was pleased. He and Bobby had pushed hard for the civil rights plank. Several of JFK's men were on the platform committee that drafted it, and several lines from Jack's speeches were included in it.

A news analysis piece that appeared the next day in the *New York Times* called the Democrats' civil rights position "astonishing."

Interviewed in his hotel room in Los Angeles after the passage of the civil rights plank, Dr. King said, "I think it's the most positive, dynamic, and meaningful civil rights plank that has ever been adopted by either party, and I'm sure if the party goes through with the implementation of it, we will go a long, long way toward solving the civil rights problems of the United States."[9]

The civil rights protesters who had picketed outside the Sports Arena every day during the convention may not have known it at that moment, but they had a powerful new ally in Jack Kennedy and the Democratic Party. Civil rights were coming to America.

The First TV Debate

While Guenther Reinhardt was visiting Richard Nixon's psychotherapist in New York City on the afternoon of September 7, 1960, John F. Kennedy was delivering an impassioned campaign speech in Portland, Oregon.

Kennedy had been suffering from laryngitis on this swing through the Western states, and Nixon operatives, who'd been sent out to reconnoiter JFK's campaign stops and to write up reports about them, were shocked at how weak he appeared onstage.

"If Kennedy doesn't do something about his voice projection and learn to speak correctly, he will not last another week," wrote a Nixon operative after watching Jack speak in at the Shrine Auditorium in Los Angeles. "His voice failed him at least twice and he was very husky after the first few minutes."[1]

But in Portland, Kennedy's voice was strong and he was in fine form. He told the wildly enthusiastic crowd there that it was time for new leadership that would "rebuild our defenses, until America is once again first in military power across the board; revamp our goals in education and research, until American science and learning are once again preeminent; renew our leadership for peace, until we have brought to that universal pursuit the same concentration of resources brought to the preparation of war; and remold our attitudes toward the aspirations of other nations, until we have a fuller understanding of their problems, their requirements, and their fundamental values."[2]

Nixon, meanwhile, was still laid up in Walter Reed Army Hospital, receiving treatment for the infection in his left knee. The injury, and his two-week hospital stay in the middle of the campaign, had been a crippling blow—both literally and figuratively.

When Nixon got out of the hospital two days later, he was behind in the polls, two weeks behind schedule, and aware that his most closely held secret—that he had been seeing a psychotherapist—was no longer a secret. Any hope of using Kennedy's medical secret against him was now probably lost.

Nixon's best chance to regain the momentum he'd lost was coming up in Chicago on September 26, when he'd face Kennedy in the first of four presidential debates—the first televised presidential debates in American history. More than 70 million Americans would be watching the first encounter—two million more than would actually cast ballots.

It was a make-or-break moment for Nixon, but he didn't seem to realize it.

A few days after speaking in Portland, Jack Kennedy flew to Chicago to meet with Don Hewitt, the producer and director of the upcoming debate telecast, to go over the ground rules. They met in a hangar at Chicago's Midway Airport. Knowing the importance of the debate, Kennedy was filled with questions for Hewitt, who years later would gain fame as the creator and executive producer of *60 Minutes*.

"He was curious," Hewitt recalled. "'Where do I stand?' 'Do I stand?' 'Do I sit?' 'How much time do I have to answer?' 'Can he interrupt?' 'Can I interrupt?' He wanted to know everything."[3]

Nixon, however, thought the debate with Kennedy was going to be a cakewalk. With his naturally mellow, baritone voice, he'd been a champion debater from the fifth grade through college. Kennedy had the good looks and the charm, to be sure; but in a debate format, Nixon felt he couldn't be beat. After all, he'd made Nikita Khrushchev, the head of the Soviet Union, look like a fool the year before in their impromptu Kitchen Debate, and Jack Kennedy was no Nikita Khrushchev. Besides, he hadn't lost an election in 30 years—not since high school.[4]

Rather than waste time with Don Hewitt going over the

debate format, Nixon stuck firmly to his rigorous campaign schedule, trying to make up for lost time.

"Nixon I never saw until he arrived that night in the studio," Hewitt later recalled. "Kennedy knew how important this television appearance would be. Nixon kissed it off as just another campaign appearance."[5]

On the night of the first televised debate, Nixon arrived before Kennedy at the studios of WBBM-TV, the CBS affiliate in Chicago, and got off to a bad start before the debate even began. Getting out of his limo to go into the studio, Nixon bumped his bad left knee—the same knee that had landed him in the hospital for two weeks—and nearly keeled over in pain.

"Getting out of the car...he banged his knee so bad he could hardly stand up," recalled CBS president Frank Stanton. "Nixon looked like warmed-over death. He'd been in the hospital, his color was bad...He was not a well man."[6]

Then Kennedy arrived.

"I was standing there talking to Nixon, and all of a sudden I noticed out of the corner of my eye Jack Kennedy arrived," Hewitt recalled. "And it was awesome. Here was this guy running for president of the United States who looked like a matinée idol: well-tailored, well-tanned, in command of himself...I guess I'd never seen a matinée idol president before."[7]

Nixon, still nursing his re-injured left knee, was sitting in a chair beneath a large boom-microphone when Kennedy walked onto the stage. Nixon leapt to his feet to greet his rival, but hit his head hard on the overhead microphone.

"It sounded like somebody dropped a watermelon," Stanton said. "It was terrible."[8]

An hour or so before airtime, Hewitt asked Nixon and Kennedy if they'd like some makeup for the cameras. He'd brought one of the best makeup artists in the business, Frances Arvold, to Chicago for just that purpose.

"I said, 'Would you like some makeup?'" Hewitt recalled. "Kennedy, who didn't need any, said, 'No, thank you, not really.' Nixon, who needed makeup, also said no. I'm convinced he didn't want history to record that that night he was made up and Kennedy wasn't. So they took him back in an office and the guys that were with him, his handlers, made him up with something called Shave Stick, to cover his beard stubble—and badly. He looked awful."[9]

Just before the debate was about to start, as Kennedy and Nixon took their places onstage, Hewitt looked at the two candidates on camera and was shocked by what he saw.

"Kennedy looked great. Nixon looked terrible," Hewitt recalled. "So I called Frank Stanton into the control room, and I said, 'Frank, you better look at this.' He took one look and he called in a guy named Ted Rogers, who was Nixon's television advisor. And Stanton said, 'Are you satisfied with the way your candidate looks?' And Rogers said, 'Yeah, we think he looks great.' So Stanton took me out in the hall and said, 'It's none of our business. That's the way they want it…And we put them on that night, and that's all anybody remembers about that night is makeup."[10]

That first televised encounter, which Don Hewitt later described as more of a "joint press conference" than a debate, focused on domestic issues.

The main thrust of Kennedy's remarks that night was that America "can do better."

"The question before the American people is: Are we doing as much as we can do?" Kennedy asked, looking straight into the camera at the American people. "Are we as strong as we should be? Are we as strong as we must be if we're going to maintain our independence, and if we're going to maintain and hold out the hand of friendship to those who look to us for assistance, to those who look to us for survival? This is a great country, but I think it could be a greater country; and this is a powerful country, but I think it could be a more powerful country."

"I'm not satisfied," he said, going on to cite several key areas of American life that needed improvement. "I think we can do better. I don't want the talents of any American to go to waste."[11]

Kennedy's charm, ease, and striking good looks may have won

the debate and won over many undecided voters that night, but it was his powerful words, heralding a call to action and an embrace of the civil rights struggle then sweeping the country, that would win the hearts and votes of millions of black, Hispanic, and poor white Americans.

Nixon, counter-punching with facts and figures, argued that night that America was moving forward on all fronts, and had seen much more progress during the Eisenhower/Nixon administration than during the previous administration of Democrat Harry Truman.

"When we compare these two records," Nixon said, staring earnestly into the camera, "I think we find that America has been moving ahead." He went on to point out that more schools, hospitals, and highways had been built in the past seven and a half years than during the Truman administration, and that wages and prices had also improved.

"Now, this is not standing still," Nixon said. "But, good as this record is, may I emphasize it isn't enough. A record is never something to stand on. It's something to build on. And in building on this record, I believe that we have the secret for progress—we know the way to progress."[12]

For all his talk about progress, Nixon, sweating profusely under the hot studio lights, was really trumpeting the status quo, urging Americans who had prospered in the 1950s to embrace a candidate who would extend those good times into the 1960s.

It was a great debate—two different visions of America's future from two very different points of view. And despite Kennedy's eloquence, Nixon, a champion debater, battled him to a draw. Several studies found that a majority of those who heard the debate on the radio that night thought that Nixon had won, while a majority of those who watched it on television thought that Kennedy had won. Most experts attribute this to the makeup issue, and to Kennedy's polish and Nixon's grim countenance.

But Dr. Arnold Hutschnecker, who watched the debate on television that night, thought he saw something else, something troubling. It was not Nixon's makeup or his manner that defeated him that night. It was his mother.

Many years later, Hutschnecker received permission from Nixon to write a book about him. The unpublished manuscript, titled *Richard Nixon: His Rise to Power, His Self-Defeat*, offers a revealing glimpse into Nixon's psyche.

Nixon's real problem the night of the debate, Hutschnecker wrote, was his unconscious fear of displeasing his stern but saintly mother, Hannah.

Sure enough, the day after the first debate, Nixon's mother telephoned her son to tell him "how terrible he looked" on TV.[13]

From the first time he saw Nixon on television in 1952, Hutschnecker said he was convinced that Nixon subconsciously associated the eye of the camera with the eye of his domineering mother, and that it was the transferred image of her stern and disapproving face that defeated him more than anything else.[14]

CHAPTER 31

The Apt Pupil

Arnold Hutschnecker had long been aware of the dangers involved in mixing politics and psychiatry. He once recalled a prominent psychiatrist asking him if he would join him in setting up an institute of political psychology that would help political candidates win elections.

"Absolutely not," Dr. Hutschnecker had replied, shocked at the very idea.

"I strongly oppose the formation of an institution which aims to use the experience of a psychiatrist to help candidates' election to political office," he later wrote. "This might lead to incompetent and corrupt individuals learning enough psychological gimmicks and salesmanship to be elected."[1]

Hutschnecker might as well have been talking about his own relationship with Richard Nixon.

A fast learner, Nixon had long used psychology to size up his opponents—going back to his poker-playing days in the navy.

"I learned," Nixon wrote in his memoirs, "that the people who have the cards are usually the ones who talk the least and the softest; those who are bluffing tend to talk loudly and give themselves away."[2]

Yet, despite Dr. Hutschnecker's concern that a corrupt politician might use psychiatry to pick up enough psychological gimmicks to win an election, he still counseled Nixon on how to use psychology to do just that.

"He encouraged me to profile political leaders, asking me to give examples of hostile or aggressive personalities," Dr. Hutschnecker wrote of his talks with Nixon.[3]

Hutschnecker did so willingly, often drawing psychological portraits of other politicians for Nixon.[4]

Unwittingly, Dr. Hutschnecker had done just what he said he would never do—teach a devious politician how to use psychological tricks to get elected. Perhaps that was the role Nixon had chosen for Dr. Hutschnecker all along.

"Over time," Dr. Hutschnecker recalled, his discussions with Nixon "became more about the psychology of other leaders."[5]

It was during these talks with Nixon that Dr. Hutschnecker developed his concept of "psychopolitics," a theory he formed to study the mental stability of political leaders—ideas he was all too eager to talk about with Nixon. Dr. Hutschnecker wrote that he shared these thoughts with Nixon because he felt that perhaps the only way Nixon "could get closer to grasping the subtle imprints and conditioning that affect all of us in life was to be open enough to listen to my observations."[6]

Throughout the 1960 campaign, Hutschnecker gave Nixon insights into Jack Kennedy's psychology, sharing his analysis that Kennedy, despite his charisma, charm, and quick wit, was a man who had a "constant need to prove his masculinity and his courage" to a "hard-driving, power-hungry, ruthlessly determined and overly aggressive father."[7]

After the first disastrous TV debate between the two candidates, the doctor offered Nixon instructions on how to use psychology to win his next televised debates with Kennedy.

"Many undecided voters will be less affected by *what* someone says and more by *how* it is said," he wrote in a note to Nixon shortly after the first debate. "They must be reached and stirred, which means not only on an intellectual response, but an emotional swinging along. Often, it is the heart [that] decides an issue and not the head. As your friend, I feel at this time that it is my duty to offer you all of my knowledge and experience."[8]

Armed with this advice and Hutschnecker's knowledge of the human psyche, Nixon fared considerably better against Kennedy in their second, third, and fourth televised debates.

CHAPTER 32

The Second TV Debate

leven days after the first televised debate with Kennedy, Nixon and his advisors were holed up at the Wardman Park Hotel in Washington, D.C, preparing for the second. This time Nixon was taking it seriously. He wasn't going to be beaten by a bad makeup job. This time he'd have a professional do it, and he'd be wearing a dark suit instead of the gray one he'd worn for the first debate, which on black-and-white TV made him appear to blend into the background.

Foreign affairs, Nixon's strong suit, would be the topic of the second debate, which was to be held October 7, 1960—the 102nd anniversary of the fifth Lincoln-Douglas debate—at the studios of WRC-TV, the NBC affiliate in the nation's capital. As usual, Nixon, the champion college debater, was well prepared; his advisors had peppered him with possible questions from the moderators, and he had his answers down pat. That may just have been his undoing. Or so he thought.

Many years later, Nixon would come to believe that Kennedy had bugged his room at the Wardman, and that Jack had known his talking points and strategy in advance. There is no proof of this, but the allegation would surface 13 years later, when Nixon's presidency was sinking into the quagmire of Watergate.

On July 24, 1973, the day after the Senate Watergate Committee subpoenaed President Nixon to turn over the now-famous White House tapes, Nixon's loyal servant, George H. W. Bush, whom Nixon had appointed chairman of the National Republican Committee to help him manage the Watergate scandal, held a press conference. Bush accused Carmine Bellino, the Senate Watergate Committee's chief investigator, of wiretapping Nixon's hotel suite the night before the second 1960 TV debate.[1]

As the Watergate Committee's chief sleuth, it was Bellino's job to track down evidence for all the various crimes President Nixon and his White House cronies were accused or suspected of.

Bellino was very good at his job. Nearly all the evidence to support the wide-ranging charges that would eventually be leveled against Nixon during the committee's probe was either dug up or substantiated by Bellino. A longtime friend of the Kennedy family and a former administrative assistant to FBI director J. Edgar Hoover, Bellino had been JFK's ace investigator when Jack was a senator investigating Jimmy Hoffa for the Senate rackets hearings in the 1950s. During the 1960 presidential race, Bellino worked for Jack as an investigator for his campaign. The full extent of Bellino's work during the 1960 campaign is unknown because his personal papers, which were donated to the John F. Kennedy Presidential Library in Boston, are permanently sealed.*

But we do know a little about Bellino's work for Jack Kennedy during the 1960 election. That year, one of Jack Kennedy's biggest obstacles to winning the White House was his religion. There had never been a Catholic president, and anti-Catholic sentiment was not uncommon, particularly in the South. The Fair Campaign Practices Committee, a nonpartisan, nonsectarian organization,

---

*The Kennedy Library website states that Bellino's personal papers "consist of correspondence, press releases, publications, telephone records, etc. relating to his investigation of Jimmy Hoffa and the Teamster's Union, John F. Kennedy's presidential campaign (1960), Robert F. Kennedy's Senate campaign (1964), and U.S. attorneys. Closed." Generally, libraries are repositories of information that is made available to the public and to researchers. In this case, however, the JFK Library is a vault that keeps information from being seen by the public. A call by the author to an archivist at the library to see if there is any process by which an appeal can be made to unseal the Bellino papers was answered with a single word: "No."

found that 392 different anti-Catholic hate pamphlets had been distributed to more than 20 million voters during the campaign.

One of Bellino's jobs for the Kennedy campaign was to track down the source of this hate literature, which he traced to a Protestant minister, a former Republican congressman from Missouri. Bellino followed the minister from Missouri on his travels around Washington, D.C., trying to determine if Republican officials were directing this anti-Catholic hate campaign.[2]

But Nixon and George H. W. Bush, a future president and father of a future president, accused Bellino of doing much more than that.

During his hastily-called press conference in July 1973, Bush, who had been put up to it by Nixon, produced affidavits from three convicted wiretappers who claimed they'd been hired by Bellino to bug Nixon's hotel room before the second TV debate in 1960.

"The Nixon-Kennedy election was a real cliffhanger," Bush told reporters at the press conference, "and the debates bore heavily on the outcome."[3]

Bellino, who had the determination and grim countenance of a bulldog, angrily denied Bush's charges, insisting that he had never engaged in any surveillance of Nixon, and denying that he had ever used electronic surveillance during his long career as an investigator.

"I think it was a terrible thing that George Bush did," Bellino said many years later. "His charges were absolutely false. Bush was doing the bidding of the White House."[4]

Leading figures on the Watergate Committee agreed that the Bush/Nixon charges against Bellino were false, and that the allegations were just an extension of the policy of dirty tricks that had gotten Nixon into trouble in the first place.

"It was a frame-up," said Sam Dash, the Watergate Committee's chief counsel. "We were all angry about it. We thought Bellino was a man of great integrity, and we thought the charges against him were an effort by people who thought they could harm the integrity of the committee by harming its chief investigator. Both Sam Ervin [the Watergate Committee chairman] and I believed then that this was a Nixon dirty trick."[5]

During his press conference, Bush sheepishly acknowledged that the evidence supporting his allegations against Bellino was "incomplete," but said, "I'd like to see somebody develop it further."

And develop it they did. Senate Republicans demanded that Bellino be taken off the Watergate investigation, and that he be investigated himself—and he was, for the next two and a half months. In the end, the investigation found no evidence to support Bush's reckless charges.

After Bellino was cleared, the chairman of the Watergate Committee declared him to be "an honorable and faithful servant," adding that "there was not a scintilla of competent or credible evidence" to sustain the charges against him.[6]

Nixon, hovering behind the scenes while Bush did his dirty work, was still obsessed with the belief that Kennedy had cheated him out of the 1960 election, even while his own presidency was crashing down all around him in 1973. That belief, whether true or merely part of Nixon's paranoia, may explain why he felt so free to cheat, lie, and steal to win the White House in 1968, and four years later, to cover up—and probably conceive—the break-in at the Democratic Party's headquarters at the Watergate office complex to win reelection in 1972.

CHAPTER 33

The Doctor's Past Is Uncovered

Guenther Reinhardt not only uncovered Richard Nixon's most closely guarded secret, he also uncovered Dr. Hutschnecker's.

Hutschnecker's 1943 arrest and indictment on charges that he'd helped Gert von Gontard dodge the draft during World War II was the most embarrassing secret of his life. He rarely spoke about it, and in the course of a long secondary career as a prolific author, he never wrote about it. Whether Richard Nixon, his most famous patient, ever knew about it is not known; he doesn't mention Hutschnecker in any of the ten books he authored. But one thing is certain: Guenther Reinhardt found out about it.

"Records show that the doctor was arrested on November 11, 1943," Reinhardt wrote in his 12-page confidential memo shortly after visiting Dr. Hutschnecker at his Park Avenue office on September 7, 1960.[1]

That Reinhardt was wrong about the date of Hutschnecker's arrest, and about so many other details in his report, belies the fact that he got the basic fact right; that Nixon was a patient of Hutschnecker's. That, and the fact that Reinhardt tipped Nixon off that his secret had been uncovered five days earlier with his phone calls to Nora de Toledano, was enough to forestall any attempts Nixon might have made to unveil Jack Kennedy's medical secret—that he had Addison's disease.

Many of the findings Reinhardt presented in his confidential report about Dr. Hutschnecker were partly right and partly wrong. For the most part, he got the basic facts right, but fabricated the details. He had always been more of a stickler for the *appearance* of truth than for the truth itself.

Fact-checking his report demonstrates the curious blend of fact and fiction that Reinhardt was famous for.

WHAT REINHARDT WROTE IN HIS REPORT	THE FACTS
"It appears that this physician is a native of Germany. He was born in 1898 and is therefore 62 years of age."	Dr. Hutschnecker *was* born in 1898, but in Austria, not Germany.
"Dr. Hutschnecker is married. His wife is the former Florita Weiss."	His wife's first name *was* Florita, but her maiden name was Platterings.
"They were married in 1932 in Berlin. No children issued from this marriage."	They were married in Berlin in 1934, not 1932. They did not have any children.
"Dr. Hutschnecker graduated from the medical school of the University of Berlin in 1923."	He graduated with a medical degree from the Friedrich Wilhelm University in Berlin in 1925, not 1923.
"Being of Jewish origin, he found himself exposed to the restrictive decrees of the National Socialist government and decided to immigrate to the United States. He arrived in New York in August 1938."	Dr. Hutschnecker *was* Jewish. But he fled Nazi Germany in 1936, not 1938, arriving in New York on January 21 of that year.

"His license to practice medicine was issued to him in 1940."	His license to practice medicine in the state of New York was granted four years earlier, on May 23, 1936.
"Dr. Hutschnecker did not see military service."	He did not serve in the U.S. military, but he *did* serve in the German army during World War I.
"Records show that the doctor was arrested on November 11, 1943."	Actually, Dr. Hutschnecker was arrested on December 22, 1943.
"He was charged with conspiracy to obtain a draft deferment for the playboy Gert Hans von Gontart, heir to the Anheuser-Busch Brewing fortune."	Reinhardt was right about all this, except he misspelled von Gontard's last name.
Describing the doctor's office, Reinhardt noted that "there was a sketch of the late Albert Einstein, who was evidently one of the doctor's patients."	Dr. Hutschnecker did indeed have a signed sketch of Albert Einstein on his wall, but Einstein was not one of his patients.

The most glaring error in Reinhardt's report was his assertion that Dr. Hutschnecker had been convicted of helping Gert von Gontard dodge the wartime draft.

"Dr. Hutschnecker was convicted and received a suspended sentence of one year and a day," Reinhardt wrote in his report.

In fact, after a six-week trial, Dr. Hutschnecker was acquitted on June 12, 1944, and received no prison sentence, suspended or otherwise.

But Reinhardt also got quite a few things right about Hutschnecker, including:

1. "His wife acts as a part time receptionist in his office."
2. "Dr. Hutschnecker's office is located at 829 Park Avenue in apartment 1-A, which is a luxurious duplex apartment on the ground floor of this rather elegant building."
3. "Dr. Hutschnecker...specializes in the practice of psychosomatic medicine."
4. "Dr. Hutschnecker is a prolific writer of texts on psychosomatic and related matters."
5. "Arrested with Dr. Hutschnecker was a military intelligence lieutenant and a clerk of a draft board."
6. Hutschnecker's "license to practice medicine was withdrawn and he was barred from membership of professional societies."
7. "The doctor is known to have entertained many people of prominence, not only at his city home, but at a very elaborate summer residence which he owns on Cozier Road in Sherman, Connecticut. He and his wife travel to Europe at least once a year."
8. "The physician is a small man, wiry and of slight build. His facial features are amazingly oriental."
9. "Dr. Hutschnecker is a man of considerable charm and has a very preposssessing personality. He is quite loquacious."

There were many things in Reinhardt's confidential memo, however, that simply cannot be verified, and which should therefore be disregarded.

For instance, Reinhardt's report claims that Hutschnecker's arrest came as the result of "certain public exposures made by a Canadian physician." In fact, there is nothing in the public record to substantiate his claim that a Canadian physician tipped off authorities to the case. All that is known for sure is that the FBI got involved in the case when they received an anonymous complaint that von Gontard had paid a different doctor—not Hutschnecker—$500 for advice to help him evade induction.

Another even more important claim is that Hutschnecker inadvertently let Reinhardt know the exact location of Nixon's patient file when he "patted his hand against the left lower drawer of his office desk" to indicate where it was kept, and then left Reinhardt in the office alone with it when he left the room to answer a phone call. This seems highly unlikely, and given Reinhardt's propensity for lying, should be viewed with great skepticism or disregarded entirely.

But there is no doubt—and all the evidence supports this—that Reinhardt had found out Nixon was seeing a psychotherapist only two months before the 1960 election, and then turned that information over to the Kennedy campaign.

CHAPTER 34

The Secrets
Are Revealed

Richard Nixon was in a panic. With only five days to go before the 1960 election, he was trailing in the polls and appeared to be headed for a narrow but certain defeat. But he had one last card to play. It was a gamble, he knew, but Nixon was a gambler, and now was the time to raise the stakes.

Throughout the campaign, both the Kennedy and Nixon camps feared that each had obtained damaging medical information about the other. The Kennedy campaign believed that Nixon had come into possession of Jack's stolen medical records showing that he had Addison's disease, and Nixon knew that someone—probably the Kennedys—had hired a private detective and discovered that he'd been a patient of Dr. Arnold Hutschnecker, the famed author and psychoanalyst.

With this knowledge, a certain balance had been achieved, one that, in a sense, mirrored the nuclear standoff then in effect between the Russian and the American armed forces—a type of mutual assured destruction. And throughout the general election, the question of the candidates' health never came up—not until the very last days of the race, when both sides edged toward the brink of all-out medical war.

Desperate and trailing in the polls in the last days of the campaign, Nixon decided that now was the time to reveal Kennedy's medical secret, even though he risked exposure of his own.

The brinksmanship began on November 3 when Nixon got

John Roosevelt, the youngest son of the late Democratic Party icon, President Franklin D. Roosevelt, to strike the first blow.

Campaigning for Nixon that day in Michigan, Roosevelt, a staunch Republican, issued a challenge to both candidates "to disclose any medical difficulties that might impair their ability to serve as president."[1]

Nixon, of course, had put him up to it.

The next day, just four days before the election, Nixon raised the stakes again. This time, he had Roosevelt send telegrams to himself and Kennedy, demanding that they make public all medical reports on any ailments that they may have had, and to disclose any treatments they may have been receiving.

In his telegram to Nixon, Roosevelt tossed the vice president a softball, saying that Nixon should come clean on the condition of his knee, which he'd injured during the campaign. No threat to Nixon's campaign there, since his knee injury had already been covered by the press.

But in his telegram to Kennedy, Roosevelt went for the jugular. He told Kennedy that a medical report released at the time of the Democratic National Convention—the one Jack had Dr. Travell write up for him—"notably failed to disclose the extent of your adrenal insufficiency and what drugs you are taking to compensate for this insufficiency."[2]

At a news conference later that day in Syracuse, where Roosevelt was stumping for Nixon, the question of Jack Kennedy's Addison's disease was brought up for the first time during the general election.

There have been "rumors," Roosevelt told reporters, "that Senator Kennedy…has or has had Addison's disease."[3]

But Nixon wasn't done yet. The next day, November 5, he raised the ante again when he tried to draw President Eisenhower into the fray. Nixon was campaigning that day in California, but he got another of his surrogates, Walter Williams, formerly President Eisenhower's undersecretary of the Commerce Department, to try to get Ike to release a statement calling for the candidates to release their medical reports.

Early that morning in Washington, Williams went to see Ann Whitman, Eisenhower's personal secretary, and pleaded with her to ask Ike to help Nixon out by calling for Nixon and Kennedy to both make public the results of their latest physical examinations. Nixon, he told Whitman, would do so as soon as Ike issued the statement.

Williams then gave her a statement, drawn up by Nixon, that he wanted President Eisenhower to sign that day and issue as his own. It read: "In response to inquiries, I (Dwight D. Eisenhower) am glad to restate my previous position regarding information about the health of candidates for the presidency. In 1956, before the election, I asked my physicians to make available for public information full and complete records on my health. I believe that all candidates for the presidency have an obligation to do this."[4]

Ann Whitman gave the statement to President Eisenhower and appended a postscript of her own, saying that a "note of desperation in Nixon camp prompted the attached suggestion to the president."[5]

Whitman jotted down in her White House diary that day that Jim Hagerty, President Eisenhower's press secretary, was none too happy about Nixon's last-minute ploy. "Jim Hagerty," she wrote, "called it a 'cheap, lousy, stinking political trick.'"[6]

She also noted in her diary that when Captain Evan Aurand, Ike's naval attaché, tried to intervene on Nixon's behalf, "the president would not let Captain Aurand tell him all of it and said, 'I am not making myself a party to anything that has to do with the health of the candidates.'"[7]

This was obviously not the answer Nixon wanted to hear from Eisenhower, but he shouldn't have been surprised; Ike never really liked him that much anyway.

Eisenhower, Dr. Hutschnecker later wrote, "was decidedly lacking in warmth or acceptance toward Nixon; as a former army general, he rarely took anyone's advice, let alone Nixon's."[8]

Rebuffed by Eisenhower, Nixon decided it was time to play the last card up his sleeve.

Campaigning that last Saturday up and down his home state of California, Nixon flew into Oakland International Airport later that afternoon, and in the pouring rain, rode in a motorcade to Oakland City Hall, where a crowd of 15,000 supporters waited to greet him. The rain had stopped before he started speaking, but many in the crowd still had their umbrellas up.

Nixon, the *New York Times* reported, "expressed his willingness to make public his full medical records in answer to health questions raised about him and his Democratic rival."[9]

He didn't mention that the "health questions" had been raised the day before by one of his own surrogates, John Roosevelt, or that President Eisenhower had that very day refused to play Nixon's game.

After the speech in Oakland, Herb Klein, Nixon's press secretary, told reporters that Nixon would make his records available "if it is agreeable to Senator Kennedy."[10]

The *Times* also reported that Klein "suggested that the information be made public at 10:00 AM Monday, and said Mr. Nixon's doctors had been instructed to have the vice president's records ready for release then."[11]

Of course, "Mr. Nixon's doctors" would not include Dr. Arnold Hutschnecker. Nixon was still trying to keep *that* a secret.

TV and radio stations around the country reported on Nixon's challenge that the candidates' medical records be made public the next Monday, the very last day before voters would go to the polls.

So there it was. Nixon had made his move, and now it was time for the Kennedy camp to make theirs.

That same night, Arnold Hutschnecker and his wife Florita were watching an old black-and-white movie on TV at their vacation home in Connecticut when the phone rang. It was 9:30 PM.

Dr. Hutschnecker answered the phone. "Hello?" he said.

"This is the Associated Press," said the voice on the other end of the line. "Dr. Hutschnecker, did you by any chance hear the announcement that on Monday there will be a statement about the health and fitness for office of the two presidential candidates?"[12]

"Yes," Hutschnecker replied. "I heard it on the radio, on the two o'clock news."

"We have been informed," continued the reporter, "that you are Vice President Nixon's doctor, and we would like a statement from you about his health."

Hutschnecker was dumbfounded. He knew that none of *his* medical files on Nixon were going to be made public on Monday, and he couldn't imagine how anyone could have connected him to the vice president, tracked him down in Sherman, Connecticut, and then called him on his unlisted, private phone number.[13]

He knew, of course, about the rumors that had been going on for years that Nixon was seeing a "shrink." Five years earlier, legendary columnist and famed Nixon-hater Walter Winchell reported that Nixon was seeing a psychiatrist. But Winchell hadn't learned the doctor's name, and no reporters had ever connected the dots—until now.

Of course, there had been *one* other inquiry—not to Dr. Hutschnecker, but to Nixon's friend, Nora de Toledano, back in September when Guenther Reinhardt had called and asked about Nixon and Hutschnecker. Nixon had been in the hospital, laid up with his bad knee, but his secretaries had gotten word to him when Nora called to alert him. And while there is no record of whether Nixon ever told Hutschnecker about the private detective's inquiries, it's hard to imagine that Nixon wouldn't have warned the doctor that someone had discovered his most politically damaging secret. Either way, it's clear that Hutschnecker didn't make the connection between the questions this "reporter" was asking him and the consultation he'd had in September with a private investigator looking for a psychosomatic specialist.

"You can't be serious," Hutschnecker told the reporter huffily. "In the entire United States there isn't one physician who would give a shred of information about a patient, much less to a stranger over the phone who might be anybody."[14]

The reporter, who indeed might have been anybody, continued to ask questions. He even asked Dr. Hutschnecker who he was going to vote for on Tuesday. Finally, getting no information out of the doctor, the reporter asked: "Could you just say yes or no if I ask you this simple question? Is Mr. Nixon in good health?"

Hutschnecker hesitated for a moment, but stood his ground and refused to confirm or deny that Nixon was one of his patients—a decision that would haunt him.

Many years later, Hutschnecker came to believe that if he *had* confirmed that Nixon was his patient and told the reporter that Nixon was in good health, that might have forced a showdown over the question of the candidates' health, and tipped the election to Nixon.

"I pondered how this particular problem would be resolved long after I hung up," he recalled. "After Election Day, considering the narrow margin by which President Kennedy won—0.2 percent—I could not help but wonder how the election might have turned out had President Kennedy been obliged to give a statement of his Addison's disease, had I given Mr. Nixon a clean bill of health."[15]

Hutschnecker wrote that Nixon had known Kennedy had Addison's disease since 1954, and that Nixon's advisors had urged him to use it against Kennedy in the 1960 election, but that Nixon had refused to do it.

"Nixon's closest advisors urged him to make use of it," Dr. Hutschnecker wrote. "Nixon refused, saying, 'Anybody who can go through a presidential campaign is healthy enough to be president...Nixon's sense of fair play may have cost him the election."[16]

But Dr. Hutschnecker, always giving his friend and most illustrious patient the benefit of the doubt, didn't know when he wrote this that Nixon had already tried to make Kennedy's Addison's disease an issue during the final desperate days of the campaign. He also didn't know that it was not Nixon's sense of "fair play" that held him back from bringing up Kennedy's disease, but the fear, and perhaps even the certain knowledge that if he did, the Kennedy camp would retaliate by making public the fact that Nixon had been seeing a "shrink."

Even though he later thought that by answering the reporter's question he might have helped Nixon win the election—and Dr. Hutschnecker wanted him to win—he knew that in good conscience he could not interfere with the election that way.[17]

But Hutschnecker also didn't understand that the phone call he'd received that night from the reporter had not been made to gather information, but to convey it—to let Nixon know that the Kennedy camp would reveal his secret if Nixon and his henchmen insisted on making Jack's health a last-minute campaign issue. Whether the call had come from a real reporter or not, someone had tipped him off that Hutschnecker was Nixon's doctor. Not surprisingly, no story moved on the AP wire the next day about Nixon being a patient of Dr. Hutschnecker's; it would be another eight years before that story would be uncovered by a real reporter—muckraking columnist Drew Pearson.

The call from the "reporter" that night to Dr. Hutschnecker on his unlisted phone number at his vacation home in Connecticut did the trick. Nixon shut up about Jack's health, and, as Hutschnecker noted, "The anticipated statement on the health issue of both candidates did not take place on Monday, and it did not become an election issue."[18]

CHAPTER 35

Election Day

On November 8, 1960, more than 68 million Americans went to the polls to cast their votes for president of the United States. Mobbed by jostling reporters, Jack Kennedy voted early that Tuesday morning at the Boston Public Library, the polling place for the Third Precinct, then caravanned—trailing three busloads of reporters and a fleet of security cars—to the Boston airport. A short 25-minute flight took him to the Kennedy compound in Hyannis Port, where he watched the returns on TV with his family and chief advisors.

Richard Nixon voted that morning in his hometown of Whittier, then spent the afternoon in Tijuana.

"To ease the tension," Nixon later recalled, he and two of his campaign aides, Don Hughes and Jack Sherwood, went for a drive in an open-air convertible down the scenic Pacific Coast Highway. Not a single reporter or photographer followed them on their lonely ride down the coast. After awhile, Nixon recalled, "Hughes remarked that he had never been to Tijuana, so we continued all the way to Mexico."[1]

They had lunch in downtown Tijuana at the Old Heidelberg, a German restaurant shaped like a low-rent, neon-lit castle, and then headed back to election headquarters, the Ambassador Hotel in Los Angeles, where JFK's brother, Bobby, would be assassinated eight years later.

They'd turned the radio off on their long drive back to Los Angeles, and hadn't heard any of the early election returns until they got to Nixon's suite at the Ambassador and turned on the TV. It was 3:45 PM. Election results were just starting to come in from the East Coast, and Nixon was already trailing.

The first results came in from Campbell County, Kentucky, at 3:25 PM West Coast time—6:25 in the East. Population 86,000, Campbell County in northern Kentucky had voted with the winning presidential candidate as far back as anyone could remember, and the early returns gave Kennedy the lead—5,300 votes to Nixon's 4,100.[2]

Five minutes later, the first complete vote came in from a precinct in Cleveland, Ohio: 158–121 for Kennedy.

But that narrow early lead, and the euphoria it created inside the Kennedy compound, vanished a few minutes later when the Associated Press moved a story showing Nixon leading nationwide, 203,628 to 166,963.

At 7:15 the news got even worse for the Kennedy camp when CBS News, using a brand new IBM 7090 punch-card computer to collate election data, predicted Nixon to win in a landslide: 459 electoral votes for Nixon, 78 for Kennedy.[3]

But something had gone haywire with the computer, the first ever to be used to project a presidential election. Forty-five minutes later, the computer switched sides and projected Kennedy to win with 51 percent of the vote.

"All of the computing machines," reported CBS election night news anchor Eric Sevareid, "are now saying Kennedy."

It was going to be that kind of a night.

In Hyannis Port, Jackie Kennedy, eight months pregnant, leaned toward her husband as they watched the latest CBS projection and whispered, "Oh, Bunny, you're president now!"

"No, no," he told her quietly. "It's too early yet."[4]

Downstairs at the ballroom of the Ambassador Hotel, the "standing room only" crowd of Nixon supporters was going through wild mood swings as television sets stationed around the room updated the latest returns. Ohio was leaning toward Nixon; Kennedy was leading in Pennsylvania; Texas was going back and forth.

"Any election night is an emotional roller coaster," Nixon

recalled in his memoirs, "but election night in 1960 was the most tantalizing and frustrating I have ever experienced."

As election night wore on, Kennedy's lead began to grow steadily, and by 10:30 the networks were saying he was ahead by 1,500,000 votes.

By midnight, Kennedy had won enough states to collect 265 electoral votes, just four short of victory. Nixon wasn't ready to concede, but he and his wife, Pat, took the elevator down to the ballroom to make what one aide called a "half-concession" speech. Sensing defeat, most of the people downstairs had already left, but there were still enough die-hard supporters on hand to send up a mighty roar when Dick and Pat Nixon entered the ballroom. But they wouldn't like what he would have to say.

"If the present trend continues," Nixon told his supporters, "Senator Kennedy will be the next president of the United States."[5]

Nixon's raucous supporters, however, weren't ready to concede. "We want Nixon!" they chanted. "We want Nixon!"

Then someone from the crowd yelled, "Don't give up!" But the look on Nixon's face suggested that he already had.

Pat Nixon, who always seemed to have a pained expression on her face, looked especially gaunt that night as she stood there smiling weakly next to her husband, gamely blinking back tears.

Back in Hyannis Port, it was past three o'clock in the morning when the networks aired Nixon's "half-concession" speech. Several of Kennedy's aides angrily grumbled that Nixon should have conceded, but Jack scolded them: "Why should he concede? I wouldn't."[6]

Jack was right; it wasn't over yet.

As the minutes ticked by and the numbers continued to pour in, Kennedy's lead began to disappear. The networks' tote boards showed that Kennedy's lead in the nationwide popular vote had slipped to 800,000, then 600,000, then to less than 500,000. California, Illinois, and Minnesota were too close to call, and if Nixon won them all, *he* would be president.

Nixon and Kennedy both went to bed at about the same

time—1:00 AM in Los Angeles and 4:00 AM in Hyannis Port. Neither knew who would be president when they awoke.

Nixon got the news when his daughter Julie woke him up at 6:00 AM. Kennedy had won by a margin of only 114,673 votes.[7]

It was the closest election in U.S. history. If he'd won Illinois, which he lost by only 9,000 votes, and Texas, which he lost by 46,000, Nixon would have been president.

But Nixon wasn't sure if he should concede. Rumors were already circulating that there'd been widespread voting fraud in Illinois and Texas, and many top Republicans were urging Nixon to contest the election.

Nixon called President Eisenhower later that morning to talk it over with his boss. In his memoirs, Nixon claimed that Eisenhower had "urged" him to challenge the election, saying that Ike had even offered "to help raise the money needed for recounts in Illinois and Texas."[8]

But Nixon claimed that he went against Eisenhower's advice and decided not to demand a recount. "There is no doubt that there was substantial vote fraud in the 1960 election," he wrote, noting that he decided not to challenge the results because "the effect would be devastating" to the country. Besides, he wrote, he didn't want to be seen as a "sore loser."[9]

But Nixon *was* a sore loser.

"We won, but they stole it from us," Nixon said as he greeted a guest at a Christmas party not long after the election.[10]

He was also a liar.

Nixon's longtime friend, Ralph de Toledano, later discovered that it was Nixon, not Eisenhower, who wanted to contest the election, and that Eisenhower had talked him out of it.

"This was the first time I ever caught Nixon in a lie," de Toledano recalled glumly.[11]

After hanging up with Eisenhower, Nixon quickly dictated a telegram and sent Herb Klein, his press secretary, downstairs to read it to the assembled press.

A hush fell over the ballroom at the Ambassador Hotel as

Klein approached the podium. Surrounded by reporters, photographers, and three huge television cameras, he looked up into the bright camera lights and read the telegram Nixon would later send to Kennedy. "I know," Klein intoned solemnly, "that you will have the united support of all Americans as you lead the nation in the cause of peace and freedom during the next four years."[12]

It was over. Nixon had conceded.

Back in Hyannis Port, Jack Kennedy and his own press secretary, Pierre Salinger, watched Klein read the telegram on TV. Jack had just won the election, but he was not happy; he was disgusted. He thought Nixon should have delivered his own concession speech.

"He went out the same way he came in," Kennedy muttered. "No class."[13]

CHAPTER 36

The Pack Rat

Milt Ebbins says he first saw Richard Nixon's stolen patient file not long after Kennedy was inaugurated—in May or June of 1961. He was standing in Frank Sinatra's old offices at the William Morris Agency, which were now the offices of Chrislaw Productions, the film and TV production company that Joe Kennedy had set up as a joint partnership for Milt and Peter Lawford. Chrislaw, which they incorporated in May of 1961, had a production deal with United Artists that Joe had arranged through his old friend, Arthur Krim, the head of United Artists.

"Joe Kennedy made the deal all by himself with Arthur Krim," recalled Ebbins, Lawford's longtime manager. "Joe called Arthur on the phone and said, 'This is it.' It took two seconds. UA financed us. Joe Kennedy worked that out. He put it on a platter."[1]

Joe had been Peter's father-in-law since Lawford married Pat Kennedy in 1954. Joe, who had run RKO Pictures in the '20s, was always trying to make his daughter happy by helping her husband with his Hollywood career.

After Joe made the call to Arthur Krim, Lawford and Milt had a production deal but no office space. But that was about to change.

Frank Sinatra, Lawford's buddy from the Rat Pack, had been a client of the William Morris Agency for years, but in 1961 Frank decided it was time for a change. He told his agent that he was leaving William Morris, but that he still wanted to keep his office on the second floor of the William Morris building in Beverly Hills.

Frank's office was one of the coolest hangouts in town, and it was certainly the nicest office in the William Morris building.

"It was built for him," Milt recalled. "It had a full bar, a shower, and the only private toilet in the building. And in the living room, he had a heavy punching bag that hung from a hook in the ceiling. Frank had all this built in, and he was there all the time with Hank Sanicola, his right-hand man, and his secretary, Gloria Lovell, the very young, very attractive wife of Jack Dawn, the head of makeup at MGM. She was Frank's secretary and mistress for a while."

Sinatra was changing agents, but he still wanted to keep his swank office at the William Morris building. When Milt, a long-time manager at the agency, learned that Frank was leaving William Morris, he went to his old friend and boss, Morris Stoller, who ran the agency's Beverly Hills office, and asked if he and Lawford could have it.

"I understand Frank's leaving," Milt told Stoller.

"Yeah," Stoller replied.

"We'd like to have his office," Milt said, matter-of-factly.

"Let me see what I can do," Stoller said.

A few days later, Stoller called Milt and said, "You got it."

Needless to say, Frank Sinatra, who had one of the shortest fuses in Hollywood, was not happy about not getting what he wanted.

"They told him, 'Frank, your lease is up,'" Milt recalled. "And Frank was very pissed off. Morris Stoller told him, 'Frank, you left the office, what do you expect?' But Frank was pissed at them and he was really pissed off at us for moving into his office. That's one of the reasons Frank didn't talk to Peter for a long time after that."

Milt and Lawford had the office completely redecorated when they moved in that May. The only thing left to remind them of Frank was the hook in the ceiling where he'd hung his punching bag.

One day, not long after they moved in, Milt was standing in Peter's office when Lawford nonchalantly handed him some papers. Milt looked them over, casually at first, and then with growing interest as he began to realize what they were: a psychiatric report about Richard Nixon.

"Where did you get this fuckin' thing?" Milt asked after looking at the three-page, typewritten report.

"This was in the file that the guys broke into," Lawford said with a laugh.

"Broke into?" Milt asked incredulously. "How did you get it?"

"The old man gave it to me," Lawford replied casually, referring to Joe Kennedy.

"What are you trying to tell me?" Milt said, still amazed at the document he was holding in his hands. "Are you saying that the old man engineered this?"

"Of course," Lawford scoffed. "How else did he get it?"[2]

Many years later, Milt still remembered the gist of the document.

"It was a complete report of Nixon's visits with Hutschnecker," he recalled. "It was three pages, typewritten on very thin paper. It said he was depressed and paranoid. And the last line said, 'In my opinion, this man should be confined to a mental institution for at least six months.'"[3]

If something like that had been made public on the eve of the 1960 presidential election, it could have destroyed Nixon's chances for the White House—not only in 1960, but in 1968 as well, and he might *never* have been elected president. But according to Milt, Jack Kennedy told his father no; it was wrong and he wouldn't allow it.

"Joe wanted to surface it, but Jack stopped it," Milt recalled. "Joe wanted to get it out but Jack wouldn't do it. He thought it was dirty pool. He didn't like it at all."[4]

Besides, how could Nixon's stolen psychiatric file be made public without boomeranging on the Kennedys? Wouldn't everyone assume that the Kennedys were behind it somehow? Jack's presidential hopes would certainly have been dashed if the alleged break-in was linked to his father, and Joe would have probably been sent to federal prison by the newly elected President Nixon's attorney general.

But as Jack would learn during the Cold War and the Cuban Missile Crisis, an atom bomb doesn't have to be dropped to have a deterrent effect.

Did Guenther Reinhardt really steal Nixon's psychiatric file? He doesn't say so in his 12-page confidential report, but he implies it. He claims that, during his meeting with Hutschnecker, the doctor inadvertently gave away the location of Nixon's patient file, and then left the detective alone in the office with it.

According to Reinhardt's report, the doctor told him, "Those files never get out of my hand. I have his file right in my desk." Reinhardt wrote that Dr. Hutschnecker then "patted his hand against the left lower drawer of his office desk," indicating the exact location of the Richard Nixon's patient file.

Then, Reinhardt wrote, one of his associates made a prearranged call to Dr. Hutschnecker's office that drew the doctor out of the office, leaving Reinhardt alone in the consulting room with Nixon's medical records.

According to his report, Reinhardt claims that he'd made "arrangements to have one of his assistants place a call to Dr. Hutschnecker while the investigator and Dr. Hutschnecker were in conference. The pretext for the call was an inquiry about the doctor's house, fees, etc., and the purpose of the call was to give the investigator an opportunity to look around the doctor's office."[5]

Is that when he stole Nixon's patient file?

Perhaps, but it seems highly unlikely that Dr. Hutschnecker would have been so careless and unprofessional as to let a perfect stranger know where he kept his most famous patient's file, and then leave him alone in his office with it. Judging from his many years of warm correspondence with Nixon—and from his unpublished book *about* Nixon—it is even more unlikely that Dr. Hutschnecker ever thought he "should be confined to a mental institution." That's just not the way the doctor felt about his friend and favorite patient.

But Milt Ebbins swore to his dying day, in 2008 at age 96, that not long after the election, Lawford handed him a copy of Nixon's stolen psychiatric file. And Milt Ebbins was a truthful and honorable man with a remarkable memory, so his account cannot be dismissed out of hand.

There is another possibility that could account for both scenarios—that Lawford showed Nixon's stolen patient file to Milt, and yet, Reinhardt didn't steal it. And that possibility is that Guenther Reinhardt fabricated a psychiatric file and then passed it off to Sinatra as Nixon's, which was then handed over to Joe Kennedy, who sent it on to Lawford, who in turn showed it to Milt Ebbins.

Given Reinhardt's history of lies and deception, this is perhaps the most likely scenario. With a man like Guenther Reinhardt, you never knew for sure.

Milt Ebbins never saw Nixon's stolen psychiatric file again. He said that Lawford had also shown it to their secretary, Joan Arnold, but she's been dead now for many years. Milt always thought that Lawford simply stashed the papers away in the business files they shared, where they would never be seen again.

When their partnership dissolved in the 1970s, Lawford, embittered and broken, gave the files to Milt.

"What do you want me to do with the files?" Milt asked him.

"Burn them, for all I care," Peter said. "Do anything you want with them. I don't want them. I don't care."[6]

But Milt, a pack rat who kept receipts for flashlight batteries he'd bought 20 years ago and warranties for electric shavers he'd bought in the 1960s, didn't burn the files. He kept them in his garage, under a blue plastic tarp, locked away in four large, four-drawer metal filing cabinets, the contents of which are today a treasure trove of Kennedy-era memorabilia.

An exhaustive search through tens of thousands of pages of business and personal papers contained in those files failed to turn up Richard Nixon's stolen patient file. They did, however, contain three copies of Reinhardt's confidential report on his surveillance of Dr. Hutschnecker, and the gray envelope, addressed to Joe Kennedy, that Lawford was supposed to send them back to Joe in, but never did. The files also contained stacks of correspondence from the Kennedy clan and letters from dozens of A-list celebrities, plus numerous one-of-a-kind documents, such as the original handwritten ransom note from the kidnappers of Frank Sinatra

Jr. There was also a typed, eight-point "to do" list written in advance of President Kennedy's arrival at Lawford's Santa Monica beach house in 1962, including "Item 1: Check food for President's House," and in a handwritten note, added at the last minute: "Item 8: Marilyn Monroe."[7]

CHAPTER 37

Marilyn

Milt Ebbins paced the floor backstage at Madison Square Garden, waiting for Marilyn Monroe to arrive to sing "Happy Birthday" to President Kennedy. It was the night of May 19, 1962, and as usual, Marilyn was late. If she didn't show up pretty soon, Peter Lawford, the evening's emcee, was going to have to sing the song himself.

Suddenly, the stage door opened and in walked Marilyn, dressed in a tight, floor-length, sequined gown.

"Is everything okay?" she asked Milt vaguely.

"Marilyn, for Christ's sake, you're on!" Milt blurted. "Peter's out there ready to announce you.'"

"Okay, I'm ready," she said, completely oblivious to the whirlwind around her. "Just let me fix my hair."

As Marilyn disappeared into a dressing room, Milt looked out onstage and caught Peter's eye.

"She's here," he mouthed, and with his hands motioned for Peter to stretch out her introduction.[1]

A few minutes later, Marilyn emerged from her dressing room, her hair no different than when she'd arrived, and as she sauntered slowly past him, Milt gave her a little shove onto the stage.

As Peter saw her thrust forward, he announced to the expectant crowd, without any sense of prophecy, "And now, the late Marilyn Monroe!"

Afterward, Jack came onstage and joked about Marilyn's breathy song, saying, "I can now retire from politics after having had 'Happy Birthday' sung to me in such a sweet, wholesome way."

Less than three months later, on August 4, 1962, Milt was on the phone with Peter the night Marilyn died.

Earlier that day, still woozy from the pills and booze she'd downed the night before, Marilyn had called her psychiatrist, Dr. Ralph Greenson, and told him she was worried and anxious. She'd been fired from her last job as the star of the 20th Century Fox film "Something's Got To Give," after repeatedly failing to show up for work. Now she had nothing to do and nowhere to go.

Dr. Greenson suggested that she take a walk on the beach, so she reluctantly drove over to see Peter and his wife, Pat, at their beach house in Santa Monica. She parked at their house, said hello, and then went for her last lonely stroll, wearing sunglasses and a scarf to conceal her identity. She walked anonymously along the shoreline for a while, oblivious to the beachgoers enjoying a glorious Saturday afternoon in Southern California. It must have seemed like she was the only one on the beach who was depressed.

At the same time, three thousand miles to the east, Jack Kennedy was enjoying a beautiful Saturday afternoon with his family at the seaside in Hyannis Port, Massachusetts. The Cuban Missile Crisis was two months away, and a famous photo of Jack that day shows him posing happily with Jackie and the children. It's the picture of a man without a care in the world.

Peter, an old friend of Marilyn's, had introduced her to Jack earlier that year, and they had had a brief affair. But Marilyn was becoming more and more erratic, and it was left to Jack's brother, Bobby, to tell her that Jack couldn't see her anymore. It was a terrible blow to Marilyn, who loved Jack dearly, and he would be much on her mind the day she died.

Later that afternoon in Santa Monica, Peter called Milt and invited him over.

"Milt, why don't you come to the house for dinner?" Peter asked. "We're gonna have Chinese food."

Over the years, Peter had become completely dependent on Milt's advice and company, and couldn't do anything without him. Whenever Peter was invited anywhere—even to the White House—Milt went along, too. When Peter flew on Air Force One, Milt flew, too. Milt accompanied Peter to Jack's inauguration and to his funeral, and to just about every other White House and Kennedy family function in between. So inseparable were Peter and Milt that Jack came to refer to them affectionately as "Tweedledee and Tweedledum."[2]

But Milt was tired that night, and begged off.

"Peter, I really can't make it," Milt said. "I'm bushed."

"Come on, Milt, Marilyn's here," Peter cajoled.

Milt rarely said no to Peter, but that night, he held firm. "I'll see you tomorrow," he said.

Marilyn wouldn't be there for dinner, either. After her walk on the beach, she went back to the house, said goodbye to Peter and Pat, and drove back home to Brentwood.

At around five o'clock that evening, Peter called Marilyn to see how she was doing.

"Why don't you come back?" he asked her. "It'll do you good."

"Peter, I'm really too tired and I'm really mentally exhausted, so I want to take a rain check," she said. Her soft voice was kind, but weary. "I think I'm gonna take a couple of sleeping pills and go to bed early."

"Okay," he said. "You take it easy. Right?"

Peter called her back three hours later, and she was despondent. It was just after 8:00 PM on the evening of August 4, 1962, and Marilyn was drunk and slurring her words badly. He tried to talk her into coming over to the house, but she didn't seem to hear what he was saying. And he could hardly make out what *she* was saying—her voice was becoming less and less audible. He began to yell at her over the phone, trying to revive her.

"Marilyn!" he screamed into the phone. "Marilyn! Listen to me, Marilyn!"

But she didn't seem to hear that, either.

Then she said something that Peter would never forget.

"Say goodbye to Jack," she said. "Say goodbye to Bobby. And

say goodbye to yourself, because you're a nice guy."

Then the phone went dead.

Peter quickly called her back, but the line was busy. He redialed, but it was still busy. Worried, he called the operator, who checked the line and told him the phone was off the hook.

This was nothing new; Marilyn had done this before. She would drink too much, take a few downers, and then pass out while talking to somebody on the phone. But this time, Peter recalled later, he had "a gut feeling that something was wrong."

Three weeks earlier, he and Pat had taken Marilyn to the Cal-Neva Lodge in Lake Tahoe to see Frank Sinatra perform. They watched the show, went backstage afterwards and talked to Frank, and had a great time together. When Peter awoke the next morning, Pat told him that Marilyn had overdosed the night before. She'd fallen out of bed and they had to call paramedics to revive her.

What if that had happened to her tonight, Peter thought, and there was no one around to revive her?

Now he was really beginning to worry, so naturally, he called Milt.

"Listen," he told his friend, panic rising in his voice, "come and pick me up. I'm goin' to see if Marilyn's okay."

"Wait a minute, wait a minute," Milt said, thinking on his feet. "Before you go over there, let's find out if she's okay. Let's call Mrs. Murray."

Eunice Murray lived with Marilyn as her "housekeeper," but she was actually a trained psychiatric nurse whom Dr. Greenson had hired to watch over the actress.

"But I can't get her on the phone, either," said Peter.

"Okay, let me see what I can do," Milt said.

Milt hung up and immediately put in a call to Mickey Rudin, Marilyn's manager and attorney. According to the files of the Los Angeles Police Department, Milt called Rudin's service at 8:25 PM and left a message. Five minutes later, the telephone service reached Rudin at a cocktail party, and Rudin called Milt back at 8:45.[3]

"Mickey, Peter's getting ready to go over to Marilyn's house,"

Milt told Rudin.

"Milt, just hold off," Rudin said above the din of the cocktail party. "Let me check with Mrs. Murray and I'll get back to you."

Rudin had a private number for Mrs. Murray. He dialed the number and asked the nurse to check on Marilyn. Mrs. Murray put the phone down, went out to the front of the house, peeked in through a crack in the curtains of Marilyn's bedroom window, and then came back to the phone to tell Rudin that Marilyn was fine.

"She takes the pills, she's talking to somebody, and then she drops the phone," Mrs. Murray said. "She's in bed. The lights are on, the radio is on, and she's locked all the doors. She looks fine to me. She does this every night."

A few minutes later, Rudin called Milt back and told him everything was all right.

"She's okay," he told Milt. "Don't worry. You don't have to go over there. Tell Peter."

The LAPD report on their official investigation into the death of Marilyn Monroe determined that Rudin, "believing that Miss Monroe was suffering from one of her despondent moments…dismissed the possibility of anything further being wrong."[4]

Milt called Peter back and told him what Rudin had said. But by this time, Peter was pretty drunk himself.

"I want to go over there," he told Milt, slurring his words.

"So why don't you go?" Milt snapped, exasperated that his efforts hadn't done anything to calm Peter down. "I'm not gonna drive out there. You wanna go, get in your fuckin' car and go."

"Well, I think I ought to go," Peter replied petulantly.

"Look, why don't you talk to Mickey Rudin?" Milt said.

"Yeah, let me talk to Mickey."

Milt called Rudin and said, "Mick, you better talk to this guy cause he's loaded and he wants to go over there."

So Rudin, still at the cocktail party, called Peter and convinced him that Marilyn was fine.

"She's okay," Rudin reassured Peter. "You know I wouldn't let anything happen to her. She's fine. She does this every night. Mrs.

Murray said she's okay. She's all right."

"Okay," Peter said, not really feeling okay about it at all. "I think I should go anyway, but I won't go."

At around midnight, comedian Mort Saul, whom Milt also managed, dropped by Milt's place for a late night talk. Milt, who was famously late to bed, let him in and they talked for hours. But it wasn't long before Peter started calling again, wanting Milt to take him over to Marilyn's.

"I think we ought to go over there," Peter slurred on the phone.

"For Christ's sake, go to bed," Milt told Peter. "Mort Saul's here. I can't take you over there."

Milt and Mort went back to talking. About an hour later, Peter called again. Milt told him the same thing, but Peter called back yet again at 2:00 AM. Exasperated, Milt laid the problem out for Peter in the bluntest terms possible.

"Peter, you're the president's brother-in-law, for Christ's sake," he said. "If there's anything wrong at all, you're the last guy that should be there."[5]

There was silence on the other end of the phone. Peter knew Milt was right. If there *was* anything wrong at Marilyn's, Peter's presence there might only lead to questions he wouldn't want to answer, questions that might expose a side of Jack Kennedy's private life that could end his presidency.

Peter hung up and didn't call back.

Milt and Mort were still talking at 3:30 in the morning when Mrs. Murray, worried after peeking through Marilyn's bedroom window again and seeing that she hadn't moved on the bed for over three hours—the phone still clutched in her hand—called Marilyn's psychiatrist.

Dr. Greenson pulled into Marilyn's driveway 10 minutes later.

"He broke the window pane and entered through the window and removed the phone from her hand," the LAPD report said.[6]

An hour later, Mickey Rudin called Milt.

"Mickey," Milt said. "What are you doing up at this hour?"

"I'm over at Marilyn's," Mickey said flatly.

"Really?" Milt asked, not grasping the import yet. "What's goin' on?"

"I'm here with her doctors—a psychiatrist and Dr. Engleberg, her internist—and they just pronounced her dead," Mickey said matter-of-factly. "You're the first one to know it. I called you first. I'm going to call the police right now."[7]

The files of the LAPD show that Peter Lawford had been the last person to talk to Marilyn the night she died. In the years following her death and the assassination of President Kennedy, rumors of conspiracy and cover-up would come to surround both of their deaths.

"She overdosed," Milt would say many years later. "That's how she died. All the rest is bullshit."

Milt always firmly believed that he did the right thing by keeping President Kennedy's brother-in-law from going over to Marilyn's place that night. After all, Mickey Rudin had assured him repeatedly that everything was all right. And in the end, Marilyn probably couldn't have been saved anyway. If it hadn't been that lost and lonely night, it probably would have been another one.

CHAPTER 38

Saving the World: The Cuban Missile Crisis

Three weeks after Kennedy was inaugurated, Nixon came to New York to see Dr. Hutschnecker for a "check-up." Nixon was staying at the posh Plaza Hotel, overlooking Central Park just a few blocks from Dr. Hutschnecker's office on Park Avenue.

Hutschnecker took a cab through the slushy, cold winter streets to the hotel and went up to Nixon's suite. Nixon greeted him at the door, and as was his custom, showed the doctor around the suite, pointing out its lovely view of Central Park, which was covered with a fresh blanket of snow.

"Isn't that something?" Nixon asked, staring out the window.

"Indeed it is," Dr. Hutschnecker replied, sensing that something was on Nixon's mind.

Nixon sat by the window and Hutschnecker opened his black medical bag. Taking out a syringe, he had Nixon roll up a sleeve so he could take a blood sample. He'd have the lab look at it, he said, and then suggested that Nixon get some exercise and eat more balanced meals to reduce the stress that had caused "some internal disturbances."[1]

They'd corresponded several times since the election. A week earlier, Hutschnecker had written Nixon saying he'd watched the events leading up to the election "with a heavy heart" and had noticed "certain developments which I felt would or could become fateful and about which I could do nothing...Perhaps we may someday have a chance to talk about it as far as these observations may have a meaning for the future."[2]

But the future was now. Sitting by the window overlooking the park, Nixon told the doctor that he was thinking about entering another political campaign.

"I've been asked to run for governor of California," he said. "I think I can beat Pat Brown."[3]

Concerned that Nixon "had not got past the trauma of having lost to Kennedy," Hutschnecker tried to dissuade him from running for office again so soon after such a devastating loss.

"Would entering the race for the governorship of California not be a significant step down from having run for the presidency?" Dr. Hutschnecker asked, trying an indirect way of talking him out of it.

Nixon rolled his shirtsleeve back down and stared out the window at the majestic winter landscape below. "It's all politics," he said wearily.

Hutschnecker knew then that Nixon would make a run for the governorship because he realized that now, more than ever, Nixon "needed to prove himself" by winning an election—any election.[4]

But it would prove to be a disastrous miscalculation.

Nixon's most humiliating election defeat would come just a few days after President Kennedy's greatest triumph—the peaceful resolution of the Cuban Missile Crisis.

On November 6, 1962, Nixon lost the gubernatorial race by a surprisingly wide five percent margin, receiving nearly 500,000 *fewer* votes against Pat Brown than he'd gotten in California just two years earlier against Jack Kennedy.

Angry and frustrated by the loss, Nixon famously told reporters that he'd had it, and was retiring from politics right then and there. "You won't have Nixon to kick around anymore, gentlemen, because this is my last press conference," he declared.

The next day, Dr. Hutschnecker sent Nixon a letter of condolence.

"Like two years ago, I waited for a happy outcome of a contest, which unfortunately was mixed with too much passion and emotionalism," he told Nixon. "The finality of the outcome struck me like a personal loss. There is so little I can say, but I want to reassure you and Pat of my respect and warmest regards. Hoping to see you soon."[5]

Nixon's back-to-back election losses—the first in his life—left him depressed and bitter.

At the press conference following his loss to Pat Brown, Nixon saw the reporters' questions as aggressive, insulting, and contemptuous. So he lashed out at them, but only ended up hurting and embarrassing himself even more.

As Dr. Hutschnecker would later observe, Nixon had inherited his father's temperament, and when attacked, his nature was to counterattack.[6]

Nine days before Nixon lost the 1962 governor's race and petulantly threatened to quit politics, President Kennedy saved the world.

The Cuban Missile Crisis had brought the world to the brink of nuclear annihilation in October of that year. It was only defused when Kennedy and Soviet Premier Nikita Khrushchev both refused to take the advice of their generals, who were all too eager to go to war—one that almost certainly would have meant an all-out nuclear holocaust.

In a direct response to the CIA's failed 1961 Bay of Pigs invasion early in the Kennedy administration, the Soviet Union had begun placing mid-range nuclear missiles on the island of Cuba, just 90 miles off the coast of Florida. U.S. spy planes first photographed the missile installations on October 14, only six days after Cuban president Osvaldo Dorticos proclaimed at the U.N. General Assembly: "If we are attacked, we will defend ourselves. I repeat, we have sufficient means with which to defend ourselves."

President Kennedy didn't see the photos of the missile installations until October 16, and quickly assembled the Executive Committee of the National Security Council to decide on a course of action. Some of Kennedy's advisors urged a cautious response, but the Joint Chiefs of Staff were unanimous in their recommendation for a full-scale attack and invasion of Cuba.

Defense Secretary Robert McNamara would later recall General Curtis LeMay, chief of staff of the air force, saying, "Let's go in, let's totally destroy Cuba."[7]

When President Kennedy finally told his generals that he'd decided instead to put up a naval blockade around Cuba to prevent any more nuclear missiles from being brought there, LeMay can be heard muttering contemptuously on JFK's White House tapes that "this is almost as bad as the appeasement at Munich...I just don't see any other solution except direct military intervention right now."[8]

If President Kennedy had followed the general's advice, McNamara stated later, "Nuclear war would have erupted, without any question."[9]

Instead, Kennedy chose the only path to peace. After 13 days of negotiations and brinksmanship, his decision not to invade Cuba proved to be the right one. He and Khrushchev, who also had to hold back his own military, worked out an agreement that brought the world back from the brink of disaster.

We now know that if Kennedy had gone along with his generals and authorized an attack on Cuba, the Russians would have launched their Cuban-based nuclear missiles at America.

Many years later, McNamara learned that there were 162 nuclear warheads on the island of Cuba during the crisis, and that Cuban prime minister Fidel Castro had urged Khrushchev to launch them if the U.S. attacked.

During a 1992 meeting in Cuba, Castro told a stunned McNamara, "I did recommend to Khrushchev that they be used."[10]

In his memoirs, published in 2006, Khruschev wrote that, had the U.S. attacked Cuba, he would have launched nuclear missiles at New York City.

If the missiles had been launched, that would have triggered an American nuclear counter-attack on Cuba *and* the Soviet Union.

"It shall be the policy of this nation," President Kennedy solemnly told a nationwide television audience on October 22, 1962, "to regard any nuclear missile launched from Cuba against any nation in the Western Hemisphere as an attack by the Soviet Union on the United States, requiring a full retaliatory response upon the Soviet Union."

Fortunately for every generation to come, that catastrophe was averted.

Dr. Hutschnecker later wrote that he was "completely convinced" that if Nixon had become president in 1960, "Vietnam would not have happened," and that, had Nixon won, "the bunker mentality that spawned Watergate would not have developed because desperate measures to win would not have been employed."[11]

Be that as it may, perhaps an even better hypothetical question arising from a Nixon victory over Kennedy in 1960 would have been: Would Nixon have handled the Cuban Missile Crisis as deftly as Kennedy? In the face of Soviet aggression, would he have rejected the unanimous advice of the U.S. military, as Kennedy had, to attack? Or, "imprinted with his father's volatile mood swings," as Hutschnecker observed, would Nixon have reacted to Soviet aggression as "a blind signal to counter-attack," and plunged the world into nuclear war?

The past, of course, cannot be changed, so we will never know for sure. But one thing is certain: JFK was the right man, in the right place, at the right time to make the most important decision ever made. If not for the confluence of events, and a private detective named Guenther Reinhardt, Kennedy might not have been there to make the call.

CHAPTER 39

The Arrest of Guenther Reinhardt

uenther Reinhardt's troubled life began its final downward spiral in April of 1963. He wasn't chasing Nazis or Communists anymore; he was informing on homosexuals and peddling stolen documents to organized crime figures. Or so he thought.

Six months earlier, the world had stepped back from the brink of nuclear war when President Kennedy and Soviet Premier Nikita Khrushchev reined in their generals, who were eager for a fight, during the Cuban Missile Crisis of October 1962. It was the closest mankind had ever come to an all-out nuclear war, and in a very real sense, Kennedy and Khrushchev had saved the world.

On April 5, 1963, the two leaders took another step toward keeping the peace by agreeing to the immediate installation of a first-of-its-kind direct communications link between the White House and the Kremlin for use in emergencies. On that day, the red-phone hot line, which is still in use today, was conceived.

April 5, 1963, was a good day for world peace, but it wasn't a good day for Guenther Reinhardt. In fact, it was probably the worst day of his life—a sad life that had already seen many "worst days."

That night, he was standing in front of a bar on the Avenue of the Americas in Midtown Manhattan when two mob guys walked up to him and identified themselves. Their mafia captain, John "Sonny" Franzese, who would later become a top capo in the Colombo organized crime family, had sent them.[1]

For several days, Reinhardt had been spreading the word in local taverns that he'd obtained some secret government files that might be worth something to Franzese. Word soon got back to Reinhardt that Franzese *was* interested and would send two of his men to meet him in front of a Midtown bar on the night of April 5th.

Reinhardt had stolen the files from the New York State Liquor Authority, which issues state liquor licenses to bars, nightclubs, hotels and restaurants. Hired by the Liquor Authority as an undercover informant, Reinhardt had been given access to its records, including a confidential file about Sonny Franzese's illegal activities in the liquor and nightclub businesses. As was his nature, Reinhardt stole the file and started looking for a buyer.

It was dark when the two mob guys showed up. Reinhardt had been waiting for them, chain-smoking Chesterfields. It was clear and cold, almost freezing, and Reinhardt's hands shook as he showed them the stolen Franzese file. The two mob guys thumbed through the papers for a few minutes and then told him that Sonny was interested and had authorized them to give him $150 as a down payment—about a thousand bucks in today's money. That wasn't anywhere near the $10,000 he'd asked for, but Guenther was broke and it was better than nothing.

"Okay," he said reluctantly, taking the cash in an unmarked envelope. As he counted the money there in front of the bar, the two mob guys quickly slapped handcuffs on him and told him he was under arrest. They weren't gangsters after all; they were New York City police detectives.[2]

Reinhardt was taken to jail while the cops obtained a warrant and searched his apartment at 95 Christopher Street in Greenwich Village, where they found another 188 pages of stolen Liquor Authority documents. During the search, they also found a blackjack—an illegal, easily concealed, leather-bound club, weighted at the end with buckshot. The documents and the blackjack were seized, and Reinhardt was charged with stealing state documents and possessing an illegal weapon.[3]

Reinhardt's arrest and arraignment would make the back pages of the *New York Times* for several days running.

After Reinhardt's arrest, Donald Hostetter, the Liquor Authority's chairman, told reporters that Reinhardt had been a "volunteer informant" for the agency, tipping them off about "joints where homosexuals hang out."[4]

Then Hostetter uttered the words that would sum up Reinhardt's life: "He gave us a lot of accurate information and some that was pure fantasy."[5]

Reinhardt's arrest was not only a nightmare for himself, but also for his friend, famed author and journalist Vance Packard. Packard had hired Reinhardt to help research his next book, a sure-fire bestseller about the new, dark arts of electronic surveillance and high-tech spying. But now, with this scandal, the now-infamous private eye had become a major liability that Packard feared could ruin his reputation.

By the time of Reinhardt's arrest in the spring of 1963, Packard had become one of the most popular and influential writers in America, delving deep beneath the veneer of the American myth to explore how rapidly changing social mores and the brave new world of technology were threatening to destroy the traditional American way of life. He'd written three best-selling books in a row about the dangers posed by consumerism, mass marketing, and the concentration of wealth and power into the hands of a few, and many sociologists today regard his insight into the world to come as having been remarkably prophetic.

Packard's biggest book yet, he hoped, was going to be *The Naked Society*, which was to be published in 1964. *The Naked Society* would be a classic exposé of the dangers posed to private citizens and public figures alike by the explosion of surveillance, wiretapping and other clandestine forms of information gathering.

It was going to be a great, pioneering book; but there was a problem. His secret weapon, his own private guide to the underworld of spying and intelligence gathering, had been arrested and was now threatening to reveal just how essential he'd been to Packard's new project.

The *New York Post* even mentioned that Reinhardt had worked for Packard, and now Reinhardt was threatening to tell reporters everything he knew about Packard's next book. For Packard, who desperately wanted to keep his book's subject a secret, the situation had become "a nightmare."[6]

Reinhardt told Packard that he wanted his contribution to the book "prominently recognized," a demand Packard viewed as blackmail. Backed into a corner, Packard sent his old friend and publisher, Kennett L. Rawson, to negotiate a deal with Reinhardt. After a tense meeting, Reinhardt accepted a large cash payment in return for keeping quiet, in addition to a token acknowledgment when the book was published.[7]

Buried near the end of four pages of acknowledgments, Packard wrote: "I express my appreciation to Guenther Reinhardt, who drew upon thirty years of federal and private investigative experience to help orient me, at the outset of my research in 1962, regarding modern investigative techniques and practices. Later, from time to time, he offered information."[8]

The recognition was nice, but Reinhardt needed the hush money more. At his arraignment, he'd pleaded not guilty and was released on $1,000 bail, but he would spend the next four years battling the charges. During the first year alone, he made 37 court appearances and went through three attorneys, each of whom, in succession, withdrew from handling his case. The last of the three, a former New York City assistant-district-attorney-turned-defense-lawyer, withdrew only minutes before the case was to be called to trial. Guenther Reinhardt was a very difficult man, and a very difficult client.[9]

But he still had a few friends in high places who could grease the skids of justice for him. On December 4, 1967, nearly five years after his arrest, a crooked New York state Supreme Court judge, who a few years later would be forced to step down from the bench amid corruption charges, dismissed all the charges against Reinhardt. The *New York Times* reported that "the court dismissed the indictment on its own motion"—an unusual move considering the mountain of the evidence that pointed to his guilt.[10]

Reinhardt was finally free of the charges, but he was broke—and a broken man.

"He kept going downhill," recalled his former colleague, Warner Michel. "He became completely irrational."[11]

And he didn't have long to live.

CHAPTER 40

November 22, 1963

Nearly everyone of a certain age remembers exactly what they were doing when they heard that President Kennedy had been assassinated. *Esquire* magazine, in its tenth anniversary retrospective on the assassination, said that it was "the only moment that almost every adult remembers…." Everyone, that is, except Richard Nixon.

For some reason, Nixon, who by a strange twist of fate was in Dallas on the morning of the assassination, has told two different stories about how he first learned that JFK had been shot.

Nixon had flown into Dallas from New York City two days earlier, on November 20, accompanying Pepsi CEO Donald Kendall to a meeting of the Pepsi-Cola Bottler's Association. Nixon was the senior partner in Nixon, Mudge, Rose, Guthrie & Alexander, the law firm that represented Pepsi. Kendall had gotten Nixon the partnership at the prestigious New York law firm earlier that year when he offered them a large retainer if they would hire Nixon and put him in charge of the Pepsi account. Kendall was repaying a favor; Nixon had helped him out in a big way four years earlier.[1]

They'd met at the U.S. Embassy in Moscow in July 1959. Nixon, who was then the vice president of the United States, had traveled to the Soviet Union to open the U.S. Trade and Cultural Fair in Sokolniki Park. Kendall, then the head of Pepsi's international division, was one of the exhibitors at the trade fair. His mission was to try to introduce Pepsi to the vast, untapped Soviet market. That night at the embassy, he came up with a plan. He knew that Nixon would be meeting with Soviet premier Nikita Khrushchev at the trade fair, so he approached the vice president and asked him for a favor.

"I asked him to bring Khrushchev by the next day," Kendall recalled. "I had to get Pepsi into Khrushchev's hands."[2]

The next day at the trade fair, as Nixon and Khrushchev stood in front of a replica of a suburban American kitchen, the two leaders engaged in an impromptu debate about the merits of their two countries' political and economic systems. Using humor and some considerable charm, Nixon came off as the more engaging of the two, and easily won what came to be known as "The Kitchen Debate," which was captured on film and broadcast on television in both countries.

Afterward, Nixon came through for Kendall, steering Khrushchev to him at the Pepsi kiosk, where the Soviet leader had his photo taken gulping down cup after cup of "Soviet Pepsi"—Pepsi made from carbonated Moscow water. Khrushchev loved the stuff and praised the company and its product. It was an international marketing public relations coup for Kendall, who soon rose through the ranks to become CEO of Pepsi.[3]

In 1972, when Nixon was president, Kendall struck a deal with the government of the Soviet Union that led to Pepsi-Cola being the first foreign product sanctioned for sale in the USSR.

"You never know when you're going to have an opportunity," Kendall laughed.[4]

Nixon attended the Pepsi board meeting in Dallas on Thursday, November 21, 1963, and afterward talked briefly to reporters. One of the reporters mentioned that Kennedy was coming to Dallas the next day, and Nixon called for "a courteous reception for President Kennedy."[5]

Their paths were crossing for the last time.

Nixon left the hotel early the next morning and took a cab to Love Field, where he noticed signs, banners, and flags heralding President Kennedy's arrival at the airport later that day.

"[My] flight was in the morning, but preparations were already underway at the airport for the arrival of the president early that afternoon," he told *Esquire* magazine for its tenth anniversary retrospective on JFK's assassination.[6]

Nixon left Dallas for New York that Friday morning, November 22, at 8:05 AM aboard American Airlines Flight 82, which arrived at Idlewild International Airport in New York at 12:56 PM local time. At Idlewild, Nixon was greeted by several more reporters and a UPI photographer. He answered a few questions, had his picture taken, and then left the airport by cab at approximately 1:15 PM, New York time.[7]

In Dallas, it was 12:15 PM, and President Kennedy's motorcade was winding its way through the streets of Dallas, which were packed with throngs of cheering Texans there to greet the president.

Fifteen minutes later, the motorcade entered Dealey Plaza, and as the president's open limousine passed the Texas School Book Depository, several shots rang out.

The first news report of the shooting was carried on Dallas's KLIF Radio, when newscaster Gary DeLaune interrupted *The Rex Jones Show* at 12:39 local time with a special bulletin.

"Three shots reportedly were fired at the motorcade of President Kennedy today near the downtown section," DeLaune told his radio listeners, trying to keep his voice calm. "*KLIF News* is checking out the report. We will have further reports. Stay tuned."

A minute or two later, Jay Watson, the program director of WFAA-TV, the ABC affiliate in Dallas, interrupted *The Julie Benell Show*, a taped program about women's fashion. Still winded from running back to the station's news room from Dealey Plaza, Watson broke the news on local television.

"Good afternoon, ladies and gentlemen," he said. "You'll excuse the fact that I am out of breath, but about 10 or 15 minutes ago a tragic thing from all indications at this point has happened in the city of Dallas."

Then, holding a press bulletin in his hands, Watson said, "A bulletin—this is from the United Press from Dallas. President Kennedy and Governor John Connally have been cut down by assassins' bullets in downtown Dallas."

Richard Nixon was stuck in a cab without a radio somewhere in Queens when the rest of the world started hearing the news.

It was 1:40 EST when CBS suddenly interrupted the popular soap opera *As the World Turns*. The CBS News Bulletin logo came onto television screens all across the country. With no picture, just audio, Walter Cronkite delivered the news with a rare sense of alarm in his voice.

"This is a bulletin from CBS News," he said. "In Dallas, Texas, three shots were fired at President Kennedy's motorcade in downtown Dallas. The first reports say that President Kennedy has been seriously wounded by this shooting."

At this point, still without any picture, Cronkite was handed an update. "More details just arrived," he said. "President Kennedy shot today just as his motorcade left downtown Dallas. Mrs. Kennedy jumped up and grabbed Mr. Kennedy. She called, 'Oh, no!' The motorcade sped on. United Press says that the wounds for President Kennedy perhaps could be fatal. Repeating, President Kennedy has been shot by a would-be assassin in Dallas, Texas. Stay tuned to CBS News for further details."[8]

Then, for seven long seconds, CBS cut incongruously to a commercial for Nescafé coffee, and then quickly back to the black screen and white block lettering of the CBS News Bulletin logo, with Cronkite's voice delivering updates. It would be another full minute before the control booth at CBS News could switch to a live image of Cronkite at the news anchor desk, and when the picture finally came on, there were signs of confusion in the newsroom. The picture rolled twice, the microphone squeaked loudly, and Cronkite could be seen shuffling papers in his shirtsleeves— in the rush to break the story, he'd left his coat in his office. For the next hour, he kept reporting the latest updates, including an unconfirmed report from Dan Rather, the network's bureau chief in Dallas, that a priest had just administered the last rites of the Catholic Church to President Kennedy.

Richard Nixon's cab had taken a wrong turn somewhere, and the cabbie was driving around lost in Astoria, Queens. It was at this point in Nixon's recollection of that day that his stories diverged.

In both versions of his accounts, Nixon said his cab was stopped at a traffic light in Queens when someone rushed up to the cab and said that President Kennedy had been shot.

But in one version of the story—the one he told in his 1978 memoirs—Nixon said that a man approached his cab and talked excitedly to the cabbie about Kennedy having been shot, while in another version—the one he told *Esquire* magazine in 1973—it was a hysterical woman who came up to his cab, looked directly into Nixon's face, and told him that Kennedy had been shot and killed.

Nixon wrote in his memoirs that after landing at Idlewild— later renamed JFK International Airport—he got into a cab and headed for the city.

"We drove through Queens toward the 59th Street Bridge," he wrote, "and as we stopped at a traffic light, a man rushed over from the curb and started talking to the driver. I heard him say, 'Do you have a radio in your cab? I just heard that Kennedy was shot.'

"We had no radio," Nixon wrote, "and as we continued into Manhattan a hundred thoughts rushed through my mind. The man [who had rushed up to the cab] could have been crazy or a macabre prankster. He could have been mistaken about what he heard; or perhaps a gunman might have shot at Kennedy but missed or only wounded him. I refused to believe that he could have been killed."

Nixon wrote that he only learned Kennedy was dead for sure when he got out of the cab at his apartment and was greeted by the doorman, who had tears streaming down his cheeks.

"Oh, Mr. Nixon, have you heard, sir?" the doorman asked. "It's just terrible. They've killed President Kennedy."[9]

But five years earlier, when interviewed by *Esquire*, Nixon told a slightly different story.

"On arrival in New York we caught a cab and headed for the city," Nixon recalled. "The cab had no radio on. As fate would have it, the cabbie missed a turn somewhere and we were off the high-way, somewhere in Astoria, Queens, I think. We were stopped for a red light when a woman came out of her house screaming and crying. I rolled down the cab window to ask what the matter was and when she saw my face she turned even paler. She told me that John Kennedy had just been shot and killed in Dallas. We drove the rest of the way in silence."[10]

Nixon was back home at his residence at 810 Fifth Avenue and had the TV on at 2:37 PM EST, when CBS news editor Ed Bliss Jr. handed Cronkite a wire report from the Associated Press. Cronkite put on his thick reading glasses, looked at it quickly, and read it to the national television audience. "From Dallas, Texas, the flash, apparently official: President Kennedy died at 1:00 PM Central Standard Time, 2:00 Eastern Standard Time..." Then, taking off his glasses, he looked up at the clock on the newsroom wall and continued, slowly sounding out each syllable, "...some 38 minutes ago." Slowly and deliberately, Cronkite put his glasses back on, then looked down and fidgeted with the papers on his desk for several seconds. When he finally spoke again, his voice broke, cracking with emotion. Trying to compose himself and visibly fighting back tears, he said, "Vice President Lyndon Johnson has left the hospital in Dallas, but we do not know to where he has proceeded. Presumably, he will be taking the oath of office shortly and become the 36th president of the United States."[11]

Some Kennedy assassination conspiracy theorists believe that the two stories Nixon has told about that day are a sign that he was trying to cover up his own involvement in Kennedy's murder, and point to a newspaper photograph and caption to prove that he was lying about where he was when he first heard the news.

The UPI photo, showing a somber-looking Nixon seated in an airport waiting area, was carried in several newspapers the day after the assassination. The caption read: "SHOCKED Richard Nixon, the former vice president who lost the presidential election to President Kennedy in 1960, is shown Friday after he arrived at Idlewild Airport in New York following a flight from Dallas, Tex., where he had been on a business trip."

Nixon had indeed been photographed at Idlewild after returning to New York from Dallas the day of the assassination, but the photograph was actually taken *before* he'd learned that Kennedy had been shot. The caption writer simply mistook Nixon's usual grim countenance as one of "shock," and that the photo therefore must have been taken *after* he learned of the assassination, which it was not.

There is no real evidence at all to suggest that Nixon was involved in the assassination. But some believe that he had been Lee Harvey Oswald's original target that day in Dallas. At least, that's what Nixon always said, even though he knew it wasn't true.

In his memoirs, Nixon said that FBI Director J. Edgar Hoover told him about it several months after the Kennedy assassination.

"Months later," Nixon wrote, "Hoover told me that Oswald's wife had disclosed that Oswald had been planning to kill me when I visited Dallas and that only with great difficulty had she managed to keep him in the house to prevent him from doing so."[12]

Nixon's arrival in Dallas on November 20 *had* been mentioned in the local Dallas newspapers, and it's possible that Oswald read about it. And in June of 1964, Oswald's widow, Marina, *did* tell the Warren Commission that Lee had gotten a pistol out of their bedroom closet and told her that he was going to go shoot Nixon.

Oswald had already tried to shoot one prominent American, former U.S. army general—and ultra-conservative—Edwin Walker. On April 4, 1963, after weeks of planning and reconnaissance, Oswald took a shot at Walker though the general's dining room window in Dallas. The bullet, fired from the same rifle Oswald would later use to shoot President Kennedy, ricocheted off the wooden window frame and missed, although Walker was slightly injured by flying glass fragments. News of the shooting was in all the local papers, although the attempted assassin got away. It wouldn't be until December that Oswald was positively identified as the shooter.

But Oswald's wife knew soon after the Walker shooting that her husband had done it. He confessed to her, and she made him promise that he would never, ever do anything like that again.

When Oswald told her that he was going out to shoot Nixon, she tearfully reminded him of that promise.

After reading the morning newspaper that day, Oswald put on his best suit and took a pistol out of the bedroom closet, the same handgun he would later use to shoot Dallas police officer J. D. Tippit while fleeing from the Dallas Book Depository. Then he told Marina that he was going out.

"I saw that he took a pistol," Marina later told the Warren Commission investigating the Kennedy assassination. "I asked him where was he going."

"Nixon is coming," he told her. "I want to go and have a look.'" Then he confided that he was going to shoot Nixon if he could get a clear shot at him.[13]

Marina pleaded with him not to do it, reminding him of his promise after the Walker shooting, but he wouldn't listen. He was going to go shoot Nixon, he told her.

"I called him into the bathroom," she told the Warren Commission on June 11, 1964, "and I closed the door and I wanted to prevent him and then I started to cry. And I told him that he shouldn't do this, and that he had promised me...I remember that I held him. We actually struggled for several minutes and then he quieted down."[14]

It's a good story, but actually, Oswald was lying to her. He was leaving town in a few days—perhaps for good—and for whatever reason, he was only trying to provoke her. Nixon wasn't even in Dallas that day; he hadn't been, and wouldn't be, for months. It was April 1963, seven months before Nixon would come to Dallas for the Pepsi-Cola Bottler's Association meeting. And Marina was sure of the timeframe. She told the Warren Commission that Lee had made the threat to shoot Nixon just a few days before he moved to New Orleans on April 24, 1963, to go there to look for work.

It was just a bluff.

There had been no newspaper reports for Oswald to read in April about Nixon being in Dallas, and Nixon later advised the

Warren Commission that the only time he'd been in Dallas in 1963 was in November.

"Regardless of what Oswald may have said to his wife," the Warren Commission rightly concluded, "he was not actually planning to shoot Mr. Nixon at that time in Dallas."[15]

Nixon certainly knew when his memoirs were published in 1978 that he had never actually been Oswald's intended target that November day in Dallas. The Warren Commission report and the depositions of 552 witnesses, including Marina's, were published a year after the assassination and were there for everyone to read. But Nixon's claim "that Oswald had been planning to kill me when I visited Dallas," as he wrote in his memoirs, made for a much better story; it made it seem as though it could have been either him or Jack Kennedy assassinated that day in Dallas, and that fate had simply chosen Jack.

Never mind that it was a lie. It made for a better story.

Jack Kennedy's assassination shocked the nation and changed the world. The only thing that remained the same was Nixon.

CHAPTER 41

Vietnam

Daniel Ellsberg was a high-ranking civilian on his first full day of duty at the Pentagon when North Vietnamese torpedo boats allegedly attacked two U.S. destroyers, the *Maddox* and the *Turner Joy*, in the Gulf of Tonkin off the coast of North Vietnam. When the first coded dispatches about the attack came into the Pentagon that day, Ellsberg rushed the message to Defense Secretary Robert McNamara.

That night, August 4, 1964, President Lyndon Johnson went on national television to tell the American people that he had just ordered the first U.S. bombing raids against North Vietnam in response to "unequivocal evidence" of an "unprovoked" attack on U.S. ships.

Watching his television at home that night, Ellsberg was shocked by what the president was saying.

"Already that night I knew, along with many other Pentagon insiders, that each of these statements was a lie," Ellsberg would say many years later.[1]

There was no "unequivocal evidence" because there had been no "unprovoked" attack that day on American warships.

"I had personally read," Ellsberg recalled later, "10 hours before our bombers were launched, a 'flash' cable from Captain John Herrick, commanding the destroyers, which put in doubt all of his cables that had crossed my desk earlier that day reporting up to 21 torpedoes fired at his ships. Attributing the prior reports to 'freak weather effects and an overeager sonar man,' Herrick recommended that no further action be taken until there had been complete evaluation, including daylight reconnaissance."[2]

But waiting for daylight was not an option. The Pentagon had been conducting clandestine military operations against North Vietnam since February 1964, and by April, the Joint Chiefs of Staff had already drawn up 94 targets in the north for massive aerial bombing.

President Johnson and the Pentagon brass were looking for a pretext for war, and this was it. Six days later, Congress obligingly passed the Gulf of Tonkin Resolution, which authorized President Johnson "to take all necessary steps, including the use of armed force...in defense of [South Vietnam's] freedom."[3]

Based on a lie, the U.S. phase of the war in Vietnam had begun in earnest.

Once known as French Indochina, Vietnam had been a colony of France for nearly a century when Japan took it away from them in 1941. Four years later, in September 1945, a month after Japan's surrendered ended World War II, Hô Chi Minh, the popular hero of Vietnam's liberation, declared his country's independence.

France, however, had other ideas.

Hô, a Communist revolutionary, had been the leader of the Việt Minh, the armed struggle for independence from the French colonialists before World War II. Then, with help from the U.S., Hô led the fight against the Japanese invaders during World War II. When the Second World War ended, however, France wanted its colony back, and President Harry Truman gave France America's blessing.

When French troops re-occupied Vietnam, Hô, who had consolidated his power in the Communist Party by purging, exhiling, and killing tens of thousands of political opponents, once again took up arms against French occupiers, leading the Việt Minh in a bloody, nine-year war.

In one of his first foreign policy missions, Vice President Nixon visited Vietnam in 1953 to show the Eisenhower administration's continuing support for France's doomed colonization of the country. A year later, the French were defeated.

As part of the Geneva Agreement that ended the fighting, Vietnam was temporarily partitioned at the 17th parallel, pending nationwide elections for reunification, which were scheduled for July 1956. Hồ took control of the north, and the Eisenhower administration threw its support to a Catholic anti-Communist in the south. His name was Ngô Đình Diệm, a pro-Western opponent of Hồ who had spent the last four years of the French occupation of his country in America, being toasted by top U.S. governmental and academic leaders as the the next democratic leader of Vietnam.

Once Vietnam was partitioned, the Eisenhower administration quickly installed Diệm in the south as the prime minister of the newly created State of Vietnam. Diệm, however, was not a very popular figure in his own country. When he arrived in Saigon on June 26, 1955, to take the reins of power, only a few hundred people turned out at the airport to greet him.

One of Diệm's first orders of business was to cancel the reunification elections, which the popular Hồ would have easily won, which in turn would have changed Vietnam into a unified, Communist-controlled country.

"President Eisenhower is widely quoted to the effect that in 1954 as many as 80 percent of the Vietnamese people would have voted for Hồ Chi Minh, as the popular hero of their liberation," the authors of the famous Pentagon Papers reported.[4]

Eisenhower and Nixon both supported the suspension of the reunification election. In fact, they insisted on it; it was part of the deal they'd made with Diệm when they put him in power.

Not surprisingly, Diệm's rule was authoritarian, nepotistic, cruel, and corrupt. It wasn't long before a low-level insurgency began taking shape in the south, and then, in 1959, the north's Communist leaders issued orders calling for armed struggle to overthrow Diệm. The civil war had begun, and a year later, when Jack Kennedy was elected president, he inherited a pot that was already coming to a boil.

The day Kennedy took office, there were already nearly 2,000 American CIA and military "advisors" in Vietnam. When Kennedy was assassinated on November 22, 1963—three weeks after Diệm was assassinated during a United States-backed military coup—there were more than 15,000 U.S. "advisors" in Vietnam. The number of troops and casualties would soon begin to escalate rapidly.

On August 4, 1964, after President Lyndon Johnson told the nation that three North Vietnamese torpedo boats had attacked U.S. destroyers in the Gulf of Tonkin—a report that turned out to be completely fabricated—he ordered retaliatory air strikes against the boats' bases in North Vietnam. Six days later, a joint resolution of Congress approved the Gulf of Tonkin Resolution.

The resolution passed in the House of Representatives by a vote of 416–0, and in the Senate by a vote of 88–2. The resolution was not an official declaration of war, but Johnson would cite it whenever he wanted to raise the stakes by expanding the air war or sending in more ground troops.

In 1965, U.S. warplanes started flying regular combat missions over South Vietnam, and in June of that year, some 23,000 American advisors in Vietnam would be committed to ground combat. By the end of the year, there would be more than 184,000 U.S. troops there.

In 1966, Johnson ordered B-52 bombing raids over the demilitarized zone that separated North and South Vietnam. Over the next two years, Johnson continued to expand the war, sending thousands of B-52 missions over North Vietnam in a bombing campaign called "Rolling Thunder," and by swelling U.S. ground forces to over 400,000 in 1966, and to over 500,000 in 1967.

By the end of the war, American warplanes had dropped more tons of high explosives on Vietnam than they'd dropped on Germany and Japan during all of World War II.

Many years later, the Vietnam War Memorial in Washington, D.C., would tell the story of the American war dead, and the price paid by each successive administration.

During the years of the Eisenhower administration, nine U.S. military advisors were killed in Vietnam: one in 1956, one in 1957, two in 1959 (killed by sniper fire while watching an outdoor movie), and five in 1960.

The first known American serviceman killed in the Vietnam War was Air Force Sergeant Richard B. Fitzgibbon Jr., who was murdered by a fellow airman on June 8, 1956. Nine years later, on September 7, 1965, his son, Marine Corps Lance Corporal Richard B. Fitzgibbon III, was also killed in Vietnam. They are one of only three American father-and-son service members killed in the Vietnam War.

During the Kennedy administration, 187 Americans were killed in Vietnam. The number rose each year, from 16 in 1961, to 53 in 1962, to 118 in 1963.

During the Johnson administration, more than 35,000 Americans died there, the number rising each year: 206 in 1964, 1,963 in 1965, 6,144 in 1966, 11,153 in 1967, and 16,589 in 1968.

During the Nixon administration, more than 21,000 Americans died in Vietnam, but the casualty numbers declined every year except the last, from a high of 11,614 killed in 1969, to 6,082 in 1970, to 2,357 in 1971, and then falling dramatically during the last three years of his presidency: 640 in 1972, 168 in 1973, and 178 in 1974.[5]

But the number of Americans killed in the war was only a small fraction of the human toll. Exact numbers are impossible to determine, but more than three million Vietnamese are believed to have been killed in the war.

The Vietnam War Memorial in Washington is engraved with the names of all 58,272 Americans killed in Vietnam. The memorial is about 500 feet long and 10 feet high at its tallest point. If a similar memorial were to be erected for the three million Vietnamese killed during the war, it would stretch nearly five miles long.

When Nixon expanded the war into Cambodia in 1969, more than two million Cambodians would be killed in the chaos of genocide and killing fields that ensued. A memorial with the names of the Cambodians killed during the war would stretch over three miles long.

On the morning of March 31, 1968, a Gallup Poll was released showing that President Johnson's approval rating had hit an all-time low, with only 26 percent of the American people approving his handling of the war in Vietnam. A few hours later, Johnson shocked the nation with the announcement that he would not seek reelection in November.

"I shall not seek, and I will not accept the nomination of my party for another term as your president," Johnson told the American people in a televised speech from his desk in the Oval Office.

Staring straight into the television camera, Johnson said that he would dedicate the last ten months of his presidency to finding a peaceful solution to end the war in Vietnam.

"With American sons in the field far away," he said, "with the American future under challenge right here at home, with our hopes and the world's hopes for peace in the balance every day, I do not believe that I should devote an hour or a day of my time to any personal partisan causes or to any duties other than the awesome duties of this office."

Achieving peace in Vietnam, he said, would require "concessions and compromises which would subject a candidate for public office to the charge of appeasement, surrender, and being soft on the Communists."[6]

At the same time, Johnson announced a partial bombing halt over North Vietnam, and called for North Vietnam to join the U.S. and South Vietnam in peace talks.

Johnson had given up on a second term, but he still hoped to help his vice president, Hubert Humphrey, win the Democratic nomination, and then the general election in November. But 1968 was not a year that would go according to anyone's plans.

Four days after Johnson's "I shall not seek" speech, Martin Luther King Jr. was assassinated in Memphis, followed by a week of rioting all across the country. Two months later, on the night he won the California Democratic primary, Robert F. Kennedy was shot in Los Angeles and died the next day. Two months later, Humphrey won the Democratic Party's nomination at the riot-torn 1968 Democratic Convention in Chicago.

The first session of the Paris peace talks began on May 13, 1968, and right away, Richard Nixon, the favorite to win the race for the Republican Party's presidential nomination, began running his own clandestine foreign policy, in direct violation of U.S. laws, to sabotage the peace talks.

Nixon believed that President Johnson's peace initiative was purely and cynically political, that Johnson was going to try to pull off an "October surprise" that would force a peace agreement down the throats of the South Vietnamese in late October, swinging the election to Humphrey in early November.

But Nixon had a surprise of his own up his sleeve—a November surprise.

CHAPTER 42

"This Is Treason!"

Spiro Agnew's campaign plane touched down at the Albuquerque International Airport at 11:15 on the morning of November 2, 1968. Agnew, the corrupt and fiery Governor of Maryland whom Nixon had picked as his vice presidential running mate, had just flown in from Los Angeles, where he'd accused leaders of the Democratic Party of having more affinity with "totalitarian dictatorships" than with America. Now, with the 1968 presidential election only three days away, he was on his way to Albuquerque's Highland High School, where he would give it to the Democrats some more.[1]

Agnew's plane taxied down the runway and then rolled to a stop near a bank of pay phones next to the terminal. Airport workers rolled out a portable staircase and one of Agnew's campaign aides got out and went down to the phones. Pulling a roll of quarters from his coat pocket, the aide inserted the coins and started dialing.

According to declassified FBI reports, the aide, whose identity has been kept a secret to this day, made five calls from the phone booth at the airport, the purpose of which was to sabotage the Paris peace talks and thus help Richard Nixon win the election.

A few minutes later, at 1:41 PM EST—11:41 AM in Albuquerque—Anna Chennault's phone rang at her home on Virginia Avenue in Washington, D.C.

Chennault, the Chinese-born widow of American World War II "Flying Tigers" hero General Claire Chennault, was one of Washington's best-known hostesses and a top fundraiser for Richard Nixon. Dubbed the "most titled woman" in Nixon's 1968 presidential campaign, Chennault was vice-chairwoman of the Republican National Finance Committee and co-chairwoman of Women for Nixon-Agnew. Fiercely anti-Communist, she had solid connections with the like-minded leaders of Formosa, the Philippines, and, most importantly, South Vietnam.

Anna talked briefly to the caller, hung up, and then called the South Vietnamese Embassy in Washington. She talked excitedly to her old friend, Bui Diem, South Vietnam's ambassador to the United States.

Anna didn't know it, but the FBI was tapping her phone. What those wiretaps uncovered would turn out to be one of the most sordid chapters in American political history.*

Anna gave Bui Diem the message she'd just received, and then, at 1:45 PM, only four minutes after the first call came in, she left her residence, got into her chauffeur-driven Lincoln Continental, and drove away, tailed by FBI agents.

An FBI report noted that her car "proceeded to the Baltimore–Washington Parkway, where it was last observed heading north at 2:15 PM." Anna was headed for New York City, where more FBI agents would pick up the surveillance there.[2]

---

*The secret FBI documents and internal White House memos cited in this chapter are contained in a package called "The 'X' Envelope," which Walt Rostow donated to the Lyndon Johnson Presidential Library on June 26, 1973, with an accompanying note to the library's director, Harry Middleton, saying that the file should not be opened for 50 years. Rostow's note, which itself was classified as "secret" and "literally eyes only," gave the history of the file and how it came to be donated to the library.

Rostow's note stated: "Sealed in the envelope is a file President Johnson asked me to hold personally because of its sensitive nature. In case of his death, the material was to be consigned to the LBJ Library under conditions I judged to be appropriate. The file concerns the activities of Mrs. Chennault and others before and immediately after the election of 1968. At the time, President Johnson decided to handle the matter strictly as a question of national security; and, in retrospect, he felt that decision was correct. It is,

The year 1968 had gotten off with a bang—literally. January 31, the Vietnamese New Year, saw the launch of the Tet Offensive, a coordinated assault on American military positions all over South Vietnam.

Tactically, the Tet Offensive was a disaster for the Viet Cong, who suffered tens of thousands of casualties. But strategically, it was a resounding success for them. Network news broadcasts showed wild gun battles raging in cities and hamlets all over South Vietnam, and the American people were shocked. More and more of them were coming to the conclusion that this was not a good or winnable war.

A few weeks after Tet, Walter Cronkite declared the war a lost cause.

"We are mired in a stalemate," he declared solemnly in a special CBS News broadcast on the night of February 27, 1968. "It is increasingly clear to this reporter that the only rational way out then will be to negotiate—not as victors, but as an honorable people who lived up to their pledge to defend democracy, and did the best they could."[3]

Two weeks later, on March 16, the frustrated and angry men of Charlie Company, First Battalion, 20th Infantry Regiment, 11th Brigade, American Division, entered the village of My Lai and massacred more than 400 unarmed civilians, many of them women,

---

therefore, my recommendation to you that this file should remain sealed for fifty years from the date of this memorandum. After fifty years, the director of the LBJ Library…may, alone, open this file. If he believes the material it contains might be opened for research, he should consult the then-responsible security officials of the Executive Branch to arrange formal clearance. If he believes the material it contains should not be opened for research, I would wish him empowered to re-close the file for another fifty years when the procedure outlined above should be repeated."

Twenty-one years later, on July 22, 1994—exactly three months after Nixon's death—"The 'X' Envelope" was opened by Regina Greenwell, senior archivist at the LBJ Library, and, on the instructions of the library's director, Harry Middleton, made available to researchers.

children, and babies. Dozens of people were herded into an irriga-
tion ditch and killed with automatic weapons. Many of the dead
had been beaten and tortured first, and some of the bodies were
found mutilated.

Two weeks after that, President Johnson went on national television and announced that he wouldn't seek a second term, and
that in order to get peace talks started, he had ordered a partial
and immediate bombing halt over most of North Vietnam. This
step was greeted positively by most Americans, but the leaders of
South Vietnam were highly suspicious. They thought Johnson had
lost his nerve, that he was going to throw them to the wolves. They
wanted the bombing, and the war, to continue.

A month after LBJ's announcement, South Vietnam president
Nguyen Van Thieu told cheering May Day ralliers in Danang that
South Vietnam would never negotiate with the Viet Cong and
would not cede "even one centimeter" to the Communists in North
Vietnam.[4]

South Vietnamese leaders feared a sellout at the peace talks;
they weren't even going to have a seat at the negotiating table. North
Vietnam, which refused to recognize the legitimacy of the South
Vietnamese government, said it would not come to the peace talks
if South Vietnam was represented. The U.S. reluctantly agreed,
and on May 6, at a cocktail party in Vientiane, the capital of Laos,
North Vietnamese representatives formally accepted Paris as the
site for the peace talks.[5]

Paris, however, would prove to be an ironic site for the peace
talks because at that moment in French history, the city was at
the epicenter of a series of sometimes violent and bloody strikes
and protests that would lead to the fall of the government under
Charles de Gaulle.

Amid this chaotic backdrop, the Paris peace talks began on May
13, but were immediately deadlocked over the American position
that North Vietnam should begin withdrawing its troops from the
south, and Hanoi's insistence that the U.S. halt all aerial bombing of the north. The talks would go on for another five months

without making any progress. Which is just what Richard Nixon wanted. A peace agreement, he calculated, would assure that the Democrats would retain the White House.

"Johnson was making the one move that I thought could determine the outcome of the election," Nixon wrote in his memoirs. "Had I done all this work and come all this way only to be undermined by the powers of an incumbent who had decided against seeking reelection?"[6]

On July 12, 1968—two months after the peace talks started—Nixon had a few friends over to his apartment in New York City to advance his plot. Joining Nixon were Anna Chennault, who would be the go-between; John Mitchell, Nixon's campaign manager, who would be Anna's handler; and Bui Diem, South Vietnam's ambassador to the U.S., who would be their link to President Thieu in Saigon.

Only later would President Johnson and his inner circle learn the sinister purpose of their meeting—to stall the peace talks while Johnson was president by offering South Vietnam a "better deal" if Nixon were elected in November.

William P. Bundy, who was then President Johnson's assistant secretary of state for East Asian and Pacific affairs, later wrote that to this end, the meeting at Nixon's apartment was held "with Mr. Nixon presiding and laying down that Mrs. Chennault would be his channel to Mr. Thieu via Bui Diem."[7]

Not surprisingly, Nixon doesn't even mention Anna Chennault in his memoirs. But in *her* memoirs, Chennault wrote that, as the 1968 election approached, John Mitchell said to her: "Anna, I'm speaking on behalf of Mr. Nixon. It's very important that our Vietnamese friends understand our Republican position and I hope you have made that clear to them."[8]

Three weeks after meeting with Chennault at his apartment in New York, Nixon was nominated to be the Republican Party's presidential candidate, with Agnew as his running mate. In his acceptance speech that night in Miami Beach, Nixon promised "an honorable end to the war in Vietnam."

But what he had in mind was anything but honorable.

Nixon's main rival in the presidential contest would be Johnson's vice president, Hubert Humphrey, who would receive the Democratic Party's nomination two weeks later at a riot-torn convention in Chicago. A third-party candidate had also entered the race: Alabama's segregationist governor, George Wallace, who would go on to win more than 13 percent of the nationwide popular vote. But Nixon was only worried about Humphrey. Polls showed them in a dead-heat, but a last-minute peace agreement would almost certainly catapult Humphrey into the White House.

Nixon's plan was to make sure that didn't happen.

The peace talks in Paris had been grinding on for months without making any headway, but a breakthrough came in mid-October, when Hanoi finally agreed to allow South Vietnam to come to the bargaining table if President Johnson called a complete halt to the bombing of the north.

Briefed on the developments, South Vietnam President Thieu reluctantly agreed on October 22 that he would drop his opposition to a bombing halt "when there is good reason to believe" that the north would talk directly to the south and join the U.S. in scaling down the level of war operations.

The next day, Thieu received a cable from Bui Diem, his ambassador in Washington. "Many Republican friends have contacted me and encouraged us to stand firm," Diem told Thieu. "They were alarmed by press reports to the effect that you had already softened your position."[9]

On October 27, Anna Chennault gave Diem another "Republican message," this time urging Thieu to cripple the peace talks by refusing to participate in them. Later that day, Diem sent Thieu another cable, urging him to go slow. "The longer the present situation continues, the more we are favored," he told Thieu, adding conspiratorially: "I am regularly in touch with the Nixon entourage."[10]

The next day, Thieu kept up the pretense of wanting to join the peace talks by informing Ellsworth Bunker, the U.S. ambassador to South Vietnam, that he had selected a negotiating team for the talks in Paris and would send them there if Hanoi agreed to accept the latest U.S. proposal for a bombing halt.

The American election was only eight days away.

President Johnson first learned of Nixon's treachery on October 29, when he was shown the most recent cables that Diem had sent to Thieu—messages that had been intercepted by the CIA. Outraged by this betrayal, Johnson deemed it a matter of national security and brought in his top cabinet officials, the secretary of state and secretary of defense, to help him deal with it. And he ordered the FBI to bug Anna Chennault's phones and the offices of the South Vietnam Embassy in Washington. Cartha "Deke" De-Loach, the FBI's deputy director and LBJ's personal liaison to the Bureau, was put in charge of the surveillance operation.[†]

"Thus alerted, Johnson requested Federal Bureau of Investigation surveillance of Mrs. Chennault and the embassy, and the results amply confirmed her activity," recalled Johnson's aide, William Bundy, many years later.[11]

After that, the FBI followed Chennault everywhere she went—even to the movies and the theater. She wasn't hard to follow; she was the one traipsing around Washington in elegant Chinese-style, formfitting dresses that showed off her tiny waistline, colorful chiffon scarves trailing along behind her as she walked.

The next day, October 30, the foreign minister of Thailand told reporters he'd learned that the U.S. and North Vietnam had

---

[†] Cartha "Deke" DeLoach would later claim in an oral history interview for the LBJ Library that there was "no evidence to indicate" that Nixon or Agnew were involved in the Chennault affair. Perhaps coincidentally, DeLoach left the FBI twenty months later, on his fiftieth birthday, July 20, 1970, and then went directly to work for Richard Nixon's old friend, PepsiCo CEO Donald Kendall—the same Donald Kendall that Nixon had introduced to Nikita Khrushchev at the trade fair in Moscow in 1959, and the same Donald Kendall whom Nixon was with in Dallas on the morning of November 22, 1963.

entered the "final stages" of bargaining for a halt to U.S. bombing of North Vietnam, and that full-scale peace talks to end the war were about to begin.

That same day, Deke DeLoach gave J. Edgar Hoover a summary of the phone call Chennault had made that morning to Ambassador Diem.

At 7:40 AM, DeLoach told his boss, Chennault had contacted Ambassador Bui Diem.

"What's the situation?" she had asked the ambassador.

"Just among us," Diem had told her confidentially, "something is cooking."[12]

Diem hadn't wanted to be any more specific on the phone, and had invited Chennault to come by the embassy to talk in private, not knowing that his office was bugged.

In his report to Hoover, DeLoach wrote, "She said that she will drop by after the luncheon for Mrs. Agnew today."

The FBI followed Anna to her lunch date with Agnew's wife, Judy, and then to the South Vietnamese embassy, which she entered at 3:26 PM.

"She was still there at 4:30," DeLoach told Hoover, who immediately passed the information along to Johnson.

The next day, October 31, Johnson ordered the halt to the bombings of North Vietnam, and announced that representatives of South Vietnam and the Viet Cong would be joining the U.S. and North Vietnam negotiators at the peace talks in Paris. The new round of talks, with all sides present for the first time, were scheduled to begin Wednesday, November 6, the day after the election, which was now only five days away. If all sides kept their word and joined the talks as they'd promised, an agreement to end the war in Vietnam might be only days away.

The next day, November 1, Agnew flew to Los Angeles to rally the party's base there. That same morning, the *Washington Post* ran a story on the back pages of its style section that profiled Washington hostess Anna Chennault. The story was mostly fluff and background, but it carried some interesting news that Johnson and his top aides found very revealing—and infuriating.

Noting all her various campaign titles, the *Post* article called Anna "the most titled woman in the Nixon campaign," and "the top woman fundraiser in Richard M. Nixon's campaign for the presidency." (By her own account, Chennault raised more than $250,000 for the Nixon/Agnew campaign that year.)

The article also noted that she had "an office in Nixon campaign headquarters," but the most interesting part of the story, at least to Johnson and his inner circle, was a brief mention of the fact that Anna would be watching the election returns with Nixon on November 5.

Chennault, the article said, was "one of the select group invited to watch the election returns Tuesday night in the Louis XVI suite at the Waldorf Astoria with top members of the Nixon team."

"The only thing we're interested in now is getting Mr. Nixon in the White House," Chennault had told the reporter.[13]

By this time, Anna Chennault had picked up various nicknames among the top Johnson advisors who were following the FBI's updates on her intrigues. Clark Clifford, the secretary of defense, referred to her as "the little flower." Walt Rostow, Johnson's special assistant for national security affairs—the post now known as national security advisor—referred to her in his many memos to LBJ as "the lady." But Johnson, who despised her for her interference in the delicate peace process, scornfully called her "that woman."[14]

On November 2, Agnew's plane landed in Albuquerque, New Mexico. One of Agnew's aides got out and called Anna, who then called Bui Diem.

Later that night, J. Edgar Hoover sent a classified dispatch to the White House Situation Room that detailed Anna's conversation with Diem.

"Mrs. Anna Chennault," Hoover wrote, "contacted Vietnamese ambassador Bui Diem, and advised him that she had received a message from her boss, which her boss wanted her to give personally to the ambassador. She said the message was that the ambassador is to 'hold on, we are gonna win,' and that her boss also said, 'hold on, he understands all of it.' She repeated that this is the only message: 'He said please tell your boss to hold on.' She advised that her boss had just called from New Mexico."[15]

Spiro Agnew didn't know it, but the FBI was watching his plane, tapping Chennault's phones and intercepting Diem's cables to President Thieu. And now the FBI knew that Agnew was "her boss."

"The plane taxied up to a pay phone," recalled Deke DeLoach. "We were asked to find out if members on the Republican side asked Mrs. Chennault to do this. We looked at phone records. They found records of five different phone calls. Somebody on Agnew's plane had called five different places."[16]

The calls were not made by Agnew himself, DeLoach recalled, but by "one of his aides."[17]

After reviewing the FBI's records on the surveillance of Agnew's plane, Walt Rostow told President Johnson that one of the calls that "the gentleman in Albuquerque" made from the phone booth had been to "the lady," who a few minutes later called Bui Diem and told him to "hold on."[18]

After his aide had made his phone calls, Spiro Agnew left the airport in a motorcade and drove to Highland High School for a campaign rally. FBI records show that after speaking at the high school, Agnew returned to the airport and then flew to Texas at 4:00 PM.

Later that night, the bell began ringing on the secure Teletype machine at the LBJ ranch just outside of Houston. It was 8:34 PM, and an "eyes-only" message was coming in from Walt Rostow.

Johnson read the message a few minutes later. It contained Hoover's report on Chennault's phone conversation with Bui Diem and the message she'd given him from her "boss" in New Mexico, as well as a note from Rostow that read: "The New Mexico reference may indicate Agnew is acting."[19]

After talking to Anna earlier that morning, Diem cabled President Thieu and gave him the message from her "boss," which was to "hold on" and wait for Nixon to win.

Later that day, Thieu informed Ambassador Bunker that

South Vietnam would not be joining the Paris peace talks after all.

"The government of South Vietnam deeply regrets not to be able to participate in the present exploratory talks," Thieu said, feigning deep regret.[20]

That same day, 11 South Vietnamese senators sent Nixon a telegram, telling him that his election was "keenly awaited for the safeguard of South Vietnam."[21]

The peace talks had been killed, and the war would go on for another seven years.

Outraged by Nixon's treachery, Johnson got on the phone and called Everett Dirksen, the Senate Minority Leader and a strong Nixon-backer, and told him that he knew what Nixon had done.

"If Nixon keeps the South Vietnamese away from the [peace] conference, well, that's going to be his responsibility," Johnson told Dirksen emphatically.[22] "I really think it's a little dirty pool for Dick's people to be messin' with the South Vietnamese ambassador and carryin' around messages to both of them. And they ought not to be doing this. This is treason!"[23]

Dirksen called Nixon immediately and told him what President Johnson had told him.

White House phone records note that the next day, November 3, "Richard Nixon called the president from Los Angeles—no subject indicated."[24]

In fact, White House tapes of that conversation reveal that the subject was Nixon's treachery. But Nixon told Johnson he knew nothing about any plans to sabotage the peace talks.

"Any, uh, rumblings around about, uh, somebody, uh, tryin' to, uh, sabotage the Saigon government's attitude—they certainly have no, absolutely no credibility as far as I'm concerned," Nixon stuttered, lying directly to the president of the United States.[25]

"I'm very happy to hear that, Dick," Johnson replied, knowing the truth full well.[26]

"My God," Nixon lied, still stammering, "I would never do anything to...to...to encourage Hanoi—I mean Saigon—not to come to the table."[27]

But Johnson knew that was exactly what Nixon had done.

William P. Bundy later wrote that Nixon had denied any connection to the affair in that conversation, which Bundy concluded was "almost certainly a lie."[28]

On November 4—the day before the election—Johnson asked his three top advisors, Walt Rostow (his national security advisor), Secretary of State Dean Rusk, and Defense Secretary Clark Clifford, to give him a recommendation about whether or not he should go public with Nixon's betrayal.

"Before the election," Rostow later wrote, "President Johnson asked Rusk, Clifford, and me to consider the question of whether the story should be made public. On November 4 we recommended unanimously against that course."[29]

Johnson took their advice.

"In a decision filled with consequences for the election and for history," Clark Clifford wrote in his 1991 book *Counsel to the President*, "President Johnson, although furious at Mrs. Chennault, decided not to use the information or make it public in any way."[30]

There were several reasons they decided not to go public with it, the most important being that it might undermine the peace talks that Johnson still hoped he could salvage before his term ended on January 20, 1969. Clifford noted that Rusk "was concerned that revealing the Chennault channel would reveal to Hanoi the strains between Saigon and Washington, stiffen Hanoi's position, and disrupt the negotiations."[31]

But any hope that they could revive the peace talks before Johnson left office was now doomed anyway. Johnson was a lame duck, and Thieu had already made up his mind to deal with his successor, hoping, of course, that it would be Nixon, who had offered him a "better deal."

In retrospect, Clifford wrote, salvaging the peace talks had by then become an illusion because "the president and Rusk seriously underestimated the harm the Chennault channel caused to the negotiating effort."[32]

Johnson and his top advisors were also worried about what

such a revelation might do to the presidency itself. They thought that by then, the day before the election, it would probably be too late to affect the outcome of the race. If Nixon won anyway, the disclosure of his treachery would surely destroy his presidency, and along with it, any chance of ending the war. So in a very real sense, by keeping mum, they were saving Nixon from Nixon.

The next morning, November 5, Anna Chennault voted for Nixon and Agnew at her precinct in Washington, then flew up to New York City, still being tailed by FBI agents. From the airport, she took a limo to the Waldorf Astoria, went up to the luxurious Louis XVI suite, and joined Nixon's inner circle to watch the election results.[33]

It must have been quite a celebration: Nixon defeated Humphrey in one of the closest presidential races ever, winning 43.4 percent of the vote to Humphrey's 42.7 percent—a victory margin of only seven-tenths of one percent.

Looking back on the affair many years later, Clark Clifford wrote: "The activities of the Nixon team went far beyond the bounds of justifiable political combat" and "constituted a gross, even potentially illegal, interference in the security affairs of the nation by private individuals."[34]

As for the role Anna Chennault played in sabotaging the peace talks, Clifford wrote, "...there was no doubt that she conveyed a simple and authoritative message from the Nixon camp that was probably decisive in convincing President Thieu to defy President Johnson—thus delaying the negotiations and prolonging the war."[35]

Many years after the election-eve decision was made not to go public with Nixon's treachery—and knowing all the war, disgrace, and national trauma that was to come from Nixon's presidency—Clifford said he would have made a different recommendation that day to President Johnson.

"I would have allowed the incident to become public," he wrote, "so that the American public might take it into account in deciding how to vote."[36]

Walt Rostow also had a change of heart, but his came much

sooner. Shortly after the election, Rostow wrote a "literally eyes only" memo to President Johnson, saying, "I think it's time to blow the whistle on these folks."[37]

But Johnson had already made up his mind. He was not going to expose Nixon, Chennault, Agnew, Mitchell, and the others for sabotaging the Paris peace talks. Now that Nixon was president-elect, the presidency itself would be damaged if this were to come out.

In other words, Rostow noted sourly, "They got away with it."[38]

In the end, despite his promise of a "better deal," Nixon double-crossed South Vietnam anyway. For when the war ended with the panicky evacuation of the last American troops in 1975, the south got no better deal than the one they could have gotten from Johnson seven years earlier. Only the lives of several million more Vietnamese and Cambodians could have been spared, along with those of more than 21,000 American soldiers, sailors, marines, and airmen who died in the war during Nixon's presidency.

CHAPTER 43

The Last Days of Guenther Reinhardt

In October of 1968, as the presidential race between Nixon and Humphrey was coming to its dramatic finish, Reinhardt's 12-page confidential report on the relationship between Nixon and Dr. Hutschnecker would once again come into play. This time, however, it wouldn't be used in time to stop Nixon, as it had eight years earlier.

On October 29, 1968, a week before Election Day—and on the same day that President Johnson first learned of Nixon's treachery in the Anna Chennault affair—a reporter called Dr. Hutschnecker at his office to ask if Nixon was a patient of his, just as a "reporter" had called the doctor eight years earlier on the eve of the 1960 election. Only this time, it really was a reporter—famed columnist Drew Pearson—who was asking the questions.

"I understand you have been giving Mr. Nixon psychiatric treatments," Pearson told Hutschnecker, "and have been concerned as to whether he is the right man to have his finger on the nuclear trigger."[1]

Hutschnecker was flabbergasted.

The 1968 presidential election was shaping up to be a close contest between Nixon and Vice President Hubert Humphrey—almost a replay of the close election eight years earlier between Nixon and Jack Kennedy. And in 1968, as in 1960, Hutschnecker still wasn't sure what to say when reporters called, even though he'd had eight years to think about it.

"Dr. Hutschnecker confirmed that he had treated Mr. Nixon, said that it was a delicate matter and that he was reluctant to talk about it," Pearson later recalled. "He had a patient with him, he said, and asked me to call back at 4:00 PM."[2]

While he was waiting to call Dr. Hutschnecker back later that afternoon, Pearson had his legman, Jack Anderson—the same assistant Pearson had sent to ask JFK if he had Addison's disease back in January 1960—call Nixon's campaign for a comment. Herb Klein, Nixon's communications director, "flatly denied Nixon had ever consulted a psychiatrist."[3]

Technically that was true because, although Hutschnecker was a licensed doctor, psychotherapist, and psychoanalyst, he was not actually a psychiatrist, which required certification from the American Board of Psychiatry and Neurology or the American Osteopathic Board of Neurology and Psychiatry.

Later that day, Pearson called Dr. Hutschnecker back to finish up their interview.

"I called the doctor back at four o'clock," Pearson recalled, "and he said, 'It's true that Nixon did consult me,' but this was for problems of internal medicine and it was not for psychotherapy."[4]

And besides, the doctor told him, this had been years ago, in the 1950s, when Nixon was vice president.

Pearson was one of the most famous investigative journalists in America. He'd been the first reporter to stand up to the deranged Senator Joe McCarthy, and had written the exposé of HUAC chairman J. Parnell Thomas that sent him to federal prison for taking kickbacks. He was also the first to report that Attorney General Robert Kennedy had authorized electronic surveillance of the Reverend Martin Luther King Jr.

He wasn't an easy man to fool.

"I just operate with a sense of smell," he once said. "If something smells wrong, I go to work."[5]

Something certainly smelled fishy about Dr. Hutschnecker's explanation. But after writing up a story about Nixon and his psychotherapist, Pearson decided not to publish it.

"In view of Dr. Hutschnecker's statement, I killed the story I had written on Mr. Nixon," Pearson later wrote, "although it seemed to me strange that Nixon should go all the way to New York to consult a well-known Park Avenue psychotherapy specialist concerning his internal medical problems when some of the best internists in the U.S. are located at Walter Reed Army Hospital and Bethesda Naval Hospital, where the vice president could have had their services on the cuff. Perhaps I was derelict, but at that time I did not pursue the matter further."[6]

Seven days later, Richard Nixon finally won the office he'd sought for so long, defeating Humphrey in one of the closest presidential elections in American history.

But Pearson couldn't let the story go. He made some more calls, this time to people who knew Hutschnecker, and came to believe that the doctor hadn't been completely candid with him the day of their interview, a week before the election. He'd been told that Dr. Hutschnecker had confided to friends that after Jack Anderson talked to Herb Klein that day, Dr. Hutschnecker "received a call from Nixon's office between my morning call and my 4:00 PM call on October 29 which led him to change his earlier statement."[7]

Pearson, angered by the deception, went public with the story. But he didn't do it in print—he did it at a National Press Club luncheon in Washington. Pearson was the guest speaker there on November 14, 1968, and after he spoke, he took a few questions from the audience and was asked how he decided what to print in his column.

To illustrate how difficult it could be to pin down news in the heat of a political campaign, Pearson cited the conversation he'd had with Dr. Hutschnecker about Richard Nixon, and how he had decided to sit on the story because he felt he didn't have enough hard facts.

On that day, in that place, Richard Nixon was first publicly identified as having been a patient of Dr. Hutschnecker's.

Pearson told his audience that he decided to come forward with the story now because since the election, he'd learned that

Dr. Hutschnecker "has told others and confirmed the fact" that he'd changed stories after "he got a call from the Nixon office," and that the doctor had subsequently confirmed "to others that he had treated or advised Nixon over psychiatric problems" and had "expressed some worry privately that Nixon had problems—or did have a problem—of not standing up under great pressure."[8]

Pearson's comments, picked up by UPI and carried in newspapers across the country, touched off a whirlwind of controversy.

Dr. Hutschnecker, outraged by Pearson's account, vehemently denied the reporter's version of the story, saying that he had "never received any such phone call from Nixon headquarters," and that he had never treated Nixon for "psychiatric problems," or that he had ever told anyone privately that he worried that Nixon had problems that made it hard for him to function under pressure.[9]

President-elect Nixon was plenty mad about it, too. After the UPI story ran, Ron Ziegler, Nixon's press secretary, was asked to comment on Pearson's remarks.

"I won't be drawn into a discussion of a Pearson utterance that is totally untrue, as most of his statements and utterances are," he told reporters huffily.[10]

Pearson's speech at the National Press Club also angered many of his editors and readers, who wondered why he hadn't come out with this story in print *before* the election, when it might have done some good.

Pearson tried to explain it to them in a column he co-authored with Jack Anderson on November 20, six days after his speech at the Press Club.

"Several of my editors," he wrote, "have been complaining that I should have written the account of Mr. Nixon's psychotheraputic treatments in the column before the election, instead of talking about the matter at the National Press Club after the election."

Much of the information he'd picked up about the true nature of Nixon's relationship with Dr. Hutschnecker, he wrote, was obtained in the very last days of the campaign.

"I could have published it at the last minute," he wrote, "but, as

I explained at the Press Club luncheon, I decided it was unfair to use it so late. It was one of those difficult decisions a newspaperman has to make."[11]

For the rest of his life—he died a year later—Pearson wondered if Nixon would have still won if he'd published his story before the election.

"It is true," he wrote, "that if this had been published before the election the outcome might have been different."[12]

Nixon spokesman Herb Klein agreed. Had Pearson run the story, he said, it "probably would have changed the results of the election."[13]

But it wasn't for Guenther Reinhardt's lack of trying. He'd helped stop Nixon in 1960, and his confidential report nearly derailed him again in 1968.

A few days after Pearson wrote his column trying to explain why he hadn't gone with the story before the election, *Newsweek* at least gave the columnist credit for having brought the Nixon/Hutschnecker relationship to light.

"The doctor-patient relationship probably would never have got out of Hutschnecker's consulting room," *Newsweek* reported, "had columnist Drew Pearson not followed up a tip and nosed into the matter during the 1968 campaign."[14]

Pearson's papers, which are collected at the Lyndon Johnson Library, don't mention who supplied him with the tip, but it was almost certainly his old pal and former employee, Guenther Reinhardt.

Reinhardt, of course, still had a copy of his report about Nixon and Hutschnecker, and it would have been just like him to try and sell it to Pearson just before the election. If he did so, it must have been particularly heartbreaking for him when it turned out that all his work, all his efforts to stop Nixon from becoming president, had been for naught.

On December 2, 1968, less than a month after Nixon was elected president, Reinhardt died. His life had been surrounded by controversy, and so too was his death. Some say it was a heart attack; others say it was a suicide. He was 63 years old and died alone.

His crippled wife, Helen, had pre-deceased him by several years.

The *New York Times* reported that Reinhardt died of a heart attack at St. Vincent's Hospital in Manhattan, but many of his friends—or former friends, who were far more numerous—believed he killed himself.

"We were told he committed suicide," said his former colleague Werner Michel. "He just couldn't cope."[15]

CHAPTER 44

"The Peace President"

During their many years together as patient and psychotherapist, Dr. Hutschnecker tried to mold Richard Nixon into the man they both wanted him to be—a man of peace. But like the fictional Dr. Frankenstein, Hutschnecker's experiment failed terribly and a monster was created instead.

"When Nixon originally appeared in my office," Hutschnecker recalled, "I hoped that I might interest him in my views: peace, ending the Cold War, social reform. One of the most consistent subjects Nixon and I spoke about was the subject of peace."[1]

"Our political discussions were emphatic," he recalled, "though on opposite sides. I suspect he must have felt trapped by his sincere desire for peace, and his need to win."[2]

Dr. Hutschnecker believed that everyone had within him or herself "a drive for power—a force that can help unfold the potentials inherent in a personality."

Because of this, he believed, everyone also has "the power to contribute to the advance of civilization—or to its destruction. For it is the direction of the power drive that leads one man to create—and another to kill."[3]

Dr. Hutschnecker tried mightily to nurture Nixon's potential for peace, but as much as Nixon admired the doctor and sought his counsel, his personality was too rigid to allow him to take the doctor's best advice. Instead, Nixon chose a path of war, death, and his own destruction.

Early in their relationship, Dr. Hutschnecker saw Nixon as "a man of destiny" who would achieve his greatest fame as a man of peace, and he actively tried to put Nixon on that path. But Nixon decided to go down a different road. Years later, as president, Nixon would kill millions of people with his merciless bombing of North Vietnam and Cambodia.

"The bastards have never been bombed like they're going to be bombed this time," Nixon would declare regarding his decision to renew B-52 raids over North Vietnam.[4]

But at least Dr. Hutschnecker had tried.

In 1955, with the U.S. and the Soviet Union building and testing their nuclear arsenals at a nightmarish rate, Dr. Hutschnecker risked losing his relationship with then-Vice President Nixon by writing him a letter that he hoped would put him on the path to peace. He'd given the letter a lot of thought, writing it while finishing work on his second book, *Love and Hate in Human Nature.*

"Please believe me," Dr. Hutschnecker wrote in the letter, "when I say I had to summon a great deal of courage to write this letter...for fear...that it may appear that I am overstepping a cordial doctor-patient relationship."[5]

In the letter, Hutschnecker urged Nixon to consider what the doctor humbly called a "blueprint of peace."

"Once," Hutschnecker told the vice president, "at the arrival of the president of Turkey here in New York, we had a brief discussion about 'chance' and 'destiny' when I, as you may perhaps remember, referred to you as a Man of Destiny."

People everywhere, Dr. Hutschnecker told Nixon, "are frightened, insecure, frustrated. All over the world millions look for hope and a new leadership that possesses daring of thought and freedom from concepts that are still hangover ideas of the post-Victorian power policies. In recorded history few men, I daresay, have achieved distinction through their devotion to the sake of peace and the advancement of man based on human rights and respect for the individual. Most men history calls great have gained their fame on battlefields—that is, by leading a successful war."

But Dr. Hutschnecker believed that Nixon had a chance to change all that and write a new history based on peace.

"While there always had been talk about the fruits of peace, its desirability, its richness and accomplishments, its full potentiality has never been exploited," he told Nixon. "So far as I know, no one man has diligently and honestly worked for or exploited these possibilities of peace, its full challenges and promise for all the people everywhere. This to me seems the only mature answer to all the '-isms' that plague our world today.

"I feel, Mr. Vice President, that you not only have the strength and ability, but also the imagination and idealism which are prerequisite attributes for a man of destiny."[6]

Four years later, in his last few months as vice president and shortly before he declared his candidacy for president, Nixon came to New York and met for lunch with Dr. Hutschnecker, who urged him to establish a Department of Peace.

"Nothing would serve the interest of peace more than the creation of a Department of Peace," he told Nixon. "Not only would such a move immensely increase the prestige of the country throughout the world, but it would be to the credit of this administration to have created an innovation of historical and far-reaching significance. All governments have general staff, and strategic commands for war or defense. Ours would be the first to have a governmental body to devote part of its efforts to explore and to develop the potentials of peace, as it is done in other departments, whose concern is to safeguard the welfare, the freedom, the health, and the justice of all its citizens. The banning of war does in principle not differ from the banning of hunger and the plagues."[7]

But Nixon, who called Dr. Hutschnecker an "ardent dove," just laughed him off.[8] Hutschnecker's idea for a Department of Peace—later proposed by Ohio Congressman Dennis Kucinich in 2001—was 40 years ahead of its time.

Ironically, nine months later, it would be Jack Kennedy—not Nixon—who would call on the nation to "renew our leadership for peace, until we have brought to that universal pursuit the same concentration of resources brought to the preparation of war."[9] To that end, Kennedy created the Peace Corps when he became president.

In 1968, when Nixon announced that he would make another run at the presidency, Dr. Hutschnecker wrote him another "peace letter," urging him to run on a campaign of ending the Vietnam War, which had been going on for years.

In his letter, Dr. Hutschnecker reminded Nixon that Eisenhower had won the 1952 election in a landslide because "he promised us peace and indeed he did go to Korea and ended a not-too-popular war. And nobody considered him weak or unpatriotic because of this."[10]

During the 1968 campaign, Nixon took at least part of Dr. Hutschnecker's advice. Nixon proclaimed that, if elected, he would be the "Peace President" and would end the war in Vietnam. That helped Nixon win the election, but once in office, he kept the war going for another six years, at the cost of several million more lives.

But Dr. Hutschnecker continued to press him to become a man of destiny, the man of peace they both wanted him to be.

"I did not want anything from Nixon," he recalled, "but I do confess to having one agenda: the Vietnam War. Despite the prolongation of Vietnam, I never stopped believing that his essential being was dedicated to the cause of world peace."[11]

When he couldn't see President Nixon in person, Dr. Hutschnecker inundated him with more letters, urging him to end the war.

Dr. Hutschnecker, who thought Nixon would end the war shortly after he took office in January 1969, was shocked when on May 8 he read a *New York Times* front page story about the "secret" B-52 bombings of Cambodia—massive air raids that were only a secret to the American people, not the Cambodians.

"I was, like many other people, horrified," he later wrote. "This was a widening and not a winding down of the war. What had happened to my Peace President?"[12]

So Dr. Hutschnecker sat down and wrote President Nixon still another letter, this time requesting just 20 minutes of his time. To his surprise, he got a prompt response; Rose Mary Woods, the president's secretary, called to say "the Boss" would see him. She scheduled an appointment with him and mentioned that, because of "media sensitivity," he would have to register at the White House as a "visitor of Rose Mary Woods" and she would then take him secretly to see the president.[13]

Everything, it seemed, was a secret now.

Dr. Hutschnecker prepared all that weekend to talk to Nixon about ending the war, but only many years later would he learn that Nixon had really only wanted to see him for a medical consultation. Nixon was depressed and couldn't sleep, and he was trying to cure both with large amounts of Scotch.[14]

That Monday morning, Dr. Hutschnecker went to the White House. He signed in and was taken directly to see Rose Mary Woods, who greeted him warmly; they'd known each other many years. They chatted for a while, and then a small green light, unseen by Dr. Hutschnecker, went on under her desk.

"Let's go," she said curtly. "The president is ready for you."[15]

She escorted him quickly down a long corridor to the Oval Office, where a soldier in dress uniform stood guarding the door, his white-gloved hands folded behind his back. Rose Mary nodded, the door opened, and Dr. Hutschnecker entered.

Nixon greeted him as he always did when they met, pointing out some interesting historic object or a particularly pretty view, and there were plenty of both in the Oval Office. It was the first time Dr. Hutschnecker had been there, and outside the windows, on the White House lawn, the dogwood and cherry trees were in bloom.

As always, Nixon was cordial, but formal. The two old friends sat down, and Dr. Hutschnecker immediately began "pitching peace," as he called it. Nixon listened intently, never mentioning his own pressing medical problems, as Dr. Hutschnecker once again besieged him to end the war and establish a Department of Peace.

After the doctor finished his pitch, Nixon leaned back in his chair behind the desk that had once been Abraham Lincoln's and said: "The Department of Defense *is* a Department of Peace."[16]

Dr. Hutschnecker respectfully reminded the president that up until World War I, what we now call the Department of Defense was then called the Department of War.

Nixon frowned and reflected on that for a moment, then asked: "How do you envision this Department of Peace?"

Dr. Hutschnecker quickly explained that he thought it should be a cabinet-level department, equal to all the others. "So at a cabinet meeting," he said, "the Department of Peace would have an equal voice."

"That would mean erecting another bureaucracy," Nixon said brusquely. "I might not be able to push it through Congress."[17]

So Hutschnecker decided on another approach. How about an agency to study the psychodynamics of peace?

This seemed to completely baffle Nixon, and there followed an awkward silence.

Perhaps he had chosen the wrong word, Dr. Hutschnecker thought. Perhaps "psychodynamics" smacked too much of psychiatry and Sigmund Freud.

Nixon leaned back in his chair and closed his eyes, giving the doctor no hint of the real reason he had wanted to see him. Then Nixon straightened up, gave Hutschnecker a slight nod, and said he might be able to do something like that.

Dr. Hutschnecker was elated. He thanked the president, shook his hand, and left the White House, euphoric.

Only later did he learn that Nixon had just been placating him. There would be no agency to study the psychodynamics of peace, much less a Department of Peace.

Afterward, Dr. Hutschnecker thought he understood why: Nixon was too conflicted to end the conflict in Vietnam.

"It is sadly ironic," he later observed, "that Nixon's profound dedication to world peace came from a man who warred within himself."[18]

Nixon had once promised to be "the Peace President," but now, searching for "the Man of Destiny," Dr. Hutschnecker found only empty slogans.[19]

And yet, even though 21,000 more Americans and millions more Vietnamese and Cambodians would die in the war while he was president, Nixon still, to the very end, thought of himself as a man of peace. The inscription on his black granite tombstone in Yorba Linda, California, reads, without any sense of irony: "The greatest honor history can bestow is the title of peacemaker."

Those words, which Nixon spoke at his first inaugural address in 1969, proved to be decidedly un-prophetic—but not for Dr. Hutschnecker's lack of trying.

CHAPTER 45

The Reckoning

The 1972 Watergate break-in is by far the most famous burglary of the Nixon presidency, but it wasn't the only one; the first came a year earlier. Reminiscent of the 1960 break-ins at Jack Kennedy's doctors' offices, its target was the doctor's office of another Nixon adversary—Daniel Ellsberg, the former Defense Department official who leaked the Pentagon Papers to the *New York Times.*

Ellsberg had been a rising star in the defense establishment who later turned against the war in Vietnam. Perhaps more than any other American, he helped bring an end to the war.

A Harvard graduate, Ellsberg joined the Marine Corps in 1954 and served for three years as a rifle platoon leader and company commander. He left the Corps in 1957 and went back to Harvard, earning his Ph.D. in economics. In 1959 he joined the Rand Corporation, a think tank in Santa Monica, California, that specialized in military studies for the Pentagon. As Rand's foremost expert on Vietnam, Ellsberg was put in charge of a study to explore the various paths the U.S. government could take in dealing with the burgeoning hot spot.

In 1964, he was hired as a special assistant to the assistant secretary of defense, working in the Pentagon on the "Vietnam problem." On his first day on the job, the U.S. launched its first wave of bomber attacks over North Vietnam. A year later, Ellsberg volunteered to go to Vietnam, where he spent two years working as a civilian at the U.S. embassy in Saigon.

Returning to the Pentagon in 1967, Ellsberg was assigned to

the McNamara Study Group, which in 1968 produced the top secret, 8,000-page *History of Decision-Making in Vietnam, 1945-1968*—better known as the Pentagon Papers.

By this time, though, Ellsberg had become disillusioned with the war and thought the Pentagon Papers should be made public. So he secretly gave a copy to Senator William Fulbright, chairman of the Senate Foreign Relations Committee and an outspoken critic of the war. But when Fulbright balked at going public with it, Ellsberg took it to the *Washington Post*, which also turned him down. So Ellsberg went to the *New York Times*, which began publishing excerpts on June 13, 1971.

The first *Times* article not only documented decades of lies the American people had been told about the war in Vietnam, but also contained specific allegations of war crimes that had been committed in Vietnam since 1954, when Nixon was vice president. This was explosive stuff.

Although the *Times* didn't disclose how it had obtained the document, Ellsberg didn't think it would take the government long to figure out that he was the source, and prosecute him to the full extent of the law.

"I was clear that it would involve going to prison for the rest of my life," he recalled, "but I was ready to do that for a small chance of ending the war. By 1971 I was ready to do it for a miniscule chance."

Nixon learned that Ellsberg was responsible for the Pentagon Papers leak on almost the same day the *Times* ran the first article.

At the White House four nights later, Henry Kissinger, who had mentored Ellsberg at Harvard, gave President Nixon and his top advisors, Bob Haldeman and John Ehrlichman, a full briefing on Ellsberg, whom he called "bright but emotionally unstable."[1]

After the first story ran, Nixon and his attorney general, John Mitchell, filed and obtained an injunction barring the *Times* from printing any more of the Pentagon Papers, but the *Times* appealed and the case quickly found its way to the U.S. Supreme Court.

Meanwhile, an increasingly paranoid President Nixon, who

had begun secretly taping his own conversations and telephone calls in the White House, believed that Ellsberg had given other secret documents to the Brookings Institution, including documents detailing war crimes in Vietnam during Nixon's time as president.

On June 30, just hours after the Supreme Court ruled that the *Times* had the right to publish the Pentagon Papers, Nixon ordered Haldeman to break into the Brookings' safe and steal those documents.

"The way I want that handled, Bob..." Nixon stammered, "I want Brookings...just to break in. Break in and take it out! You understand?"

"But who do we have to do it?" Haldeman asked.

"Well, don't discuss it here," Nixon angrily replied. "You talk to...You're to break into the place, rifle the files, and bring me... Just go in and take it!"

"I want a break-in," Nixon bellowed later the same day, pounding on his desk in the Oval Office. "Get it done...I want the Brookings safe cleaned out. And have it cleaned out in a way that makes somebody else [look responsible]."[2]

The White House Plumbers hadn't been formed yet, and the mission was never carried out. But a few days later, Chuck Colson, Nixon's chief counsel, came up with another bright idea—to firebomb the Brookings Institution.

"Chuck Colson had called in a private eye," recalled John Dean, who was then the White House counsel to Nixon. "[The private eye] came in and said, 'Chuck Colson wants me to firebomb the Brookings Institute.' I said, 'What?' He said, yes, when the fire department comes, to send some burglars to get into the safe at the Brookings Institute and take out these papers the president wanted."[3]

"They were going to rent a fake fire truck and go in as fake firemen," Daniel Ellsberg said in a radio interview.[4]

Dean thought they had all gone mad.

"Hey, don't do anything," he told Colson's detective, a private investigator named Jack Caulfield, and got on the next flight to California to see his boss, John Ehrlichman, at the Western White

House in San Clemente.

Arriving at La Casa Pacifica, Nixon's secluded, oceanfront villa later that same day, Dean went into Ehrlichman's office and told him he had to put a stop to this.

"This is insane!" he told Ehrlichman, the surf pounding on the beach just outside the window. "I mean, if somebody were to die during this, it's a capital offense in the District of Columbia. It's surely going to get traced right back to the White House. Do you really want us having anything to do with something like this?"

Ehrlichman thought for a second, picked up the phone, and dialed the staff operator. "Get me Chuck Colson," he said, and put the phone back on its cradle.

A few minutes later, Colson came in.

"Young Counsel Dean is out here," Ehrlichman calmly told Colson, "and he doesn't think the Brookings plan is a very good idea. Cancel it." Then, turning to Dean, he said: "Anything else, Counsel?"

"That'll take care of it, John," Dean replied, relieved that this crazy idea had finally been put to rest.[5]

They never broke into the Brookings Institution, but a few weeks later, on July 24, Nixon approved the creation of the White House Plumbers, a White House Special Investigations Unit whose initial job was to stop the leaking of classified information to the media—a direct result of Ellsberg leaking the Pentagon Papers to the *New York Times*.

Three days later, Nixon's White House tapes recorded Henry Kissinger telling the president that something had to be done about Ellsberg.

"Daniel Ellsberg is the most dangerous man in America," Kissinger said in his thick, deep German accent. "He must be stopped at all costs...Once we've broken the war in Vietnam, then we can say this son of a bitch nearly blew it. Then we have...Then we're in strong shape—then no one will give a damn about war crimes."[6]

Logs of the White House tapes show that Nixon, Ehrlichman, and Haldeman discussed what to do about Ellsberg again on

August 2, and that Kissinger joined them to talk about Ellsberg yet again on August 12.

Three weeks later, on September 3, 1971, two members of Nixon's newly formed Plumbers unit, former CIA agent E. Howard Hunt and former FBI agent G. Gordon Liddy, supervised a break-in at the offices of Dr. Lewis Fielding, Ellsberg's former psychiatrist, where they photographed Ellsberg's patient file in hopes of blackmailing and discrediting him.

Nine months later, Hunt and Liddy would mastermind the break-in and bugging of the Democratic National Committee's headquarters at the Watergate complex.

Everyone but Kissinger would go down in the ensuing scandal.

The first to go were Ehrlichman, Haldeman, and Dean, all of whom Nixon fired on the same day—April 30, 1973. All three were later convicted and sent to jail for their roles in the Watergate scandal. Ehrlichman and Haldeman each spent 18 months in federal prison, and Dean, who became the star witness during the televised Senate Watergate hearings, got a reduced sentence and served only four months.

Next to go was Vice President Spiro Agnew, who had come under investigation for having taken more than $100,000 in cash bribes, some handed over to him in a brown paper bag at the White House. Agnew pleaded *nolo contendre*—"no contest"—to one count of failing to report $29,500 of income, the bribes he'd received in 1967 as Governor of Maryland. He resigned on October 10, 1973, becoming the first vice president in American history ever forced to leave office under the threat of criminal charges.

It was a fitting end for the man who had been Anna Chennault's "boss" during the 1968 plot to sabotage the Paris peace talks.

In his 1980 memoirs, *Go Quietly...Or Else*, Agnew denied taking any bribes, although the evidence is overwhelming that he did.

"I am writing this book," he claimed, "because I am innocent of the allegations which compelled me to resign from the vice presidency of the United States in 1973."[7]

In a truly startling allegation, Agnew also claimed that

President Nixon threatened to have him assassinated if he didn't resign, thus the title of his book.

The threat, Agnew wrote, came in early October, 1973, a week before he was forced to resign amid the growing scandal over the bribery charges that had been leveled against him. It came, Agnew wrote, from Nixon, who had his chief of staff, Alexander Haig, deliver it to Agnew's loyal military aide, General Mike Dunn, who then passed it on to Agnew.

"I received an indirect threat from the White House that made me fear for my life," Agnew wrote.[8] "I did not know what might happen to me. But I don't mind admitting I was frightened. This directive was aimed at me like a gun at my head. That is the only way I can describe it. I was told, 'Go quietly—or else.'"[9]

"I feared for my life," he wrote. "If a decision had been made to eliminate me—through an automobile accident, a fake suicide, or whatever—the order would not have been traced back to the White House.[10] I was just a pawn on the chessboard to be played in whatever way would help Nixon survive."[11]

According to Agnew, Nixon was worried that if he didn't resign, the House of Representatives would start impeachment proceedings against Agnew, and "there were plenty of people around who would want to make it a doubleheader."[12]

But Agnew, hated by the Democrats even more than Nixon was, quite astutely saw himself as Nixon's only hope of *not* being impeached.

"Mr. Nixon did not seem to realize that I was his insurance policy against his own ouster," he wrote. "The left-wingers who despised us both would never push him out of the White House until they were certain I would not be around to take his place."[13]

But Nixon pushed him out anyway.

Despite all his claims of being innocent of taking bribes, and of being unfairly and unjustifiably forced from office—under threat of assassination, no less—Agnew never denied that he had been part of the plot to sabotage the Paris peace talks, a plot President Johnson called "treason."

"It is known now that Lyndon Johnson put me under surveillance in October 1968, when he thought I had been in contact with President Thieu through Anna Chennault," Agnew wrote in his memoirs.[14]

Agnew said he didn't learn about the surveillance "until the truth came out several years later, but I did not resent it. If I had been president and had had the same suspicions as Lyndon Johnson, I might have done the same thing, as a national security measure."[15]

Despite his denials about everything else, Agnew went to his grave in 1996 without ever denying his involvement in the Chennault affair.

G. Gordon Liddy, meanwhile, got the stiffest Watergate sentence and served four and a half years in prison for his role in the burglary.

Chuck Colson, regarded by some as Nixon's "darkest henchman," was never convicted of any Watergate crimes, nor of his aborted plot to firebomb the Bookings Institution, but he served seven months in federal prison for his role in masterminding the break-in at the offices of Daniel Ellsberg's former psychiatrist. (On December 10, 2008, President George W. Bush presented Colson with the Presidential Citizens Medal, the second-highest civilian honor, which is given in recognition of those "who have performed exemplary deeds of service for the nation.")

John Mitchell, who resigned as U.S. Attorney General in 1972 to manage Nixon's reelection campaign, was also convicted for his role in attempting to cover up the Watergate scandal. The first former U.S. Attorney General ever to be convicted and imprisoned for criminal activities, he spent 19 months in federal prison—another fitting end to one of the ringleaders of the 1968 plot to sabotage the Paris peace talks.

Richard Nixon held out the longest, but facing impeachment in the House of Representatives and certain conviction in the Senate, he resigned as president on August 9, 1974. He was the first U.S. president ever to resign in disgrace. Before he left office, he didn't even pardon his fellow Watergate conspirators, although he gladly accepted one from his successor, President Gerald Ford.

Many years later, Nixon would try to explain why he had been such a ruthless politician—and a failed president.

"I played by the rules of politics as I found them," he wrote. "Not taking a higher road than my predecessors and my adversaries was my central mistake."[16]

To Nixon's way of thinking, it was somebody else's fault that he was a crook.

Dr. Hutschnecker thought that Nixon's loss to John F. Kennedy in the 1960 election—an election Nixon believed had been "stolen"—was the underlying cause of Nixon's downfall.

"I believe…that had Nixon won, the bunker mentality that spawned Watergate would not have developed because desperate measures to win would not have been employed," Hutschnecker wrote.[17]

Dr. Hutschnecker had tried to reach out to Nixon during the Watergate crisis, but Nixon had shunted him aside.

Nixon had found a friend whose advice might have saved him from himself. In the end, though, he wouldn't listen to Dr. Hutschnecker. He never really did.

CHAPTER 46

Why Watergate?

A few days before the Watergate break-in on June 17, 1972, President Nixon's approval rating hit 61 percent—a two-year high. He had double-digit leads in the national polls over each of the top two Democratic rivals in the upcoming presidential election and appeared headed for easy reelection in November.[1]

There was only one thing that could change that: the disclosure that Nixon and Agnew had sabotaged the Paris peace talks four years earlier.

Was that why Nixon's White House Plumbers broke into Democratic headquarters at the Watergate office complex that night? After all, they hadn't just broken in to *steal* sensitive documents; they were also there to "bug" the office in order to find out what the Democrats knew, and what their plans were.[2]

In June of 1972, there were still plenty of people around who knew about Nixon's betrayal four years earlier. Lyndon Johnson was still alive, and so were Dean Rusk, Clark Clifford and Walt Rostow. So was Hubert Humphrey, who was then in a heated race against George McGovern to win the Democratic nomination and another chance to run against Nixon. Humphrey, who had narrowly lost to Nixon in 1968, certainly knew about it.

Then there was Larry O'Brien, the chairman of the National Democratic Committee, whose office at the Watergate was the one the Plumbers had broken into. O'Brien, who'd directed Jack Kennedy's presidential campaign in 1960, LBJ's in 1964, and Humphrey's in 1968, certainly knew what Nixon had done to sabotage the Paris peace talks. But would he, or any of the others who hated

Nixon so much for what he'd done, make a campaign issue of it? They'd held back once before, but would they hold back again?

Nixon may have figured that the answer to this question, which could determine the outcome of the 1972 election, might be learned if his White House Plumbers could put a "bug" in O'Brien's office at the Watergate.

Of course, no one really knows for sure. Those who knew are either dead or aren't talking. And those who say they know only have theories. Even Nixon's own vice president, Spiro Agnew, later wrote, "The real reason for the Watergate break-in is still a mystery to me."[3]

Nixon's longtime speechwriter agreed.

"The whole thing with 'why Watergate?' remains a mystery," said Ray Price, who was Nixon's head speechwriter throughout his presidency and who wrote all of Nixon's Watergate speeches.[4]

Some theorize that the Watergate burglary was meant to find out if the Democrats had any incriminating evidence connecting Nixon to eccentric billionaire Howard Hughes. O'Brien, after all, had once worked for Hughes through his friend, Robert Maheu, and knew a great deal about the Nixon/Hughes relationship, including the fact that Hughes had once loaned Nixon's brother, Donald, $205,000 to open a chain of fast food outlets specializing in triple-decker sandwiches called "Nixon Burgers."[5]

Others believe that Watergate was just Nixon being Nixon, that "Tricky Dick" just couldn't stop cheating to win an election, even when he was miles ahead and the finish line was in sight.

But Walt Rostow, President Johnson's national security advisor, and the White House point man on the Chennault affair, believed that Nixon's treachery in sabotaging the Paris peace talks in 1968 was a direct cause of Watergate.

In his "Memorandum for the Record," which he wrote in 1973 to provide future historians with the background, and the actual FBI and internal White House memos on the Chennault affair, Rostow wrote: "I am inclined to believe the Republican operation in 1968 relates in two ways to the Watergate affair of 1972."

"First," he wrote, "the election of 1968 proved to be close and there was some reason for those involved on the Republican side to believe their enterprise with the South Vietnamese, and Thieu's recalcitrance, may have sufficiently blunted the impact on U.S. politics of the total bombing halt and agreement to negotiate to constitute the margin of victory [in the '68 election]. Second, they got away with it.

"Despite considerable press commentary after the election, the matter was never investigated fully. Thus, as the same men faced the election of 1972, there was nothing in their previous experience with an operation of doubtful propriety—or even legality—to warn them off; and there were memories of how close an election could get and the possible utility of pressing to the limit—or beyond."[6]

If Rostow was right, then Nixon's 1968 treachery may have been the *cause* of Watergate. But was the Watergate caper pulled off *because* of the '68 betrayal? Was it done expressly to cover up what had then become Nixon's deepest and darkest secret?

We may never know for sure, but the answer might still lie buried under the mountain of Nixon White House tapes that have yet to be released. The first batch of tapes was made public in May of 1980, and every few years a few more hours of his secretly recorded conversations are dribbled out to the public piecemeal. So far, only about 300 hours of the tapes have been made public, but there are more than 3,000 more hours that have yet to be released. Perhaps one day the answer to the most intriguing Watergate question of all will turn up on a scratchy tape recording of a long-ago, Scotch-fueled conversation in the Oval Office—tapes Nixon later wished he had destroyed.[7]

CHAPTER 47

Richard Nixon's
"Unforgivable Sin"

Worried that Nixon might be spiraling into depression after his fall from grace, Dr. Hutschnecker flew out to California to see him in April 1976. It was a lovely spring day as his cab pulled up to Nixon's gated compound, La Casa Pacifica, on the beach in San Clemente.

Nixon showed him into his study and, as was his custom, remarked on the beautiful views of the Pacific Ocean the room afforded.

They sat and talked for a while about old times, politics, philosophy, and the memoirs Nixon was writing. Then, taking full measure of the haggard and beaten man sitting before him, Dr. Hutschnecker spoke to Nixon more bluntly than he'd ever spoken to him before. The doctor told him that he looked depressed and suicidal.

In psychiatric slang, the phrase "couchbroken" is sometimes used to describe a patient who has accepted treatment and is willing to work with a psychoanalyst to explore the patient's unconscious mind in order to discover the root of the patient's neuroses.

Richard Nixon was never couchbroken.

All throughout their long relationship, Nixon and Dr. Hutschnecker played a cat-and-mouse game, never directly engaging in psychoanalysis—at least not in the clinical sense of the word. They did not discuss Nixon's dreams or his childhood traumas, and Nixon never revealed his innermost fears and fantasies, as is customary in a psychoanalytic setting. And although Dr. Hutschnecker was always careful to point out in his writings that he technically never psycho-analyzed Nixon, he left many clues to suggest that their relationship was much more than just that of medical doctor and patient.

Since arriving in America in 1936, Dr. Hutschnecker had been a practicing internist—a physician who can prescribe drugs and do medical check-ups, but who is generally a doctor who refers pa-tients to other specialists. There are hundreds of internists in ev-ery major American city, but Dr. Hutschnecker had a specialty few other doctors in America had when Nixon first came to see him in 1952. He was a specialist in the psychosomatic causes of illness—that is, illness caused by psychological disturbances. Having read Dr. Hutschnecker's book, *The Will to Live*, Nixon knew exactly the kind of doctor Hutschnecker was.

Nixon was in denial about receiving psychological treatment from Dr. Hutschnecker because he was in denial that he had any psychological problems. After all, a politician of his stature could not *have* psychological problems, and certainly could not be seen with a shrink. In the mind of the general public, Dr. Hutschneck-er later wrote, seeing a psychoanalyst was "a politician's unforgiv-able sin."[1]

"The American cultural prejudice against any politician in psy-chotherapy has always been swiftly punitive," Hutschnecker wrote. "Their careers are generally irreparably damaged."[2]

Nixon was vice president of the United States in 1955, the year Dr. Hutschnecker gave up his practice as an internist to be-come a psychoanalyst full-time. When gossip columnist Walter Winchell reported that year that Nixon was seeing an unnamed psychiatrist, the men around Nixon advised him to stop seeing Dr. Hutschnecker.

The doctor mentioned this briefly in his fourth book, *The Drive for Power*, a study of the mental health of political leaders. Published in 1974 while Nixon was still in the White House and reeling from the revelations of Watergate, Hutschnecker studiously avoided offering any insights into Nixon's personality for fear that it would further damage him. The book's publisher, however, sought to capitalize on Hutschnecker's relationship with Nixon, describing Hutschnecker on the book's dust jacket as "the psychiatrist who broke into national prominence when it was revealed that Richard Nixon had consulted him."

Dr. Hutschnecker, however, was not actually a psychiatrist, a title that requires certification from the American Board of Psychiatry and Neurology or the American Osteopathic Board of Neurology and Psychiatry.

In *The Drive for Power*, Dr. Hutschnecker noted that in 1955, he and Nixon "had yielded to the urging of his political advisers that he not see me anymore professionally, and yet it had been a good, that is, trusting doctor-patient relationship. How strange, I thought, that a man in public life would be allowed, even encouraged, to visit a heart specialist, but would be criticized for trying to understand the emotional undercurrent of his unconscious drives, fears, and conflicts, or possible neurotic hang-ups.[3] Any average man or woman who feels emotionally upset can go to a psychoanalyst, but a leader who might be under the greatest stress imaginable, such as the president of the United States, is denied the seeking of such help. Is this rational thinking for the last third of the twentieth century?"[4]

What Dr. Hutschnecker did not take into account was the fact that many political observers, and many more in the public at large, already viewed Nixon as crazy and dangerous, and if it came out that *he* was seeing a shrink, that view would only be reinforced. Perhaps in those days another politician could have let it be known that he had seen a psychologist—but not Nixon.

Despite the urging of his advisors, Nixon would go on seeing Hutschnecker for many more years. Nixon, it seems, had bonded with Hutschnecker and could not give up his consultations.

"I surmised that Nixon had made what is psychologically called a positive transference," Dr. Hutschnecker wrote. "In short, I may have reminded him of the real VIP in his life, his mother Hannah."[5]

Over the years, Dr. Hutschnecker would continue trying to connect with his most difficult patient.

Dr. Hutschnecker wouldn't be publicly linked to Nixon until Nov. 13, 1968—a few days *after* Nixon was elected president— when columnist Drew Pearson, speaking at the National Press Club, told the audience, "Nixon had been under the care of a psychiatrist," and identified Hutschnecker as his "shrink."[6]

Pearson told his audience that Hutschnecker had acknowledged that Nixon was a patient of his, but told Pearson that he had consulted Nixon "about strictly medical problems, not for psychotherapy."

Dr. Hutschnecker was not being candid with Pearson. His medical practice since 1955 had been strictly as a psychotherapist specializing in psychosomatic illness—ill health brought on by stress and other psychological factors—and Hutschnecker had consulted Nixon many times over the intervening years. Both Nixon and Dr. Hutschnecker, it seems, were in denial.

In 1969, Dr. Hutschnecker penned an article for *Look* magazine in which he acknowledged treating Nixon. In the article, however, he claimed that it had been "at a time when I was engaged in the practice of internal medicine," which was not exactly the whole truth, since he'd continued treating Nixon long after switching his practice exclusively to psychoanalysis in 1955.

In the article he wrote, "During the entire period that I treated Mr. Nixon, I detected no sign of mental illness in him."[7]

But could he really have said otherwise about a patient without violating doctor-patient confidentiality—especially a patient who just a few months earlier had been inaugurated president of the United States?

Dr. Hutschnecker was in the news again in 1970 when the *Los Angeles Times*, referring to him as a "former physician to President Nixon," revealed that Nixon had assigned Hutschnecker to write a report about the prevention of juvenile crime.[8]

That report caused a stir when it was leaked to the press that

Dr. Hutschnecker had recommended that all seven- and eight-year-olds be psychologically tested for "violent and homicidal tendencies," and that "daycare centers for three- to five-year-olds ought to be increased in number and quality, especially in slum areas."[9]

Caspar Weinberger, Nixon's secretary of health, education, and welfare, created an uproar when he offhandedly dismissed the report, which he hadn't read, as a recommendation that concentration camps be opened for potentially violent children.

"We don't want to send five-year-olds to camps," he flippantly told a reporter.[10]

Dr. Hutschnecker made headlines again in November 1973 when Congress called him to testify about whether or not he had been the psychologist to another high-profile politician—Gerald Ford.

Nixon's controversial vice president, Spiro Agnew, had resigned on October 10, 1973, after being criminally charged with accepting bribes while he'd been governor of Maryland. Nixon had selected the popular Michigan congressman, Gerald Ford, as Agnew's successor. But Ford would have to be confirmed by the Senate first, and during the confirmation hearings, a witness testified that Ford had been a psychiatric patient of Hutschnecker's.

Ford flatly denied it. "Under no circumstances did I see him for treatment and under no circumstances have I ever been treated by any psychiatrist," he said.[11]

Ford acknowledged, however, that he'd paid a visit to Dr. Hutschnecker's New York office on November 21, 1966. He said that he had merely dropped by the doctor's office to "say hello," and that during their meeting, "Dr. Hutschnecker gave me a lecture... about the role of leadership in the American political system."[12]

Dr. Hutschnecker was called before the Senate Rules Committee on November 7, 1973, to testify about whether or not he had ever treated Ford for psychiatric problems. He stated unequivocally that he had not.

Ford, he said, "had never been a patient of mine and had been to my office only once."[13]

Then Senator Howard Cannon asked him if he had ever treated President Nixon for psychiatric problems.

"No," Hutschnecker replied, explaining that he had treated Nixon "strictly in my capacity as an internist."

In his book, *The Drive for Power*, Hutschnecker noted that Senator Mark Hatfield then asked: "You never had an occasion to help Mr. Nixon as a patient in the field of psychiatric medicine?"

"No," Hutschnecker replied.

Thirteen days later, on November 20, Dr. Hutschnecker appeared before the House Judiciary Committee to answer the same questions—and gave them the same answers, though he did volunteer one interesting detail about Nixon's patient file.

"I kept his record apart from the other records," he testified, "and kept his record locked up someplace else."

But the members of the House committee didn't ask him the obvious follow-up question: Why would he keep Nixon's medical records under lock and key if he was only seeing him as an internist, while not similarly protecting the patient files of the many other famous people he *had* been consulting as a psychotherapist?

In his unpublished manuscript, Dr. Hutschnecker wrote that he had dropped his practice as an internist and become a full-time psychotherapist in 1955. At that point, because of the stigma attached to seeing a psychotherapist, Nixon's advisors urged him to stop seeing Dr. Hutschnecker.

But Nixon kept seeing him anyway. On Thanksgiving Day, 1957, Dr. Hutschnecker wrote a note to Nixon that read: "I had meant to write to you several times since I have had the pleasure of seeing you last in Washington on my return from Europe."

On October 9, 1959, Nixon wrote a note to his secretary, Rose Mary Woods, regarding Dr. Hutschnecker: "I want to have him come down—probably after we return—but check with me as to whether I want it before we go."

Then, on December 16, 1959, Dr. Hutschnecker wrote Nixon a note that read: "This is a belated thank-you note for the luncheon I had the pleasure of sharing with you last week."

And in February 1961, Dr. Hutschnecker came to Nixon's hotel suite at the Plaza Hotel in New York for a "check-up."

All this despite the fact that he had ceased his practice as an internist in 1955.

Ford was confirmed, and a few weeks later, Dr. Hutschnecker wrote an article for the *New York Times*, deploring the stigma attached to politicians seeing psychiatrists.

"General Pershing had a psychiatrist on his staff," he wrote. "I cannot help [but] think if an American president had a staff psychiatrist, perhaps a case such as Watergate might not have had a chance to develop."[14]

Dr. Hutschnecker had continued seeing Nixon even when he was president. But because of Nixon's fear that their relationship might be exposed, their consultations had to be conducted surreptitiously.

Hutschnecker wrote that in 1969, when President Nixon summoned him to the White House for a "medical consultation" to treat his depression and insomnia, he was listed in the White House log "as a visitor of Ms. Woods [Nixon's secretary] and shown in by a guard to her office, thereby avoiding the press."[15]

All the while they kept up their lifelong correspondence. Hutschnecker's letters to Nixon were an invitation to talk, to open up. Of course, Nixon, being Nixon, never did. But Hutschnecker, being Hutschnecker, never stopped trying.

When Nixon left the White House in disgrace, Dr. Hutschnecker visited him, although even then Nixon was worried that someone might discover the forbidden nature of their relationship.

Nixon was stunned on that spring day in 1976, when Dr. Hutschnecker told him he looked depressed and suicidal. He looked at the doctor with wide eyes, as if to say, "What do you mean? I'm doing things. I'm busy. I'm not depressed." But he didn't protest or argue; instead, he sat quietly, listening as his old friend and confidant described the psychological aspects of depression and how they manifest themselves in the body.[16]

Nixon was still in denial, but he understood that Hutschneck-er had been, over all these many years, more than a family doctor to him.

When it came time to say their goodbyes, Nixon thanked the doctor for coming to see him in California. Then, conspiratorially, he told Dr. Hutschnecker that if anyone asked, "You can say you just came to visit an old friend."

Dr. Hutschnecker was shocked.

"This absolutely startled me," he later wrote, "because I had simply assumed that it no longer mattered what people thought. But the same reality that had always hovered over us was still present: what the press would say."[17]

Nixon, Dr. Hutschnecker understood, "had not forgotten that seeing me could be detrimental to his career."[18]

Needless to say, Dr. Hutschnecker is not mentioned in the 1,122-page memoir Nixon was writing when the doctor came to visit him that day in San Clemente. To the very end, Nixon tried to hide the nature of his relationship with Dr. Hutschnecker. He knew that for a politician like him, the only thing worse than needing to see a psychiatrist was actually seeing one.

They would meet again only one more time, in June of 1993, when Dr. Hutschnecker flew back to California to attend the funeral of Nixon's wife, Pat. After the services at the Nixon Library in Yorba Linda, Hutschnecker's assistant snapped a photograph of them. It's the only photo ever taken of Nixon and Hutschnecker together.

Despite what he'd said publicly about their relationship, toward the end of his long life, Dr. Hutschnecker was more candid about it in private. When he was in his nineties, and Nixon was already dead, Hutschnecker finally told his friends the truth.

"He would say he was Nixon's shrink," recalled Squire Rush-nell, a friend of Dr. Hutschnecker's in Connecticut. "And when he said he was Nixon's shrink, he always said it with a giggle. He was a great man, very wise. He reminded me of Yoda in 'Star Wars,' the character with a million wrinkles in his face, and when he smiled, every wrinkle seemed to smile."[19]

Dr. Arnold Hutschnecker died at his home in Sherman, Connecticut, on December 28, 2000. He was 102 years old, and over his long life, he certainly expressed the will to live.

Guenther Reinhardt's Confidential Report

Two months before the 1960 election, Guenther Reinhardt wrote a twelve-page report about the relationship between Dr. Arnold Hutschnecker and Vice President Richard Nixon. Except for two pages, which contain unfounded and libelous allegations, the report is reprinted here in its entirety.

<u>CONFIDENTIAL</u> <u>REPORT</u>
REPORT ON A CONFIDENTIAL INVESTIGATION
RELATIVE TO CERTAIN ALLEGATIONS MADE
BY ARNOLD A. HUTSCHNECKER, M.D. OF
829 PARK AVENUE, NEW YORK, NEW YORK

OBJECTIVES
It is the objective of this investigation to establish the veracity of certain statements allegedly made by Dr. Arnold A. Hutschnecker to a person or persons not known to the investigator with regard to his having given professional care to a prominent Californian who, for the purpose of this report, shall be identified only as Mr. N. It is the investigator's understanding that a picture of Mr. N. is being exhibited in Dr. Hutschnecker's office and that Dr. Hutschnecker has definitely identified Mr. N. as one of his former patients.

FINDINGS
The very nature of the problem ruled out any approach other than

that of surreptitious inquiry. In order to attack the problem intelligently, it was decided to make a background investigation of Dr. Arnold A. Hutschnecker.

It appears that this physician is a native of Germany. He was born there in 1898 and is therefore 62 years of age.

Dr. Hutschnecker is married. His wife is the former Florita Weiss. They were married in 1932 in Berlin. No children issued from this marriage.

Dr. Hutschnecker graduated from the Medical School of the University of Berlin in 1923 summa cum laude. Being of Jewish origin, he found himself exposed to the restrictive decrees of the National Socialist government and decided to immigrate to the United States. He arrived in New York in August 1938. His license to practice medicine was issued to him in 1940. Dr. Hutschnecker did not see military service.

His wife also acts as a part time receptionist in his office. Dr. Hutschnecker's office is located at 829 Park Avenue in Apartment 1-A which is a luxurious, duplex apartment on the ground floor of this rather elegant building. It is an eight-room apartment. The doctor's office, as well as the examination rooms and the office of his associate, Dr. Ralph Jacoby, likewise a native of Germany, are located on the ground floor while luxuriously furnished living quarters are in the first floor section of the duplex apartment. Dr. Hutschnecker and his associate, Dr. Ralph Jacoby, specialize in the practice of psychosomatic medicine. Stedman's Medical Dictionary (19th Revised Edition) defines psychosomatic medicine as "the study and treatment of diseases of abnormal states of psychosomatic origin (*psyche* mind plus *soma* body) pertaining to the influence of the mind or higher functions of the brain (emotions, fears, desires, etc.) upon the functions of the body, especially in relation to disease."

In one of his papers entitled "Health and Wholeness," copy of which is hereto appended and made a portion of this report, Dr. Hutschnecker described the psychosomatic concept as follows:

"Psychosomatic medicine studying the effect which disturbing emotions have on the chemistry, and its effect on the physical functioning of an organism, provides us increasingly with more data of the interrelationship between soma and psyche."

Dr. Hutschnecker is a prolific writer of texts on psychosomatic and related matters. It might be stated at this juncture, parenthetically, that the investigator, in the conduct of this inquiry, had the benefit of perusing a considerable amount of dossier material on Dr. Hutschnecker which had been amassed by several agencies. As a matter of fact, it would appear that as a result of various activities in which Dr. Hutschnecker seems to have engaged, he has been for many years and is still under investigation or security by several agencies.

Records show that the doctor was arrested on November 11, 1943 following certain public exposures made by a Canadian physician. He was charged with conspiracy to obtain a draft deferment for the playboy Gert Von Gontart [sic], heir to the Anheuser-Busch brewing fortune by falsely swearing to a nonexistent medical condition of Gert Von Gontart [sic]. Arrested with Dr. Hutschnecker was a military intelligence lieutenant and a clerk of a draft board. Dr. Hutschnecker was convicted and received a suspended sentence of one year and a day. His license to practice medicine was withdrawn and he was barred from membership of professional societies. He also lost his privileges in various hospitals. He had never been on the staff of a prominent hospital, but had been given privileges at the Lenox Hill Hospital.

It seems that while Dr. Hutschnecker was barred from the practice of medicine, his associate, Dr. Ralph Jacoby, who had arrived in this country from Berlin in 1939, handled Dr. Hutschnecker's patients. Dr. Jacoby is accredited with prominent hospitals in Manhattan and Mount Vernon. As stated hereinabove, Dr. Jacoby is still associated in practice with Dr. Hutschnecker. He comes into the office on Mondays, Wednesdays, and Fridays.

On April 13, 1959 Dr. Hutschnecker achieved some newspaper notoriety following an alleged $5,000 jewelry loss through burglary at his home. When the burglary was investifated [sic] the doctor admitted that the stolen jewelry had been considerably underinsured.

Recently Dr. Hutschnecker was re-admitted to membership in the American Medical Association and the New York State Medical Society, the New York County Medical Society and the American Psychosomatic Association, as well as the Academy of Medicine, all of which had withdrawn his membership following his conviction.

Dossier references indicate that Dr. Hutschnecker's practice is enormously lucrative. An investigation which had been previously conducted by a certain agency yielded the information that "he treats notorious persons of prominence. His income is estimated as being in excess of $140,000 per annum. Dr. Hutschnecker charges a minimum fee of $100 for a consultation."

The doctor is known to have entertained many people of prominence, not only at his city home but at a very elaborate summer residence which he owns on Cozier Road in Sherman, Connecticut. He and his wife travel to Europe at least once a year.

Referring again to the dossier material, references therein indicate that many of Dr. Hutschnecker's patients are domiciled in California.

Among the known patients of Dr. Hutschnecker are the wife of the inventor and instrument builder, Paul Kollman; Arthur Kudner of advertising prominence; film actor Joseph Schildkraut and others.

While the investigation into the antecedents and activities of Dr. Hutschnecker was being made, the subject of the investigation was vacationing at his summer home in Sherman, Connecticut. He returned from his vacation on Tuesday, September 6, 1960.

With the aid of a prominent New York surgeon and a former chief of surgery of Flower Fifth Avenue Hospital, the investigator obtained an introduction to Dr. Hutschnecker. The introducing surgeon was, of course, not aware of the fact that the request for an introduction of the investigator to Dr. Hutschnecker was precipitated by this inquiry. A pretext was used to lay the foundation for the investigator's visit at Dr. Hutschnecker's office.

The pretext: The investigator, using his correct name and address and stating his profession correctly, represents a law firm in Pittsburgh who, in turn, are counsel for a very wealthy and socially and politically prominent Pennsylvanian who recently underwent a serious operation which resulted in the removal of his colon. He failed to respond properly to the postoperative treatment and to adjust himself to the new regimen which the operation demanded of him. As a result he became despondent and now suffers from acute depression. It was suggested to him that he submit himself to treatment by a psychosomatic specialist. However, the patient is hesitant to do so, feeling that should it become known to the public at large that he is under psychosomatic care, it would cast a stigma upon him which would seriously impair his political future. Therefore, his counsel suggested to him that he see a psychosomatic specialist in New York where, presumably, there is better medical talent available than in Pittsburgh. They obtained the name of Dr. Hutschnecker and instructed the investigator to make a discreet inquiry whether the physician might consider examining and, if need be, treating the patient without setting up a chart or other records showing the patient's true identity, name, and address.

Dr. Hutschnecker was visited at his office by the investigator on Wednesday, September 7, 1960 at 12:45. The ensuing interview was recorded with the aid of a surreptitious pocket wire recorder. Most of the conversation was in German. Dr. Hutschnecker received the investigator cordially and accepted the pretext story with enthusiasm. The physician is a small man, wiry and of slight build. His facial features are amazingly oriental; so much so that when the physician first entered his office, it was the instant reaction of the investigator that this man was a Chinese or Filipino house man.

Dr. Hutschnecker is a man of considerable charm and has a very prepossessing personality. He is quite loquacious. It was obvious that the physician made every effort to impress the investigator, within the limits of professional dignity, with the high plateau of his clientele. He readily agreed to a consultation with the prominent Pennsylvanian and to take him under treatment without making up a chart or any other record relative to his identity. The doctor then made the following statement: "This problem is not new to me. I am treating the No. 1 man in our federal government in Washington, or rather I should say No. 2 man. If you take another step above that you are next to God." The investigator then said, "Do you mean Eisenhower?" Dr. Hutschnecker replied, "No, the man directly under him." Dr. Hutschnecker then continued: "Those files never get out of my hand. I have his file right in my desk. (He patted his hand against the left lower drawer of his office desk.) Of course, it is very difficult to hide the fact that I am treating him because when he comes here he generally has two or four Secret Service agents preceding him. They station themselves at strategic points of the building and then comes this man in a big black-hooded State Department limousine. Of course the whole building is alerted to the fact that a very important person is in the building, but I think that so far nobody actually knows who it is. I also treat him in Washington."

The conversation then continued on the topic of the imaginary patient in Pennsylvania. Thereafter, Dr. Hutschnecker once again briefly referred to "No. 2 man in Washington" as a patient of his.

The investigator had made arrangements to have one of his assistants place a call to Dr. Hutschnecker while the investigator and Dr. Hutschnecker were in conference. The pretext for the call was an inquiry about the doctor's house, fees, etc. and the purpose of the call was to give the investigator an opportunity to look around the doctor's office. The office is expensively furnished, but in typical German taste with heavy furniture, expensive oriental rugs and its walls are lined with book shelves containing medical textbooks. It was noted that there was no picture of Mr. N. in the office. There was a sketch of the late Albert Einstein, who was evidently one of the doctor's patients; another sketch of Baron De Rothschild;

several paintings in the primitive style and an autographed color photo of a prominent New York attorney who happens to be a very close personal friend and client of the investigator. When the doctor got off the phone, the investigator mentioned that he knew the attorney quite well, which seemed to please Dr. Hutschnecker.

Before taking his leave of the doctor, the investigator had an opportunity to see the room adjacent to Dr. Hutschnecker's consultation room. This is Dr. Jacoby's office. The physician was not in at the time. There was no picture of Mr. N. in Dr. Jacoby's office. Neither was there a picture of the gentleman in the reception room. The investigator had no opportunity to look into the examination room, but it is hardly conceivable that any picture would be on display in that particular room.

In the course of the following morning, Thursday, September 8, 1960, the investigator had occasion to call the attorney whose picture appeared in Dr. Hutschnecker's office, with respect to another matter and the lawyer told the investigator that he had just come from the office of Dr. Hutschnecker and that Dr. Hutschnecker had mentioned the investigator's name and the reason for his call. The attorney seemed to be pleased that the investigator might refer a patient to Dr. Hutschnecker, to whom he referred as "Hutch." He stated he, the lawyer, had defended Dr. Hutschnecker in his trial in the Gert Von Gontart [sic] matter and that thereafter they had become very close personal friends. The attorney said that Hutschnecker had treated him, as well as members of his family, and that he was an extremely fine and reliable man and a good friend. The investigator interjected that he had called on the doctor merely to find out whether he could keep the identity of a prominent patient a secret. This brought forth an emphatic avowal from the lawyer who said, "Well, he is treating Richard Nixon, and you don't read about that in the papers." The investigator asked the attorney whether this was actually so, whereupon the lawyer said, "Well I have met Richard Nixon in Dr. Hutschnecker's office." The gentleman repeated this statement, in substance, several times during the rest of the conversation. He also said that he had seen a letter which President Eisenhower had written to Dr. Hutsch-necker thanking him for a copy of Dr. Hutschnecker's latest book (*The Will to Live*). The lawyer further said that Dr. Hutschnecker had treated Mr. N. also in Washington and that whenever N. is in New York he generally calls on Dr. Hutschnecker.

The investigator, in order to draw out the lawyer, asked him whether Mr. N. was suffering from a cancer condition, to which the attorney replied: "No, he is very often under heavy pressure and this has an influence upon his body chemistry as it would have in the case of any normal person." Whenever that is the case, he sees Dr. Hutschnecker and evidently the latter has been able to provide relief for him.

The attorney then said that as long as Mr. N. did not consider it a stigma to be treated by a psychosomatic specialist, the investiga-tor's client should have no compunction about the same treatment. The attorney explained that Dr. Hutschnecker is not a psychoana-lyst or a psychiatrist; the latter category of medical practitioners said the attorney, will try to correct or heal mental or neurologi-cal disorders while the psychosomatic specialist will endeavor to correct disorders of the physical system or the body of the patient which may have been brought on by emotional disturbances or pressure. In other words, according to the attorney, the psychoso-matic man is not concerned with the correction or adjustment of mental or psychiatric abnormalities or ailments.

The investigator plans to confirm the visits of Mr. N. at Dr. Hutschnecker's office in approximately two weeks by a surrepti-tious inquiry among the building personnel at 829 Park Avenue. Except for this phase, the investigation has been suspended.

The information contained in, or accompanying this report, or any part thereof, is CONFIDENTIAL and for the use of the cli-ent only. The report is accepted with this specific understanding. The report is accepted with the further understanding that none of the sources mentioned herein can be quoted directly or indirectly.

ACKNOWLEDGMENTS

To properly express my gratitude to all those who helped me on this book would take another whole book. But I am especially indebted to Milt Ebbins, Peter Lawford's former manager, who shared his considerable knowledge of Kennedy family secrets with me, and who allowed me to explore his vast collection of Kennedy memorabilia.

It was in Milt's underground garage, looking through tens of thousands of pages of papers crammed into the drawers of four large filing cabinets, that I found a 12-page report on the surveillance of Dr. Arnold Hutschnecker. The report was unsigned, and I would have never known who wrote it—or written this book—if it hadn't been for the extraordinarily generous staff of the Richard Nixon Presidential Library, who unsealed several never-before-seen documents that revealed the identity of the mad detective at the center of my story.

I would also like to thank the very helpful staff of the Lyndon Johnson Presidential Library, who provided me with "The 'X' Envelope"—the key to understanding the 1968 election and the collapse of the 1968 Paris peace talks—and with the correspondence of Drew Pearson, one of the greatest and bravest investigative reporters in the history of American journalism.

I would also like to thank the kind staff of the John F. Kennedy Presidential Library. This book could not have been written without access to the Kennedy Library's oral history collection.

This book also would not have been possible without the generosity of the Hutschnecker family, particularly Dorina Link, the great-niece of Arnold Hutschnecker. Dorina allowed me to quote from Hutschnecker's unpublished manuscript about his treatment of Richard Nixon.

I am also indebted to the staff of the M. E. Grenander

Department of Special Collections and Archives at the University of Albany for having accidentally—and without the authority of the Hutschnecker family—given me access to Dr. Hutschnecker's unpublished manuscript.

The Beverly Hills Public Library also deserves special thanks. Their website, and the invaluable Proquest database they subscribe to, connected me to the archives of the *New York Times* and the *Los Angeles Times*, as well as the work of hundreds of reporters who covered the events chronicled in this book.

The Richard Nixon oral history project at Cal State Fullerton was also invaluable to my better understanding of our darkest and most troubled president.

I am especially grateful to the few surviving people who knew Guenther Reinhardt and were kind enough to share their insights into his deeply disturbed personality. First and foremost, these include Werner Michel, Guenther's delightful and insightful former colleague in the Counterintelligence Corps; John Lichtblau and his wife, Charlotte, whose friendship with Guenther was betrayed in the worst possible way; and Paul Bruehl, who served unhappily with Guenther in the CIC in occupied Germany.

I would also like to extend special thanks to the many other people I interviewed for this book, including Loie Gaunt, Vice President Nixon's office manager; Squire Rushnell, Dr. Hutschnecker's former neighbor; Cartha "Deke" DeLoach, the FBI's man in charge of the investigation into Nixon's sabotage of the 1968 Paris peace talks; Carmine Bellino, the Senate Watergate Committee's chief investigator; Sam Dash, the Watergate Committee's chief counsel; and Sir Ian Kershaw, the preeminent expert on Adolf Hitler and the Third Reich.

This book, of course, would not have been possible but for the lives of two extraordinary men: Dr. Arnold Hutschnecker, who tried so gallantly to save Nixon, and Guenther Reinhardt, who tried so madly to stop him. I wish I could have met them both.

Finally, this book would not have been written at all without the love and support of my adorable wife, Eileen Kelly Robb.

CHAPTER 1

1. From a flyer for Guenther Reinhardt's lecture series, contained in the Drew Pearson Collection at the Lyndon Johnson Presidential Library.
2. From the author's interview with Loie Gaunt, March 13, 2007.
3. Memo from Loie Gaunt to Rose Mary Woods, dated November 26, 1957, from the archives of the Richard Nixon Library.
4. Memo from Charles K. McWhorter to Richard Nixon, dated August 22, 1957, from the archives of the Richard Nixon Library.
5. From Nora de Toledano's 45-page report answering charges that had been leveled against Richard Nixon, 1958, from the archives of the Richard Nixon Library.
6. Memo written by Loie Gaunt, dated August 28, 1958, from the archives of the Richard Nixon Library.
7. Memos from Loie Gaunt to Rose Mary Woods, dated September 2 and 3, 1960, from the archives of the Richard Nixon Library.
8. Ibid.
9. Ibid.
10. Memo from Rose Mary Woods to Loie Gaunt, dated September 6, 1960, from the archives of the Richard Nixon Library.

CHAPTER 2

1. Arnold Hutschnecker, *Richard Nixon: His Rise to Power, His Self-Defeat* (Hutschnecker's unpublished manuscript about his treatment of Nixon), 124; with the permission of the Arnold Hutschnecker family.
2. Arnold Hutschnecker, *The Will to Live*, (Prentice-Hall, 1951), 107.

3. Arnold Hutschnecker, *Richard Nixon: His Rise to Power, His Self-Defeat*, 50.

4. Guenther Reinhardt, *Crime Without Punishment* (Hermitage House, Inc., 1952), 10.

5. Arnold Hutschnecker, *Richard Nixon: His Rise to Power, His Self-Defeat*, 208.

6. Richard Nixon's first inaugural address, January 20, 1969.

7. Arnold Hutschnecker, *The Will to Live* (Prentice-Hall, 1951), 284.

8. Richard Nixon's farewell address at the White House, August 9, 1974.

9. Arnold Hutschnecker, *The Will to Live* (Prentice-Hall, 1951), 107, 122, and 232.

10. Ibid., 232.

11. Arnold Hutschnecker, *Richard Nixon: His Rise to Power, His Self-Defeat*, 115.

12. Ibid., 116.

13. Ibid., 123.

14. Ibid., 126–127.

15. Ibid., 125.

16. Ibid., 126.

17. Ibid., 127.

18. Earl Mazo, *Richard Nixon: A Political and Personal Portrait* (Harper & Brothers, 1959), 5.

CHAPTER 3

1. Werner Michel's interview with the author, May 20, 2008.

2. Guenther Reinhardt, *Coronet* magazine; "Hitler on Trial," April 1940.

3. Werner Michel's interview with the author, May 20, 2008.

4. Guenther Reinhardt, *Crime Without Punishment* (Hermitage House, Inc., 1952), 10.

5. J. Edgar Hoover's notes to Edward A. Tamm, November 20, 1936; from Guenther Reinhardt's FBI file, obtained under the Freedom of Information Act.

6. Guenther Reinhardt's report to the FBI, December 14, 1936.
7. Memorandum for the Director, from Edward A. Tamm to J. Edgar Hoover, dated December 16, 1936; from Guenther Reinhardt's FBI file.
8. Ibid.
9. Memorandum for the Director, from Edward A. Tamm to J. Edgar Hoover, dated December 19, 1936; from Guenther Reinhardt's FBI file.
10. Memorandum for the Director, from Edward A. Tamm to J. Edgar Hoover, dated November 20, 1936; from Guenther Reinhardt's FBI file.
11. Memorandum for the Director, from Edward A. Tamm to J. Edgar Hoover, dated December 5, 1936; from Guenther Reinhardt's FBI file.
12. Guenther Reinhardt's report to the FBI, dated December 17, 1936; from Guenther Reinhardt's FBI file.
13. Memorandum for the Director, from Edward A. Tamm to J. Edgar Hoover, dated December 17, 1936, from Guenther Reinhardt's FBI file.
14. Ibid.
15. Ibid.
16. Alan Hynd, *Betrayal from the East* (Robert M. McBride & Co., 1943), 258.
17. *New York Times*, October 5, 1938.
18. Guenther Reinhardt, "What America Teaches the Foreign Correspondent," in *You Americans*, ed. B. P. Adams (Funk & Wagnalls, 1939) 150.
19. Ibid. 159–160.
20. "Heads Foreign Correspondents," *New York Times*, October 3, 1940, 11.
21. Alan Hynd, *Betrayal from the East*, 265.
22. Ibid.
23. Ibid.
24. Ibid.
25. Ibid.

26. Walter Winchell, "Walter Winchell on Broadway," *New York Daily Mirror*, November 24, 1941.

27. "Press Group in War Move," *New York Times*, December 10, 1941, 4.

28. Walter Winchell, "Walter Winchell in New York," *New York Daily Mirror*, November 18, 1943.

CHAPTER 4

1. From the FBI's files on Richard Nixon.

2. J. Edgar Hoover's introduction of Vice President Nixon at the graduation exercises of the 53rd Session of the FBI National Academy, June 11, 1954.

3. Richard Nixon, *RN: The Memoirs of Richard Nixon* (Simon & Schuster, 1979), 80.

4. Ibid., 80–81.

5. Ibid., 81.

6. Ibid., 284.

7. Nixon's White House tapes, May 13, 1971.

8. Ibid.

9. Guenther Reinhardt's Bohemian Club membership card.

10. Ibid.

11. The author's 2008 interview with Patricia Bosworth.

CHAPTER 5

1. Arnold Hutschnecker told the story of his narrow escape from a Russian firing squad to his friend Squire Rushnell, who retold the story in his book, *When God Winks at You: How God Speaks Directly to You Through the Power of Coincidence* (Thomas Nelson, 2006),149–152.

2. Arnold Hutschnecker, *Richard Nixon: His Rise to Power, His Self-Defeat*, 119, 149, and 150.

3. Arnold Hutschnecker, *The Drive for Power* (Bantam Books, 1966), 12.

4. The author's 2008 interview with Dorina Link, Arnold Hutschnecker's great-niece.

5. From Arnold Hutschnecker's obituary, *New York Times,* January 3, 2001.
6. From the records of the University of the State of New York, State Department of Education, in the matter of the application for the revocation of the license of Dr. Arnold Hutschnecker.

CHAPTER 6

1. The events and conversation described here are based on Guenther Reinhardt's 12-page confidential report, obtained exclusively by the author, about his consultation with Dr. Arnold Hutschnecker on September 7, 1960. (See the appendix for Reinhardt's report.)

CHAPTER 7

1. Vincent Bugliosi, author of *Reclaiming History: The Assassination of President John F. Kennedy,* interviewed on *Bookmark with Maria Hall Brown,* PBS, November 19, 2008.
2. Richard Nixon, *RN: The Memoirs of Richard Nixon* (Simon & Schuster, 1978), 26.
3. Ibid., 29.
4. Ibid., 27.
5. Ibid.
6. Ibid.
7. From the Naval Historical Center's website, *John F. Kennedy's Naval Service.*
8. Richard Nixon, *RN: The Memoirs of Richard Nixon* (Simon & Schuster, 1978), 28.
9. Lance Morrow, *The Best Years of Their Lives: Kennedy, Johnson and Nixon in 1948* (Basic Books, 2005); p. 17.
10. Ibid.
11. Richard Nixon, *RN: The Memoirs of Richard Nixon* (Simon & Schuster, 1978), 29.
12. Ibid.

13. From John F. Kennedy's speech upon accepting the presidential nomination of the Democratic Party, July 15, 1960, Memorial Coliseum, Los Angeles.

14. Handwritten note from John F. Kennedy to Richard Nixon, July 1952, as cited in *RN: The Memoirs of Richard Nixon* (Simon & Schuster, 1978), 91.

15. Christopher J. Matthews, *Kennedy and Nixon: The Rivalry That Shaped Postwar America* (Free Press, 1997).

CHAPTER 8

1. Ian Sayer and Douglas Botting, *Nazi Gold* (Granada Publishing, 1984), 293.

2. Guenther Reinhardt, *Crime Without Punishment* (Hermitage House, Inc., 1952), 54.

3. Ibid., 64.

4. Memorandum for the Director, from A. Rosen to J. Edgar Hoover, May 11, 1948, from the FBI files of Guenther Reinhardt.

5. Ibid.

6. From the FBI's Reading Room Index.

7. Guenther Reinhardt, "Hitler on Trial," *Coronet*, April 1940.

8. Ibid.

9. Ibid.

10. The author's interview with Sir Ian Kershaw, May 3, 2008.

11. Guenther Reinhardt, "Hitler on Trial," *Coronet*, April 1940.

12. The author's interview with Sir Ian Kershaw, May 3, 2008.

13. Guenther Reinhardt, "Hitler on Trial," *Coronet*, April 1940.

14. The author's interview with Werner Michel, May 20, 2008.

CHAPTER 9

1. Ralph de Toledano, *One Man Alone: Richard Nixon* (Funk & Wagnalls, 1969), 53.

2. Ibid.

3. "Richard Nixon," *The American Experience*, PBS.

4. Ibid.

5. Robert Caro, *The Years of Lyndon Johnson: Master of the Senate* (Knopf, 2002), 141–45.

6. Ibid.

7. Ibid.

8. Richard Nixon, *RN: The Memoirs of Richard Nixon* (Simon & Schuster, 1978), 75.

9. Memo written by Rose Mary Woods to Richard Nixon, dated March 3, 1960, from the archives of the Richard Nixon Library.

CHAPTER 10

1. "Dies At Convention," *New York Times*, August 16, 1956.

2. "Newsman Undergoes Surgery," *New York Times*, August 16, 1956.

3. "Democrats Get Roses," *New York Times*, August 18, 1956.

4. James MacGregor Burns, *John Kennedy: A Political Profile* (Harcourt Brace & Company, 1960), 184.

5. Theodore Sorensen, *Kennedy* (Harper & Row, 1965), 85.

6. "Finish Dramatic: Bay Stater Nearly In When Stampede to Rival Is Set Off," *New York Times*, August 18, 1956.

7. Rose Kennedy, *Times To Remember* (Doubleday & Company, 1974), 329.

CHAPTER 11

1. "Brewery Heir Held in Draft Plot Here," *New York Times*, December 24, 1943, 1.

2. "Gert Von Gontard, Aided Stage Groups," *New York Times*, October 5, 1979, D19.

3. The author's interview with Adalbert von Gontard Jr., May 2008.

4. Gert von Gontard, *In Defense of Love* (Alliance Book Corporation, 1940), 29.

5. "Evidence Completed in Von Gontard Case," *New York Times*, January 6, 1944, 10.

6. From Dr. Hutschnecker's application in 1946 to the Board of Regents of the State of New York for the restoration of his license to practice medicine.

7. "Von Gontard Slap at Army Charged," *New York Times*, May 6, 1944, 9.

8. Ibid.

9. From the records of the University of the State of New York, State Department of Education, in the matter of the application for the revocation of the license of Dr. Arnold Hutschnecker.

10. Ibid.

11. Ibid.

12. Ibid.

13. "Von Gontard Free of Draft Charges," *New York Times*, June 14, 1944, 21.

CHAPTER 12

1. Anthony Summers, *The Arrogance of Power* (Penguin Putnam Inc., 2000).

2. Arnold Hutschnecker, *Richard Nixon: His Rise to Power, His Self-Defeat*, 49.

3. Richard Nixon, *RN: The Memoirs of Richard Nixon* (Simon & Schuster, 1978), 3.

4. Art Ryon, "Yorba Lindans Dedicate Nixon's Boyhood Home," *Los Angeles Times*, January 10, 1959.

5. Philip Potter, "Political Pitchman, Richard M. Nixon," in *Candidates 1960*, ed. Eric Sevareid (Basic Books, 1959), 96.

6. Interview by Richard Curtiss for the Cal State Fullerton oral history program, the Richard M. Nixon Project, February 10, 1970.

7. Interview by Jeff Jones for the Cal State Fullerton oral history program, the Richard M. Nixon Project, June 3, 1970.

8. Interview by Richard Curtiss for the Cal State Fullerton oral history program, the Richard M. Nixon Project, February 10, 1970.

9. Interview by Mitch Haddad for the Cal State Fullerton oral history program, the Richard M. Nixon Project, December 22, 1969.

10. Philip Potter, "Political Pitchman, Richard M. Nixon," in *Candidates 1960*, ed. Eric Sevareid (Basic Books, 1959), 70 and 74.

11. Interview by Frank Gannon, February 9, 1983.

12. Richard Nixon's farewell address at the White House, August 9, 1974.

13. Arnold Hutschnecker, *Richard Nixon: His Rise to Power, His Self-Defeat*, 183.

14. Ibid., 209.

15. Ibid., 169.

CHAPTER 13

1. From Guenther Reinhardt's 1948 job application for Voice of America, requesting that his wife not be interviewed as part of the background check.

2. Ian Sayer and Douglas Botting, *Nazi Gold* (Granada Publishing, 1984), 284.

3. Confidential report about Guenther Reinhardt, Office of the Army Inspector General, April 1948.

4. Ibid.

5. The author's interview with Werner Michel, May 20, 2008.

6. Ibid.

CHAPTER 14

1. *Washington Daily News*, August 16, 1960.

2. Note from Richard Nixon to Jack Kennedy, August 23, 1960, from the archives of the Richard Nixon Library.

3. Western Union telegram from John F. Kennedy to Richard Nixon, dated August 29, 1960, from the archives of the Richard Nixon Library.

4. Letter from Richard Nixon to John F. Kennedy, dated August 31, 1960, from the archives of the Richard Nixon Library.

5. John H. Fenton, "Nixon Denies Kennedy Is Soft on Reds, Repudiating New Hampshire Governor," *New York Times*, March 8, 1960, 1.

6. Typewritten statement by Herb Klein, dated March 7, 1960, from the archives of the Richard Nixon Library.

7. Speech by John F. Kennedy in Indiana, April 29, 1960, from the JFK Library.

8. "Kennedy Scores Nixon," *New York Times*, June 18, 1960, 12.

9. Speech by John F. Kennedy at the George Washington High School stadium, Alexandria, Virginia, August 24, 1960.

10. Statement by John F. Kennedy, issued in New Castle, Pennsylvania, October 15, 1960.

11. Speech by John F. Kennedy, Boston Garden, Boston, Massachusetts, November 7, 1960.

12. Richard Nixon's acceptance speech, National Republican Convention, International Amphitheatre, Chicago, Illinois, July 28, 1960.

13. "Falling Leaves," *Time*, October 31, 1960.

14. Second TV debate, Washington, D.C., October 7, 1960.

15. United Press International, "Nixon Blasts Kennedy as Enemy of State Rights in Last Dixie Foray," *Oswego Palladium-Times*, November 4, 1960.

CHAPTER 15

1. "Kennedy In Race," *New York Times*, 1.

2. Tape recording of JFK's dinner party on January 5, 1960, which aired on NBC *Nightly News*, October 13, 2008.

3. Richard Stengel, "Rich Man, Poor Man," *Time*, June 3, 1996.

4. Robert E. Gilbert, "JFK and Addison's Disease," posted on the official website of the John F. Kennedy Library and Museum, excerpted from his book, *The Mortal Presidency: Illness and Anguish in the White House* (Basic Books, 1992).

5. Ibid.

6. Robert Dallek, "The Medical Ordeals of JFK," *Atlantic Monthly*, December 2002.

7. Robert E. Gilbert, "JFK and Addison's Disease," posted on the official website of the John F. Kennedy Library and Museum,

excerpted from his book, *The Mortal Presidency: Illness and Anguish in the White House* (Basic Books, 1992).

8. Ibid.

9. Ibid.

10. Ibid.

11. Arnold Hutschnecker, *Richard Nixon: His Rise to Power, His Self-Defeat*, 141–142.

12. Ibid.

CHAPTER 16

1. Memo written by Rose Mary Woods to Richard Nixon, dated March 3, 1960, from the archives of the Richard Nixon Library.

2. Herb Klein's press statement, on behalf of Richard Nixon, September 12, 1960.

3. Ibid.

4. Arnold Hutschnecker, *Richard Nixon: His Rise to Power, His Self-Defeat*, unnumbered page.

CHAPTER 17

1. "Von Gontard Free of Draft Charges," *New York Times*, June 14, 1944, 21.

2. Ibid.

3. "Von Gontard in Army," *New York Times*, August 19, 1944, 13.

CHAPTER 18

1. The author's interview with Werner Michel, May 20, 2008.

2. Ian Sayer and Douglas Botting, *Nazi Gold* (Granada Publishing, 1984).

3. Guenther Reinhardt, *Crime Without Punishment* (Hermitage House, Inc., 1952), 230.

4. Ibid., 221.

5. Ian Sayer and Douglas Botting, *Nazi Gold* (Granada Publishing, 1984), 296.

6. The author's interview with Werner Michel, May 20, 2008.

7. Ibid.

8. Ibid.

9. Ian Sayer and Douglas Botting, *Nazi Gold* (Granada Publishing, 1984), 286.

10. The author's interview with Werner Michel, May 20, 2008.

11. The author's interview with Paul Bruehl, July 9, 2008.

12. The author's interview with Werner Michel, July 27, 2008.

13. Ibid.

CHAPTER 19

1. Thurston Clarke, *Ask Not: The Inauguration of John F. Kennedy and the Speech That Changed America* (Henry Holt and Co., 2004), 160.

2. Interview by Vicki Daitch, October 8, 2002, for the John F. Kennedy Library.

3. Kitty Kelley, *His Way: The Unauthorized Biography of Frank Sinatra* (Bantam Books, 1986), 249.

4. From the author's interviews with Milt Ebbins.

5. Arnold Hutschnecker, *The Drive for Power* (M. Evans and Company, 1974), 3.

6. Arnold Hutschnecker, *Richard Nixon: His Rise to Power, His Self-Defeat*, 146.

7. Ibid., 147.

8. From Guenther Reinhardt's 12-page confidential report about his consultation with Dr. Arnold Hutschnecker on September 7, 1960, and his follow-up conversation with Dr. Hutschnecker's attorney.

9. Ibid.

10. Ibid.

11. Ibid.

12. Ibid.

13. Ibid.

14. Ibid.

15. Kitty Kelley, *His Way: The Unauthorized Biography of Frank Sinatra* (Bantam Books, 1986), 279.

16. From the files of Peter Lawford and Milt Ebbins.

CHAPTER 20

1. From the author's interview with Milt Ebbins.
2. Doris Kearns Goodwin, *Fitzgeralds & the Kennedys: An American Saga* (Simon & Schuster, 1986).
3. Ibid.
4. Arnold Hutschnecker, *The Drive for Power* (M. Evans and Company, 1974), 54–56.
5. From JFK's speech at the Gridiron Club, Washington, D.C., March 15, 1958, from the archives of the John F. Kennedy Library.

CHAPTER 21

1. From the records of the University of the State of New York, State Department of Education, in the matter of the application for the revocation of the license of Dr. Arnold Hutschnecker.
2. Ibid.
3. Ibid.
4. Friedl Levy's letter from Berlin, dated September 22, 1945, but not received by Arnold and Florita Hutschnecker until January 1946.
5. From the application of Arnold Hutschnecker for the restoration of his license to practice medicine, June 1946.
6. Ibid.
7. Ibid.

CHAPTER 22

1. Nixon White House tapes, May 26, 1971.
2. "Character Assassins Getting an Early Start," *B'nai B'rith Messenger*, August 12, 1960, 1.
3. Ibid.
4. "Anti-Semitic Bias By Nixon Is Denied," *New York Times*, August 19, 1960, 10.
5. Nixon White House tapes, July 3, 1971.
6. Ibid.

7. Nixon White House tapes, October 19, 1972.

8. Nixon White House tapes, February 1, 1972.

9. Nixon White House tapes, September 13, 1971.

10. Nixon White House tapes, September 14, 1971.

11. Nixon White House tapes, May 26, 1971.

12. Nixon White House tapes, May 13, 1971.

13. Nixon White House tapes, January 23, 1973.

14. Douglas Dales, "Candidates Urge End to Bias in U.S.," *New York Times*, October 13, 1960, 26.

15. Ibid.

16. Edward C. Burks, "Negro in Cabinet Pledged by Lodge," *New York Times*, October 13, 1960, 1.

17. Edward C. Burks, "Pledge on Negro Diluted by Lodge," *New York Times*, October 14, 1960, 1.

18. Nixon White House tapes, November 19, 1972.

19. Paul Charles Merkley, *American Presidents, Religion and Israel*, (Praeger Publishers, 2004), 52.

20. Howard M. Sachar, *A History of the Jews in America*, (Vintage, 1993).

CHAPTER 23

1. Guenther Reinhardt's letter to Tom Agoston, February 12, 1949.

2. Ibid.

3. The author's interview with Werner Michel, May 20, 2008.

4. The author's interview with Werner Michel, July 27, 2008.

5. Ibid.

CHAPTER 24

1. Virginia Wilson (Janet Travell's daughter), "Janet G. Travell, MD: A Daughter's Recollection," *Texas Heart Institute Journal*, 2003.

2. Robert Dallek, "The Medical Ordeals of JFK," *The Atlantic Monthly*, December 2002.

3. Oral history interview by Ted Sorensen for the JFK Library on Januray 20, 1966, in which Janet Travell talks about the

break-ins and her efforts to thwart future attempts to steal Kennedy's medical files.

4. Arnold Hutschnecker, *Richard Nixon: His Rise to Power, His Self-Defeat*, 178–179.
5. Ibid.
6. Robert Dallek, "The Medical Ordeals of JFK," *The Atlantic Monthly*, December 2002.
7. John Gizzi, "Historian Dalleck Maligned Nixon's 1960 Campaign," *Human Events*, January 6, 2003.
8. From the letter written by Dr. Travell and Dr. Cohen to John Kennedy, dated June 11, 1960.

CHAPTER 25
1. Robert Caro, *The Path to Power* (Vintage, 1990), 174–180.
2. Ibid.
3. Robert Dallek, *Lone Star Rising* (Oxford University Press, 1992), 98–348.
4. *Los Angeles Times*, July 5, 1959, 1.
5. India Edwards' oral history interview for the Lyndon Johnson Library, February 4, 1969.
6. Ibid.
7. Ibid.
8. Ibid.
9. *New York Times*, July 5, 1960, 19.
10. India Edwards' oral history interview for the Lyndon Johnson Library, February 4, 1969.
11. Jeff Shesol, *Mutual Contempt: Lyndon Johnson and Bobby Kennedy, The Feud that Defined a Decade* (W. W. Norton & Company, 1998), 35.

CHAPTER 26
1. *New York Times*, July 5, 1960, 19.
2. Ibid.
3. Bobby Baker, *Wheeling and Dealing* (W. W. Norton & Company, 1978),118.

4. From Janet Travell's oral history interview, conducted by Kennedy adviser and speechwriter Ted Sorensen, January 20, 1966.
5. Ibid.
6. Ibid.
7. Ibid.
8. Ibid.
9. From the minutes of the 1960 Democratic National Convention, the John F. Kennedy Library.

CHAPTER 27

1. From a draft of Drew Pearson's lawsuit against Westbrook Pegler, February 1, 1950, later filed in the U.S. District Court for the Southern District of New York.
2. Letter of introduction written by Jack L. Kraus II, August 7, 1950, from the Drew Pearson Collection at the Lyndon Johnson Presidential Library.
3. From Drew Pearson's deposition, given September 25, 1951, in his $5.1 million lawsuit against Senator Joseph McCarthy.
4. Ralph de Toledano, *One Man Alone* (Funk & Wagnalls, 1969), 178.
5. "Pearson Helps Reds, McCarthy Declares," *Washington Post*, December 16, 1950, 6.
6. Haynes Johnson, *The Age of Anxiety* (Harvest Books, 2006), 207.

CHAPTER 28

1. John H. Lichtblau, *New York Times* review of *Crime Without Punishment*, November 9, 1952, BR62.
2. Ibid.
3. Guenther Reinhardt, *Crime Without Punishment* (Hermitage House, 1952), 92.
4. Hedda Hopper, "Looking at Hollywood," *New York Times*, March 8, 1954, B15.
5. From the author's interview with John H. Lichtblau, April 19, 2009.

6. From the author's interview with Charlotte Lichtblau, April 19, 2009.
7. Ian Sayer and Douglas Botting, *Nazi Gold* (Granada Publishing, 1984), 284.
8. "Guenther Reinhardt, 63, Dies; Was a Writer and Investigator," *New York Times* obituary, December 3, 1968.

CHAPTER 29
1. "Cheers and Boos Greet Kennedy at Rights Rally," *Los Angeles Times*, July 11, 1960, 3.
2. David Garrow, *Bearing the Cross: Martin Luther King, Jr., and the Southern Christian Leadership Conference* (Harper Perennial Modern Classics, 2004), 139.
3. "Cheers and Boos Greet Kennedy at Rights Rally," *Los Angeles Times*, July 11, 1960, 3.
4. Remarks by Senator John F. Kennedy at the Shrine Auditorium, Los Angeles, July 10, 1960, from the John F. Kennedy Presidential Library & Museum.
5. "Delegates Boo Negro," *New York Times*, July 12, 1960, 23.
6. The 1960 Democratic National Convention minutes, from the John F. Kennedy Presidential Library & Museum.
7. Ibid.
8. Ibid.
9. Martin Luther King Jr., *The Papers of Martin Luther King, Jr.: Volume V: Threshold of a New Decade, January 1959–December 1960*, ed. Clayborne Carson, Tenisha Armstrong, Adrienne Clay, and Susan Carson (University of California Press, 2005), 482.

CHAPTER 30
1. Barbara Secour, "Report on Kennedy at Shrine Auditorium," September 9, 1960, from the archives of the Richard Nixon Library.
2. W. H. Lawrence, "Kennedy Says U.S. Must Regain Lead in 'Fight for Peace,'" *New York Times*, September 8, 1960, 1.

3. Interview by Vicki Daitch on October 8, 2002, for the John F. Kennedy Library.

4. Philip Potter, "Political Pitchman: Richard M. Nixon" in *Candidates 1960*, ed. Eric Sevareid (Basic Books, 1959), 82–93.

5. Interview by Vicki Daitch on October 8, 2002, for the John F. Kennedy Library.

6. Interview by Vicki Daitch on August 26, 2002, for the John F. Kennedy Library.

7. Interview by Vicki Daitch on October 8, 2002, for the John F. Kennedy Library.

8. Interview by Vicki Daitch on August 26, 2002, for the John F. Kennedy Library.

9. Interview by Vicki Daitch on October 8, 2002, for the John F. Kennedy Library.

10. Ibid.

11. Transcript of the Nixon-Kennedy debate, September 27, 1960, from the archives of the John F. Kennedy Library.

12. Ibid.

13. Arnold Hutschnecker, *Richard Nixon: His Rise to Power, His Self-Defeat*, unnumbered page.

14. Ibid., 139–140.

CHAPTER 31

1. Arnold Hutschnecker, *The Drive for Power* (M. Evans and Company, 1974), 56.

2. Nixon, *RN: The Memoirs of Richard Nixon* (Simon & Schuster, 1978), 29.

3. Arnold Hutschnecker, *Richard Nixon: His Rise to Power, His Self-Defeat*, 134.

4. Ibid., 133.

5. Ibid., 50.

6. Ibid., 49–50.

7. Arnold Hutschnecker, *The Drive for Power* (M. Evans and Company, 1974), 52.

8. Letter from Arnold Hutschnecker to Richard Nixon, dated September 27, 1960.

CHAPTER 32

1. "'60 Spying Effort Laid To Democrats," *New York Times*, July 25, 1973, 31.
2. Ibid.
3. Ibid.
4. Carmine Bellino's interview with the author, September 21, 1988.
5. Sam Dash's 1986 interview with the author.
6. Kitty Kelley, *The Family: The Real Story of the Bush Dynasty* (Doubleday, 2004), 317.

CHAPTER 33

1. All quotes cited here are from Guenther Reinhardt's 12-page confidential report about his meeting with Dr. Arnold Hutschnecker on September 7, 1960.

CHAPTER 34

1. United Press International story, *New York Times*, November 4, 1960, 38.
2. "Candidates Pressed on Data of Any Ills," *New York Times*, November 6, 1960, 132.
3. Ibid.
4. Memo from Ann Whitman to President Eisenhower, November 5, 1960, from the archives of the Dwight D. Eisenhower Library.
5. Ann Whitman's White House diary entry, November 5, 1960, from the archives of the Dwight D. Eisenhower Library.
6. Ibid.
7. Ibid.
8. Arnold Hutschnecker, *Richard Nixon: His Rise to Power, His Self-Defeat*, 147.

9. W. H. Lawrence, "Nixon Stumps in the West," *New York Times,* November 6, 1960, 1.

10. Ibid.

11. Ibid.

12. Arnold Hutschnecker, *The Drive for Power* (M. Evans and Company, Inc., 1974), 1–4.

13. The 1960 Sherman/New Milford, Connecticut, telephone directory shows that Arnold Hutschnecker's phone number was unlisted in 1960; courtesy of the New Milford Public Library.

14. Arnold Hutschnecker, *The Drive for Power* (M. Evans and Company, Inc., 1974), 1–4.

15. Ibid.

16. Arnold Hutschnecker, *Richard Nixon: His Rise to Power, His Self-Defeat,* 141-142.

17. Ibid., 147.

18. Arnold Hutschnecker, *The Drive for Power* (M. Evans and Company, Inc., 1974), 4.

CHAPTER 35

1. Richard Nixon, *RN: The Memoirs of Richard Nixon* (Simon & Schuster, 1978), 223.

2. Theodore White, *The Making of the President: 1960* (Antheum Publishers, 1964), 11.

3. Ibid., 12.

4. Ibid., 18.

5. *Time,* November 16, 1960.

6. Theodore White, *The Making of the President: 1960* (Antheum Publishers, 1964), 25.

7. Peter Carlson, "Another Race To the Finish," *Washington Post,* November 17, 2000, 1.

8. Richard Nixon, *RN: The Memoirs of Richard Nixon* (Simon & Schuster, 1978), 224.

9. Ibid.

10. William Ewald Jr., *Eisenhower the President: Crucial Days 1951-1960* (Prentice-Hall 1981), 313.
11. David Greenberg, "Was Nixon Robbed? The Legend of the Stolen 1960 Election," *Slate*, October 16, 2000.
12. Telegram from Richard Nixon to Jack Kennedy, November 9, 1960, from the files of the Richard Nixon Library.
13. Peter Carlson, "Another Race To the Finish," *Washington Post*, November 17, 2000, 1.

CHAPTER 36
1. From the author's interviews with Milt Ebbins.
2. Ibid.
3. Ibid.
4. Ibid.
5. From Guenther Reinhardt's 12-page confidential memo about his meeting with Dr. Hutschnecker.
6. From the author's interviews with Milt Ebbins.
7. From the files of Peter Lawford and Milt Ebbins.

CHAPTER 37
1. From the author's interviews with Milt Ebbins.
2. Ibid.
3. Los Angeles Police Department report on the death of Marilyn Monroe, August 10, 1962.
4. Los Angeles Police Department report on the death of Marilyn Monroe, August 6, 1962.
5. From the author's interviews with Milt Ebbins.
6. Los Angeles Police Department report on the death of Marilyn Monroe, August 6, 1962.
7. From the author's interviews with Milt Ebbins.

CHAPTER 38
1. Arnold Hutschnecker, *Richard Nixon: His Rise to Power, His Self-Defeat*, 158.

2. Letter from Arnold Hutschnecker to Richard Nixon, February 10, 1961, from the archives of the Richard Nixon Library.

3. Arnold Hutschnecker, *Richard Nixon: His Rise to Power, His Self-Defeat*, 158.

4. Ibid., 159.

5. Letter from Arnold Hutschnecker to Richard Nixon, November 7, 1962, from the archives of the Richard Nixon Library.

6. Arnold Hutschnecker, *Richard Nixon: His Rise to Power, His Self-Defeat*, 160-61.

7. Interview by Errol Morris in the 2003 documentary film *The Fog of War: Eleven Lessons from the Life of Robert McNamara*.

8. JFK's White House tapes, October 19, 1962, from the John F. Kennedy Library.

9. Robert McNamara, speaking about the Cuban Missile Crisis at the John F. Kennedy Library, October 1, 2002.

10. Interview by Errol Morris in the 2003 documentary film *The Fog of War: Eleven Lessons from the Life of Robert McNamara*.

11. Arnold Hutschnecker, *Richard Nixon: His Rise to Power, His Self-Defeat*, 144–145.

CHAPTER 39

1. "S.L.A. Aide Held in Theft of Files," *New York Times*, April 7, 1963, 77.

2. Ibid.

3. "S.L.A. Tells Role of Theft Suspect," *New York Times*, April 9, 1963, 5.

4. Ibid.

5. Ibid.

6. Daniel Horowitz, *Vance Packard & American Social Criticism* (University of North Carolina Press, 1994), 227.

7. Ibid.

8. Vance Packard, *The Naked Society* (David McKay Company, Inc., 1964), ix.

9. "Investigator Taken To Court for 37th Time," *New York Times*, April 1, 1964, 77.

10. "Ex-S.L.A. Aide Cleared," *New York Times*, December 5, 1967, 29.
11. The author's interview with Werner Michel, May 20, 2008.

CHAPTER 40
1. Ovid Demaris, *Dirty Business: The Corporate-Political Money-Power Game* (Avon Books, 1974), 140.
2. Curt Schleier, "PepsiCo's Donald Kendall—Hard Work and Firsthand Learning Propelled His Career," *Investor's Business Daily*, June 21, 2000.
3. Ibid.
4. Ibid.
5. Letter from Rose Mary Woods to William Manchester, August 4, 1964, from the files of the Richard Nixon Library.
6. "Ten Years Later: Nobody Forgets: Where Were You?," *Esquire*, November 1973.
7. Letter from Rose Mary Woods to William Manchester, August 4, 1964, from the files of the Richard Nixon Library.
8. CBS News, November 22, 1963.
9. Richard Nixon, *RN: The Memoirs of Richard Nixon* (Simon & Schuster, 1978), 252.
10. "Ten Years Later: Nobody Forgets: Where Were You?," *Esquire*, November 1973.
11. CBS News, November 22, 1963.
12. Richard Nixon, *RN: The Memoirs of Richard Nixon* (Simon & Schuster, 1978), 252.
13. Testimony by Marina Oswald to the Warren Commission, June 11, 1964, from *The Report of the President's Commission on the Assassination of President John F. Kennedy* (also known as the Warren Report).
14. Ibid.
15. *The Report of the President's Commission on the Assassination of President John F. Kennedy.*

CHAPTER 41

1. Daniel Ellsberg, "Where Are Iraq's Pentagon Papers?" *Boston Globe*, February 22, 2004.
2. Ibid.
3. Richard Reston, "Resolution To Defend Southeast Asia Signed," *New York Times*, August 11, 1964.
4. *The Pentagon Papers* (Gravel Edition), Vol. 1, Chapter 5, "Origins of the Insurgency in South Vietnam, 1954-1960" (Beacon Press, 1971), 242-269.
5. The Vietnam Veterans Memorial, Washington, D.C.
6. Max Frankel, "Halts North Vietnam Raids; Bids Hanoi Join Peace Moves," *New York Times*, April 1, 1968, 1.

CHAPTER 42

1. Fred P. Graham, "Agnew Charges Left Is Favored," *New York Times*, November 3, 1968, 79.
2. "Secret" memo from Walt Rostow to President Johnson, November 2, 1968, which included the FBI's report on their surveillance of Anna Chennault, from "The 'X' Envelope" at the Lyndon Johnson Library archives.
3. CBS News, February 27, 1968.
4. Bernard Weinraub, "Saigon's Reaction," *New York Times*, May 5, 1968, E1.
5. Terence Smith, "Behind the Talks: A Cocktail Party," *New York Times*, May 8, 1968, 3.
6. Richard Nixon, *RN: The Memoirs of Richard Nixon* (Simon & Schuster, 1979), 80.
7. "The Real Story of '68 Vietnam Bombing Halt" (George P. Bundy's letter to the editor), *New York Times*, June 13, 1991.
8. Anna Chennault, *The Education of Anna* (Times Books, 1980), 190.
9. Bui Diem and David Chanoff, *In the Jaws of History* (Houghton Mifflin Company, 1987), 244.
10. Ibid.

11. "The Real Story of '68 Vietnam Bombing Halt" (George P. Bundy's letter to the editor), *New York Times*, June 13, 1991.
12. FBI report, written by then-FBI Deputy Director Cartha DeLoach, dated October 30, 1968, from "The 'X' Envelope" at the Lyndon Johnson Library archives.
13. Marie Smith, "A Wealth of Talent: GOP's Anna Chennault," *Washington Post*, November 1, 1968, B6.
14. From "The 'X' Envelope" at the Lyndon Johnson Library archives.
15. J. Edgar Hoover's secret dispatch to the White House Situation Room, dated November 2, 1968, from "The 'X' Envelope" at the Lyndon Johnson Library archives.
16. The author's interview with former FBI Deputy Director Cartha "Deke" DeLoach, June 18, 2008.
17. The author's interview with former FBI Deputy Director Cartha "Deke" DeLoach, December 1, 2008.
18. Walt Rostow's "eyes only" memo to President Johnson, November 12, 1968, from "The 'X' Envelope" at the Lyndon Johnson Library archives.
19. Walt Rostow's report to President Johnson at the LBJ Ranch, November 2, 1968, from "The 'X' Envelope" at the Lyndon Johnson Library archives.
20. Gene Roberts, "Thieu Says Saigon Cannot Join Paris Talks Under Present Plan," *New York Times*, November 2, 1968, 1.
21. "11 Saigon Senators Voice Hope for a Nixon Victory," *New York Times*, November 3, 1968, 77.
22. Kelley Shannon, "New Tapes Show LBJ Worried About Vietnam, Nixon," Associated Press, December 4, 2008, from tape recordings of President Johnson's phone conversations released by the Lyndon Johnson Library, December 4, 2008.
23. "LBJ Tapes Implicate Nixon with Treason," *ABC World News*, December 4, 2008, from tape recordings of President Johnson's phone conversations released by the Lyndon Johnson Library, December 4, 2008.2

24. Lyndon Johnson's diary, November 3, 1968, from "The 'X' Envelope" at the Lyndon Johnson Library archives.

25. *ABC World News*, December 4, 2008, from tape recordings of President Johnson's phone conversations, released by the Lyndon Johnson Library.

26. Ibid.

27. Ibid.

28. "The Real Story of '68 Vietnam Bombing Halt" (George P. Bundy's letter to the editor), *New York Times*, June 13, 1991.

29. Walt Rostow, "Memorandum for the Record," May 14, 1973, from "The 'X' Envelope" at the Lyndon Johnson Library archives.

30. Clark Clifford, *Counsel To the President* (Random House, 1991), 583.

31. Ibid.

32. Ibid.

33. FBI memo from J. Edgar Hoover to President Johnson, classified as "secret," on the movements of Anna Chennault on Election Day, November 5, 1968, from "The 'X' Envelope" at the Lyndon Johnson Library archives.

34. Clark Clifford, *Counsel To the President* (Random House, 1991), 582–583.

35. Ibid., 582.

36. Ibid., 584.

37. Memo from Walt Rostow to President Johnson, November 8, 1968, from "The 'X' Envelope" at the Lyndon Johnson Library archives.

38. "Memorandum for the Record," Walt Rostow, May 14, 1973, from "The 'X' Envelope" at the Lyndon Johnson Library archives.

CHAPTER 43

1. Drew Pearson's address to the National Press Club, November 14, 1968.

2. Column by Drew Pearson and Jack Anderson, "Washington Merry-Go-Round," November 20, 1968.

3. Ibid.

4. Drew Pearson's address to the National Press Club, November 14, 1968.

5. "Querulous Quaker," *Time*, December 13, 1948.

6. Column by Drew Pearson and Jack Anderson, "Washington Merry-Go-Round," November 20, 1968.

7. Ibid.

8. Drew Pearson's address to the National Press Club, November 14, 1968.

9. Arnold Hutschnecker, *The Drive for Power*, 6.

10. United Press International, November 14, 1968.

11. Column by Drew Pearson and Jack Anderson, "Washington Merry-Go-Round," November 20, 1968.

12. Ibid.

13. Mark Feldstein, *Poisoning the Press: Richard Nixon, Jack Anderson, and the Rise of Washington's Scandal Culture* (Farrar, Straus and Giroux, 2010), 99.

14. *Newsweek*, November 25, 1968.

15. The author's interview with Werner Michel, May 20, 2008.

CHAPTER 44

1. Arnold Hutschnecker, *Richard Nixon: His Rise to Power, His Self-Defeat*, 150.

2. Ibid., 148.

3. Arnold Hutschnecker, *The Drive for Power* (M. Evans and Company, 1974), 9.

4. Nixon's White House tapes, April 4, 1972.

5. Letter from Arnold Hutschnecker to Richard Nixon, April 12, 1955, from the archives of the Richard Nixon Library.

6. Ibid.

7. Letter from Arnold Hutschnecker to Richard Nixon, December 16, 1959, from the archives of the Richard Nixon Library.

8. Arnold Hutschnecker, *Richard Nixon: His Rise to Power, His Self-Defeat*, 50.
9. W. H. Lawrence, "Kennedy Says U.S. Must Regain Lead in 'Fight for Peace,'" *New York Times*, September 8, 1960, 1.
10. Letter from Arnold Hutschnecker to Richard Nixon, February 14, 1968.
11. Arnold Hutschnecker, *Richard Nixon: His Rise to Power, His Self-Defeat*, 50.
12. Ibid., 171.
13. Ibid., 172.
14. Ibid., 173.
15. Ibid., 174.
16. Ibid.
17. Ibid.
18. Ibid., 175.
19. Ibid.

CHAPTER 45
1. White House tapes, June 17, 1971.
2. White House tapes, June 30, 1971.
3. From Amy Goodman's radio interview with Daniel Ellsberg and John Dean, *Democracy Now!*, April 27, 2006.
4. Ibid.
5. Ibid.
6. White House tapes, July 27, 1971.
7. Spiro Agnew, *Go Quietly…Or Else* (William Morrow and Company, 1980), 9.
8. Ibid., 186.
9. Ibid., 190.
10. Ibid.
11. Ibid., 104.
12. Ibid., 141.
13. Ibid., 130.
14. Ibid., 106.
15. Ibid.

16. Richard Nixon, *In the Arena* (Pocket, 1991).
17. Arnold Hutschnecker, *Richard Nixon: His Rise to Power, His Self-Defeat*, 145.

CHAPTER 46

1. "Gallup Poll Gives President Widest Lead Over 2 Democrats," *New York Times*, June 11, 1972.
2. Alfred E. Lewis, "5 Held in Plot to Bug Democrats' Office Here," *Washington Post*, June 18, 1972.
3. Spiro Agnew, *Go Quietly...Or Else* (William Morrow and Company, 1980), 106.
4. Ray Price, interviewed by Brian Lamb on "Q & A," C-SPAN, December 28, 2008.
5. Leon Friedman and William F. Levantrosser, ed., *Watergate and Afterward: The Legacy of Richard M. Nixon* (Greenwood Press, 1992), 41.
6. Walt Rostow, "Memorandum for the Record," May 14, 1973, from "The 'X' Envelope" at the Lyndon Johnson Library archives.
7. Walter Pincus and George Lardner Jr., "Nixon Order to Destroy Tapes Surfaces," *Los Angeles Times*, October 30, 1997.

CHAPTER 47

1. Arnold Hutschnecker, *The Drive for Power* (M. Evans and Company, 1974), 11.
2. Arnold Hutschnecker, *Richard Nixon: His Rise to Power, His Self-Defeat*, 196.
3. Arnold Hutschnecker, *The Drive for Power* (M. Evans and Company, 1974), 5.
4. Ibid., 15.
5. Arnold Hutschnecker, *Richard Nixon: His Rise to Power, His Self-Defeat*, 149.
6. "Psychiatric Aid To Nixon Denied," *New York Times*, November 14, 1968, 34.

7. "Doctor Discusses Treatment of Nixon," *New York Times,* July 1, 1969, 25.

8. Stanley Willford, "James Farmer Lauds Stand on Child Tests," *Los Angeles Times,* April 17, 1970, B5.9

9. Arnold Hutschnecker, "Nixon-Era Plan for Children Didn't Include Concentration Camps" (letter to the editor), *New York Times,* October 15, 1988.

10. Ibid.

11. Arnold Hutschnecker, "The Stigma of Seeing a Psychiatrist," *New York Times,* November 20, 1973, 39.

12. Ibid.

13. Ibid.

14. Ibid.

15. Arnold Hutschnecker, *Richard Nixon: His Rise to Power, His Self-Defeat,* 36–37.

16. Ibid., 44.

17. Ibid., 51.

18. Ibid.

19. From the author's 2008 interview with Squire Rushnell.

INDEX